Field, Forest, and Family

Field, Forest, and Family

Women's Work and Power in Rural Laos

Carol J. Ireson

WestviewPress

A Division of HarperCollins*Publishers*

Copyright © 1996 by Westview Press, A Division of HarperCollins Publishers, Inc.

Published in 1996 in the United States of America by Westview Press, 5500 Central Avenue, Boulder, Colorado 80301-2877, and in the United Kingdom by Westview Press, 12 Hid's Copse Road, Cumnor Hill, Oxford OX2 9JJ

Library of Congress Cataloging-in-Publication Data
Ireson, Carol J.
   Field, forest, and family : women's work and power in rural Laos /
by Carol J. Ireson.
    p.   cm.
    Includes bibliographical references and index.
    ISBN 0-8133-8936-4 (hardcover)
    1. Women, Hmong—Social conditions. 2. Women, Lao—Social
conditions. 3. Women, Khmu'—Social conditions. 4. Sex role—Laos—
Louangphrabang (Province) 5. Social change—Laos—Louangphrabang
(Province) 6. Louangphrabang (Laos : Province)—Social conditions.
7. Louangphrabang (Laos : Province)—Economic conditions.
I. Title.
DS555.45.M5I74   1996
305.4'09594—dc20   96-27143
                                                                                                      CIP

All photos by Carol and Randy Ireson. Editing by Virginia Bothun, Randy Ireson, and Helen Takeiuchi. Typesetting by Elsa Struble and Layla George. Indexing by Anthony Laffrenz of Catchword, Inc.

10   9   8   7   6   5   4   3   2

To my parents,
Eddie and Barbara Jean Doolittle

Contents

Tables and Illustrations

Tables

Preface

Field, Forest, and Family is the culmination of work in Laos ranging over more than a quarter of a century of my life. My research and experience in Laos form the basis for much of the book, though I rely more heavily on existing literature for Khmu and Hmong comparisons and I draw liberally on other published and unpublished sources when relevant. I gathered the information about rural women from several years of development project work in Laos. In all I have worked in Laos for five years (1967-69, 1984-86, 1988-89) and have made several shorter visits. I was fortunate to be able to travel and carry out research in Laos during these times. Foreigners not from socialist bloc countries were rarely granted permission by communist government authorities to travel to rural areas for research purposes alone. Thus, data on the social and economic impacts of events like agricultural cooperativization, economic liberalization, or the removal of restrictions on family planning education and birth-control devices have usually been gathered by foreigners primarily in the context of development project planning, implementation, and evaluation. Furthermore, there were no Laotian social science researchers who were carrying out research during the time periods covered in this book.

I first worked in Laos in the late 1960s as a volunteer on the rural development team of International Voluntary Services (IVS). At that time I learned to speak Lao and became acquainted with Lao culture and customs. In 1968-69 I designed and, with the support of the Royal Lao Government and the United States Agency for International Development, implemented a study of the diet of twelve families in each of six villages from northern to southern Laos. War interfered with the study, but my six research teams (home economists from the Ministry of Agriculture and their counterpart IVS home economists) were able to interview household members and to record and weigh the food prepared over a three-day period during at least two of the three seasons in most selected village households. With the help of a nutritionist from the World Health Organization (WHO), research teams also weighed and measured children in these households, noting obvious signs of nutritional deficiencies (C. Ireson 1969). Some of this information is included in Chapters 2 and 7.

I was delighted to return to a peaceful Laos in 1984 to work as co-director of the American Friends Service Committee (AFSC) development program, especially since my mandate from AFSC included the creation of a women's project. Working for a non-governmental organization (AFSC), focusing on developing small-scale, often village-based projects in conjunction with the government, I frequently traveled to remote districts and spoke with a variety of province, district, and village officials, though travel and communication restrictions on Westerners restricted my access to villagers. In this way, I encountered women's union officials in one province, Luang Prabang, who were interested in implementing a project to benefit provincial women. Many of the main ideas and examples in Chapters 4 through 7 are drawn from the data collected during project design and evaluation activities conducted with the Luang Prabang Women's Union (in 1986 and 1990, respectively) in seven project villages in Luang Prabang Province. In both cases project teams, including me, met village women's union officials with no men present and interviewed a number of women in each village. During the project design study, the research team was composed of a department head of the National Lao Women's Union (Davone, profiled in Chapter 1), the then-president of the Luang Prabang Women's Union and former head of the provincial agriculture office, and me. In our two-week project design trip, we traveled together, stayed in villages together, and together gradually began to understand the needs of village women as they told us and showed us about their lives. Since the Lao Women's Union is closely connected to the government and to the Lao People's Revolutionary Party (Davone has been an alternate member of the governing Party Central Committee since 1991), village women's responses were probably biased toward "political correctness." However, daily work, crops grown, animals raised, number of children borne, and other objective data were probably reported as accurately as respondents' memories permitted. The research process during the project evaluation study was similar, though the research team included Bandith, a more junior member of the Lao Women's Union who had become a deputy department head by 1993 (see Chapter 8); Soumountha, a doctor/development worker from AFSC in Laos who is a Khmu woman originally from Oudomxay, a northern province adjoining Luang Prabang Province (see Chapter 2); and me.

I have augmented these data with information gathered from a 1989 interview study, sponsored by the Forestry Department of the Ministry of Agriculture, Irrigation and Forestry and funded by the Swedish International Development Authority, of 200 women in Bolikhamsay Province. The research team randomly selected 120 women farmer/gatherers, ages 20 to 55, from eight villages and 80 women residents of two timber company towns for 40 to 60 minute interviews. Most respondents were ethnic Lao. Villages were of two types: villages with access to mature forest and villages with access only to degraded forest. Survey villages ranged in size from 35 to 160 households, and in age from 6 to 150 years. All villages had at least a few grades of school. Besides the author, the research team consisted of a Lao social scientist; four women interviewers, including a trained forester; and the vice president of the provincial women's union. Districts and villages provided us with officials to facilitate survey implementation. All instruments were jointly constructed by research team members. The main instrument, the structured interview schedule, was constructed, pretested, revised, and implemented completely in the Lao language, thus avoiding a variety of translation problems. The women sampled were interviewed in their homes. Information from these interviews formed the heart of this study, though supplementary information was gathered from provincial, district, and village officials, and by observation and conversation with women and other villagers. Members of the research team also accompanied women skilled in forest work into their gathering forest to observe the process of gathering, to see the products gathered, and to examine the types of forest available to the women of each village. Findings from this study are presented primarily in Chapter 6.

In addition to these studies, I draw on interviews with Lao refugees to the United States. The study, "Patterns of Cooperation in Rural Laos," was carried out with funding from the Social Science Research Council under the Indochina Studies Program, a program specifically oriented toward "culture-saving." The program supported research projects that documented pre-1975 Indochinese cultural patterns and artifacts, using recent refugees from Laos, Cambodia, and Vietnam as cultural informants and sources of information. At that time, all three countries were nearly completely closed to Western researchers. "Patterns of Cooperation in Rural Laos" was organized by Carol and Randall Ireson, with the collaboration of four Lao-American social service professionals: Kham-One Keopraseuth, Chansouk Meksavanh, Tou Meksavanh, and Chareundi Vansi (1988). All four were born and raised in Lao villages during their early years, though all left the countryside to continue their education.

The study draws on semi-structured interviews of 40 ethnic Lao adult informants (21 men, 19 women) who lived in a Lao village for at least part of their adulthood, actively participating in traditional village life. The informant pool included former villagers from northern (n=5), central (n=14), and southern (n=21) provinces. Interviews were conducted in Lao, usually by two team members, and covered a standard list of topics. Interviews lasted from forty-five minutes to three hours, with shorter follow-up interviews of a few informants. The sections of the recorded interviews pertaining to village work were transcribed into Lao and translated into English. Taped interviews, Lao transcriptions, and English translations are archived in the Library of Congress in Washington, D.C., in the study "Traditional Cooperation Patterns in Rural Laos." These data include information about ethnic Lao women's work before 1975.

I also draw from other development project experience of my own, from government statistics, and from the mainly unpublished development and aid agency reports of others. Since 1984, I have been gathering relevant information from Lao government ministries, the National Women's Union, foreign aid agencies working in Laos, and from local officials and villagers.

For example, one study I discuss was carried out by the Lao government with the support of the Commission of the European Communities. This study included seven villages in an area 15 kilometers southwest of Luang Prabang town. The villages were selected for participation in a variety of rural micro-projects (Luang Prabang Rural Micro-Projects 1990, 1991). Another included study was undertaken by the Swedish International Development Authority in conjunction with their upland agriculture project in the province and contains information from nine villages in two southern districts of the province—Luang Prabang and Muang Nan (see Map 4.1)(Håkangård 1990). As with the data from the Luang Prabang Women's Project, the villages were not chosen to be representative of all Luang Prabang villages. Furthermore, the data were gathered during relatively short field visits of one or two days per village, and data quality depends on the goodwill and good memory of individual villagers and, for some items, on the good record-keeping of the village administrative committee. Both of these studies are included in Chapter 4.

Results of project-related research form the basis for many of my examples and for my assessment of rural women's responses to economic liberalization. The data I collected during these years were necessarily limited by the focus of the projects and the political sensitivity of research itself. However, I often was able to learn a great deal about women's work, especially once I began working with the National Women's Union in 1985. Most of my data are qualitative, though some economic data from particular villages are quantitative.

I introduce the reader to this study of women's work and power in rural Laos in Chapter 1 by presenting the conceptual framework of the analysis and by locating the study in the context of women's experiences in other socialist Third World and Southeast Asian countries. In Chapter 2 I introduce the reader to the Lao People's Democratic Republic, focusing particularly on the recent history of macro-level shifts during socialist reorganization and economic liberalization and on the situation of women in Laos. Changes in economic policies have partially opened the Lao economy to neighboring capitalist entrepreneurs and to the international flow of resources and capital. In the countryside this is most visible in the reinstatement or creation of local markets selling imported goods. But one can also see evidence of increased logging and contract agriculture, with the promise of increased exploitation of other natural resources like oil, gems, and hydropower. Women are economically active but subject to poor health conditions, many pregnancies, and less education and political involvement than men.

In Chapter 3 I analyze the traditional sources of power and subordination for village women of three major ethnic groups: the ethnic Lao, the Khmu, and the Hmong. In Chapter 4 I present women from Luang Prabang Province, the source of many illustrative examples. Descriptions of the daily lives of women from different villages and ethnic groups illustrate social, cultural, and individual variations in activities that directly affect women's power. Village descriptions and individual profiles enrich the general picture of women's traditional activities and provide the basis for the succeeding chapters.

Chapters 5 and 6 present rural women's economic activities and sources of power. This is the one arena from which nearly all women traditionally derive at least some power. Women's rural economic activities from which they may derive some economic power include agriculture, forest gathering, cloth production, and commerce. For both post-1975 time periods (socialist reorganization and economic liberalization), I consider how women's work in each area translates into economic power and how macro-level policies and practices influence women's work and power in each area. I also analyze how women's domestic and reproductive responsibilities shape their involvement in each of these economic activities. Chapter 7 considers women's domestic responsibilities in greater detail. Women's continuous child-bearing and household labor withdraw time and energy from their economic activities and limit their economic power in each ethnic group in all time periods explored.

Chapter 8 focuses on the evolution and recent transformation of the Lao Women's Union. The Lao Women's Union, a national mass organization with branches in villages, neighborhoods, and work places, was responsible for women's political education and for mobilizing all women for the building of socialism. With economic liberalization and increasing Western foreign aid, the women's union was able to broaden its mission to include training and assistance projects targeting village women. The transformation of the women's union, from a political arm of the Party to a political *and* development organization, mirrors other broad economic and political changes and parallels the changes experienced by rural women themselves. Chapter 9 summarizes the main findings of this study, noting the effects of macro-level changes of socialist reorganization and economic liberalization on the lives of village women, the changing relationship between women's productive and reproductive work, and the factors that conditioned ethnic group differences in response to these changes.

Carol J. Ireson

Acknowledgments

How *did* it begin, my connection with the land and people of Laos? It began in 1967 with a phone call by undersea cable and radio-phone to my fiancé in Los Baños in The Philippines (where he had just plowed with a water buffalo for the first time). I was calling to tell him I would delay graduate school so that I could join him in Southeast Asia. A few months later, my adventures in Laos began with a wedding in Vientiane, language training in Sayaboury Province, and a posting in Khammouane Province.

Since then, many people and organizations have helped me in my work and play in Laos, in my growth as a social scientist, and in my thinking and writing about Laos. My mentors have been a diverse group. Jamie Bell, an agronomist and development specialist extrordinaire who has been active in projects in Southeast Asia well into retirement, encouraged and supported my first research on nutritional needs in rural Lao households. Judy Long, a feminist scholar actively working to change conditions that oppress women, encouraged and critiqued my early academic attempts to understand power and the politics of everyday life. David Elder, a perceptive observer of Southeast Asia and China who is committed to conflict resolution and to grassroots development, challenged me to put my theories and academic knowledge into practice in Laos and offered creative ideas and home-office support along the way. Charles "Biff" Keyes, an outstanding scholar of mainland Southeast Asia, enticed me into further exploring—and writing about—Lao culture in the mid-1980s and introduced me to specialists in Southeast Asia (before I became one myself).

In recent years, many friends and fellow workers in Laos shared their stories, their perceptions of events, and their project information. Several have been central to my learning about rural Lao women, especially Ng Shui Meng, Davone Vongsack, Sombath Somphone, Douang Deuane Viravong, Bouaphet Khotnhotha, and Jacqui Chagnon. Lao-American families, especially the Phommachanhs and the Temmerajs, have welcomed my family to their homes and cultural events. Daroun and Boualoy Phommachanh revived my dormant knowledge of the Lao language before I returned to Laos in 1984.

I especially appreciate the rural Laotian women who have opened my eyes to other ways of living through conversations, interviews, participation in local events, and guided visits to fields, gardens, and gathering forests. Sometimes shy, sometimes lively, sometimes troubled, sometimes content, but invariably friendly, the testimony of these women forms the heart of *Field, Forest, and Family.* My interpretation of their lives is simply that—my interpretation.

Several organizations have hired me for development work or supported my work "in the field," either in Laos or with Laotians in North America. These organizations include the American Friends Service Committee (AFSC), International Voluntary Services, the Social Science Research Council, and the Swedish International Development Authority. Of this group, AFSC has made the largest contribution to the information in this book. AFSC works in difficult situations throughout the world, attempting to facilitate war reconciliation and the empowerment of the powerless. By the time I began working with AFSC in Laos in 1984, AFSC staff had already identified rural women as a disenfranchised group and encouraged me to do what I could to facilitate grassroots development through women's unions. The resulting project produced much of the information contained in Chapter 4 and influenced my later experience with rural Laotian women.

Colleagues, students, organizations, friends, and family supported me at various stages of book-writing. Shirley Harkess, Ann Stromberg, and Suresht Bald helped me formulate the initial book prospectus. Virginia Bothun's careful reading and enthusiasm, Cornelia Flora's insightful suggestions, Randy Ireson's detailed knowledge of Laotian villages, and Ng Shui Meng's understanding of the Lao Women's Union all contributed to the creation of *Field, Forest, and Family.* Monica Morris, Anita Weiss, Geraldine Moreno-Black, Irene Tinker, Gale Summerfield, and Barney Hope offered encouragement. Students studying "Women in International Perspective" at Willamette University contributed their suggestions and ideas. My students in the Spring of 1995 were especially important critics. These include Emily Anderson, Maggie Dick, Annette Dietz, Eugene Ah Kim, Jodi Leahy, Kirsten McKeraghan, Annalisa Morgan, Kevin Plechl, and Erin Sutherland.

In 1994 the East-West Center in Honolulu awarded me a summer fellowship which supported writing the first draft, connected me with other Southeast Asia scholars and development workers, and contributed to the preparation of the final manuscript. A. Terry Rambo, director of the Center's Program on Environment, was especially helpful in facilitating both the writing and editing of *Field, Forest, and Family.* In 1989 the Southeast Asia Program of Cornell University awarded me a Luce Junior Faculty Fellowship for work on Laos using the Echols Collection on Southeast Asia; a number of my references to pre-1975 Laos are from the Echols Collection. Willamette University awarded me research and writing grants at nearly every stage of my involvement in Laos-related research and writing and provided occasional release time from courses to facilitate writing. The Northwest Regional Consortium for Southeast Asian Studies supplied intellectual stimulation and a forum for my ideas.

I would never have completed *Field, Forest, and Family* without the emotional strength and spiritual power of my women's group (Jennifer Carley, Karen Craven, Susan Davis, Susan Lee Graves, Anita King, Martha Thompson, and Melanie Zermer) and the Chapman-Graves family, who gave me a temporary home and writing room. Family members provided both support and distraction. April and Fred often furnished human companionship after a long day of solitary writing. Shirley commiserated and offered hope when the going got tough. Megan knew I could do it, and baked my favorite chocolate chip cookies. Bryhn regularly provided lively breaks from writing. My parents emanated confidence in their eldest daughter. Over the years Randy and I have often shared our jobs, friendships, projects, children, and homes. We have created a jointly held archive of wonderful, shared adventures and co-written articles, as well as boxes, drawers, and shelves of photos, files, and books on Laos. I relied on the Ireson archive when creating *Field, Forest, and Family*. And Randy, thanks for the pancakes.

CJI

Field, Forest, and Family

1

Women: Power, Subordination, and Development

Phing grew rice, sesame, vegetables, fruit, and other crops in the family's hillside field in northern Laos that year. These crops fed her family and provided cotton to exchange for finished cloth. During that growing season she regularly carried the baby, a small machete, and her lunch on the ninety-minute walk to the family's field where she pulled and cut rapidly growing weeds, tending the crops as they grew. With a nursing baby, three other young children, and a husband often occupied with the business of the village cooperative, thirty-two year old Phing had little time to devote to the production of sesame and cotton for sale. Even so, sales of her cash crops through the cooperative marketing network enabled her to roof her house. Family survival depended largely on Phing's efforts. Four years later, Phing grows more subsistence and more cash crops. Her husband and older children regularly work with her in the fields. Phing's improved quality of life that year is evident in her relaxed manner, her larger sawn wood house, and her satisfaction.

Noi's husband took their two sons when he deserted her. The two teenage daughters help Noi with the farming, but she must depend on her relatives to care for the toddler while she and the girls are working. She sometimes sells bamboo shoots from the forest and corn from her field in order to buy much-needed rice, hauling these products 26 kilometers round trip to and from the nearest market. Noi must do all the work necessary for family survival, including work usually done by a man, like repairing the house, clearing the field, and chopping trees for firewood. Although traditional Lao villages have never organized cooperatives, Noi is convinced that a village cooperative would help her. She can earn rice, she says, for the work that she can contribute, while male laborers can do the field clearing and plowing. In addition, she says, the cooperative child-care center can care for her child while she works.

Davone, the daughter of nationalist and communist activists, rarely lived with her parents but was educated in Thailand and Vietnam while her parents worked for national liberation and communist revolution in Laos. Completing medical school in Hanoi, she returned to Laos, first as a physician at the Party headquarters and then as the founding director of a nursing school located in a series of caves to protect students from American bombing. Raising her children in the capital city after the communist victory in 1975, she gradually worked her way up the governmental and Party hierarchy while balancing her work and political life with her domestic responsibilities.

How are the lives of these three Laotian women alike? Each is economically productive. Each is responsible for both productive work and housework. Each is supported and constrained by family and by culture. Each is markedly affected by major social change, especially political and economic change.

Dramatic changes are occurring throughout the developing world. Changes in economy, politics, family, and worldviews strike at the heart of the lives of women like Phing, Noi, and Davone, occasionally improving their lives, but more often impoverishing and subordinating them. Even in Southeast Asia where women have commonly enjoyed a variety of economic and social rights, explosive transformations are subverting their traditional prerogatives.

The dynamics of change in the present Lao People's Democratic Republic (Lao PDR) during the last several decades provide an excellent opportunity to illustrate current ideas about women and development and to explore changing sources of women's power and status. Laotian women have traditionally sustained the household and local economy with their work in field, forest, and family, but Laos has undergone a tremendous upheaval in this century, unleashing changes that have strongly affected these women. Before 1975, Laotians experienced colonization and two protracted wars. Victory of socialist revolutionary forces in 1975 enabled the Lao Communist party to consolidate all of Laos under a socialist government (1975–88). With *perestroika* and economic changes throughout the international socialist bloc, Laotian communists subsequently moved to liberalize the Lao economy, creating changes that accelerated with the dissolution of the USSR (1988–present).

Surprisingly, Laotian women are not yet being overwhelmed by these contemporary changes. Instead, many women are maintaining their traditional sources of power and autonomy, while some women have been able to take advantage of emerging economic and educational opportunities. However, women's work roles are being affected by these national and international changes, and recent national policy decisions may yet undermine women and their families. Because Laotian women's work is an important component of their power and autonomy, changes in women's work have broader implications for all aspects of women's lives. Rural women of different ethnic groups have different levels of power and autonomy traditionally, and have responded differently to these changes.

What has happened to rural Laotian women's traditional sources of control over their own activities and the activities of others since the 1975 revolution? Have women maintained power or autonomy in traditional arenas? Have these arenas expanded with new opportunities or changed social, political, and economic conditions? Or have these arenas contracted as opportunities and conditions changed, enabling other groups to encroach on rural women's traditional arenas of power and autonomy? Have these changes had different effects on rural women of different ethnic groups and varying economic means? These are the questions I address in this study.

Since economic power is a central determinant of women's power, I focus particularly on changes in women's work and women's control over resources. I deliberately concentrate on rural women of all socioeconomic levels because the population of the Lao PDR is about 85 percent rural and most of my own observations are from rural areas. Even many women residents in nominally urban areas still carry out a variety of rural tasks like food production and animal husbandry. Because only one-half of the population is Lao in ethnicity, I also include women of other major ethnic groups.

Several theories of women's subordination are especially relevant for understanding the situation of rural Lao women. The first, Blumberg's gender stratification theory (1978, 1991a, 1991b, 1995), focuses mainly on factors enabling women to exercise power in a society. The second, Sen and Grown's analysis (1987) of what has happened to poor women with development, concentrates primarily on women's subordination.[1] Both of these perspectives rely principally on economic explanations of women's power and subordination, while acknowledging the impact of politics and ideology on women's power. Both seem to define "power" operationally in the same way. Both consider issues relevant to analyzing the situation of rural Lao women, like women's economic power, the relationship between women's productive and reproductive activities, and the impact on women's lives of the broader political, economic, and sociocultural setting. A third approach, by Carolyn Moser (1987, 1993), emphasizes women's creative initiatives in the face of difficulties, noting that women's community managing to meet practical needs may occasionally enable to them to make more fundamental changes toward greater equality. Previous research on the effects on women's position of Third World socialist political systems and of Southeast Asian economic development and change provide background information for analyzing the changing situation of rural Laotian women.

Women's Power and Subordination

What does it mean to say that women in any society have power? Or to identify a particular woman as powerful? Most women (and most men) do not command armies, direct nations, head powerful corporations, or lead major religions. Yet many women, even in strongly patriarchal societies, are able to exercise some control over their lives and sometimes over the lives of others, though these arenas of control may change dramatically with development. How can we measure women's power in a society, in a village, or in a household? Also, what factors enable these women to exercise some measure of control and how are these factors affected by development? There are many possible indicators of social power, and a variety of economic, sociocultural, political, and other factors may affect women's power. This analysis requires a clear definition of the central concepts of gender stratification and power, and a discussion of the sources of women's power or powerlessness.

Defining and Measuring Power

Definitions of Power. Differential power between women and men is the essential ingredient of the gender stratification system of a society. Gender stratification refers to the system by which a society is divided into gendered and ranked categories, with the higher ranking category(ies) disproportionately gaining access to the society's valued resources. Since gender stratification systems almost universally favor men, some authors define gender stratification as the extent to which women are systematically disadvantaged in their access to the scarce values of their society relative to men in the society (Chafetz 1991, 76; Mies 1988; Stockard and Johnson 1992).

Alice Schlegel (1977, 3–4) identifies three main dimensions of stratification: rewards, prestige, and power. When access to any of these, however defined by the society, is characteristically restricted by gender, gender stratification exists. The status of women and men within the power dimension refers to their capability to govern themselves and their own activities, and to control the persons and activities of others. Where neither sex controls the other, gender equality exists. Sexual inequality or equality in the power dimension, the critical dimension according to Schlegel, is a composite of power, authority, and autonomy operating throughout society. Power, she notes, is the ability to exert control in domestic, political, economic, or religious arenas; authority is socially legitimated power; and autonomy is the freedom from control by others (Schlegel 1977, 8–9).

In this analysis, *gender stratification* refers to the systematic way in which one gender category receives disproportionate access to the society's valued resources. Differential power between women and men is integral to a gender stratification system, and disproportionate control over valued resources by the favored gender category is an aspect of this system. *Power*, as used in this analysis, refers to the ability to exert control over self, others, and/or valued resources in economic, political, religious, domestic, or other social arenas. Other social criteria, like ethnicity, social class, and religion, combine with gender to shape the overall stratification system of a society.

Blumberg (1978, 1991b, 1995) defines women's relative status in their society's stratification system as women's control over their life options, but believes that female economic power relative to men is the most important single variable that affects overall gender stratification and has, therefore, the most profound effects on women's life options. Sen and Grown (1987, Ch. 1), for DAWN (Development Alternatives for Women for a New Era), focus on economic control and access to economic and political power, noting that with colonization, as well as with later "development," women often lost control over land, labor, and the productive process, all critical economic and social resources. Like Blumberg and Sen and Grown, this author identifies women's power in the *economic* arena as central to gender stratification systems.

Depending on the society, similarity or complementarity may be the basis for women's power. Some researchers assert that equality occurs only when women and men are equally represented, equally active, and equally rewarded for their performance in all major spheres of activity. In other words, women and men can have equal power only when they are similar (Dixon 1976; Lamphere 1977). Schlegel (1977, 8), on the other hand, notes that gender equality can occur in societies "where males and females have equal control in all spheres, or where spheres of control are different but balanced." Sacks (1979) adds that many U.S. feminists think that equality is possible only with androgyny. But equality may take other forms in nonstate societies in which women and men have separate spheres of activity and decision making that they consider of equal importance (Leacock 1978, 252). Their activities and roles are complementary and neither dominates the other. Ong (1989) maintains that gender relations in Southeast Asia are characterized by complementarity, coupled with an emphasis on rank, rather than gender, as the basis of authority. This has formed the basis for women's relatively high status in that region.

Measures of Women's Power and Autonomy. There is no single measure of "women's power" in any one society. The most common approach is to use a battery of indicators that include information about several aspects of women's lives. Unfortunately, existing data are often biased or incomplete. For example, women and children are disproportionately undercounted in farm work. Rural time-use studies of all household members show a much higher rate of participation for women and children than census data indicate (Boserup 1970, 29; Dixon 1982). Commonly available aggregate statistics distort women's productive activities. Husbands or fathers, for example, may be listed as having an occupation (e.g., farmer, fisher), while wives, who may also farm, fish, or process and sell fish, may automatically be labelled a "housewife" (Boulding 1983). More recent United Nations statistics disaggregate male and female statistical information, but problems of bias and distortion remain.

Researchers often measure women's power by a combination of several indicators of women's control over (or at least access to) economic, political, educational, legal, and other social resources (Charlton 1984; Giele and Smock 1977; Sivard 1985; United Nations 1991, 1995). Because women's power in one area may not be the same as power in another area, it seems important to specify what type of "power" one is measuring. Blumberg (1988, 54–55), who sees economic power relative to men as the most important determinant of life options, operationalizes power as control over economic resources like income/capital, property, and other means of production. Control over resources that create a surplus is more important for female economic power than control over subsistence-creating resources.

Why Is Women's Power Important? Both Blumberg and Sen and Grown argue that women's income and their related influence over household spending and other decision making directly affect the well-being of household members, especially children. Blumberg (1991b) demonstrates that women's net economic power affects their level of influence in household decisions, the nutritional status of their children, and their ability to control their own fertility. Women with independent sources of income are more likely than women with no such income to influence major household decisions (Acharya 1983 in Blumberg 1988, 66–67; Weller 1968; Benería and Roldan 1987; Roldan 1988) and decisions about their children's education (Hanger and Moris 1973; Blumberg 1988). Furthermore, income-earning women are likely to contribute a significantly higher proportion of their income to family needs than are their husbands, with men contributing 75 percent or less of their income, while women contribute 90–100 percent (Mencher 1988, 100; Blumberg 1988, 56–58; Roldan 1988).[2] Mother's rather than father's production or income is more closely related to the nutritional status of their children as demonstrated by village-based studies in India, Ghana, and Belize (Kumar 1978; Tripp 1981; Stavrakis and Marshall 1978 discussed in Blumberg 1991b, 105–7). Economically active women are also likely to exercise some control over their own bodies. For example, employed women contributing substantially to household income were more likely than other women to control the decisions to have a child or to use contraception and were more likely to have few children (Roldan 1988; Blumberg 1988, 65–66).

Sen and Grown (1987) discuss how family well-being was negatively impacted by colonial changes that deprived women of some of their traditional sources of power resulting in poorer living conditions for entire households. Colonial changes often deprived women of use rights to agricultural and uncultivated land while new cultivation techniques increased women's labor without giving them control over the products of this labor and without reducing the drudgery necessary to maintain the household. Technology, training, and credit for cash crop production were available almost exclusively to men to increase their production. Woman-produced goods for sale (like processed foods and beverages or clothing) were undercut on the local market by manufactured foods and other goods, forcing many women's micro-enter-prises out of business. While decreasing women's access to resources, these changes made it more difficult for rural women to meet the basic needs of their families by depriving them of land for subsistence cropping and access to uncultivated land for gathering of food, firewood, items for sale, or medicinal herbs (Sen and Grown 1987, 31, 34–35). Decreasing women's access to resources clearly affects the well-being of household members. Furthermore, colonial changes institutionalized with independence often reinforce women's lack of access to resources and aggravate food crises and the related crises in fuel and water (Sen and Grown 1987, 50–59; Blumberg 1991a, 119–20).

Elements of Women's Power

Women's power arises from a variety of sources. Both women's power and the sources of power may change over time. This analysis focuses on rural Laotian women's economic power and how it has changed through three time periods, beginning in the "traditional" period (before 1975), continuing through the "socialist" period (1975–88), and moving into the current period of economic "liberalization" (1988–present). My central theoretical ideas are drawn from Blumberg, Sen and Grown, and Moser though modified in light of related studies and my own research and development experience. Women may derive power, authority, or autonomy from economic, political, edu-cational, religious, or cultural sources. Autonomy and authority are both aspects of power as previously noted. Domestic organization and reproduction seem to restrict women's power, though some aspects of family organization may reinforce it. Development has affected many sources of women's power. These changes are often negative as Western- and Japanese-funded development assistance programs commonly create or reinforce local ideologies of male dominance and female domesticity (for examples, see Rogers 1980; Tinker and Bramsen 1976; Charlton 1984; Mies 1988).

Elements of Women's Economic Power. Women's economic power, the key to women's power in general, is composed of several elements. Before women can generate their own economic power, they must produce. The gendered division of labor and the technology available to women in their work were early identified as central to female power (Boserup 1970). Women's productive activity alone may generate power if their economic contribution, relative to men, is high and if their labor is perceived of as indispensable or nearly so. However, if a woman's economic contribution is relatively high and if her labor is nearly indispensable, she may also control economic resources, a second aspect of economic power. Control over economic resources involves control over one or more factors of production (land, labor, water, capital) and, especially effective for the generation of economic power, control over the distribution of income, goods, or services beyond those needed for basic subsistence. Economic control is the result of the relative contribution and indispensability of women's labor, and traditional kinship patterns (inheritance, residence, and descent) enabling women to control property (Blumberg 1978, 27–28).

A number of analysts agree with Blumberg and Sen and Grown that control of key economic resources is the basis for women's economic power, not productive work alone or ownership without control. Leacock (1978, 252), for example, states that women make important economic contributions in all societies, but "their status depends on how this contribution is structured. The issue is whether they control the conditions of their work and the dispensation of the goods they produce." Similarly, Mies (1988) notes that women's exploitation under capitalism is based on women's *lack* of control over themselves, others, and other productive assets. Women can be economically productive, however, only if their domestic and reproductive responsibilities are not too heavy or time-consuming.

Relationship Between Production and Reproduction. Women's reproductive responsibilities are central to female subordination.[3] These responsibilities include biological reproduction and maintenance of the household (housework, cooking, washing, child-rearing, health care). The rubric of "reproduction" sometimes also encompasses the maintenance of traditional social systems including maintaining traditional family patterns by setting an example, by socializing children into traditional patterns, and by following traditional inheritance patterns.[4] Some social changes damage women's reproductive capabilities and erode their traditional bases of power in the family.

Housework, cooking, washing, child-rearing, and the care of sick family members take a great deal of a woman's time. In less developed societies, cooking includes obtaining fuel and preparing the food for cooking, as well as actually cooking the meals. Washing includes hauling the wash water, often from some distance. In some societies, women care for sick family members without the assistance of adequate health services. In spite of sometimes demanding and extensive reproductive work, many Third World women are economically active, though their economic activity is often shaped by their domestic responsibilities.

Women are most likely to participate in economic activities that are compatible with child care, especially if there is a demand for their labor (Blumberg 1978, 25–27). In many societies, babies are not weaned until eighteen to twenty-four months of age. In societies like Laos, where birth control is practiced by few, women often become pregnant shortly after weaning their youngest child. So, women must be available to their babies several times a day for most of their prime labor and child-bearing years. Foraging, horticulture, small animal husbandry, cottage industries, and local trading are all activities that enable women to combine work and breast-feeding. Hunting, herding, long-distance trading, and, to a lesser extent, plow agriculture are not as compatible with child care and breast-feeding. Even if an economic activity is incompatible with child care, however, some women may do it if male labor is insufficient as in war or male out-migration (Blumberg 1978, 26–27).

Benería and Sen (1986) assert that one must examine production, repro-duction, and the relationship between the two in order to understand the nature of gender discrimination. Women's continuing responsibilities for family maintenance limit their economic contributions while the separation of economic production from other household activities renders domestic work invisible. Ideology may reinforce these restrictions. Sen and Grown (1987) place this discussion in a broader context. They assert that colonization and subsequent "developmental" change marginalized basic survival needs like food, health, housing, and other requirements for a decent life. Women, as the main providers of these needs, were similarly pushed to the economic periphery where they lost status and access to resources. The current linked crises of food, fuel, and water are the result. Women's universal association with the domestic sphere is inadequate as an explanation for the worsening situation of many Third World women.[5] Rather, the cause is the development of production structures that sharply separate production of basic domestic needs from commercial production.

Women's Other Activities and Power

A woman's level of economic power is affected by her other activities and sources of power. In particular, a heavy domestic workload with little assistance by household males diminishes a woman's economic power by cut-ting into time and energy needed for productive activities and by increasing the possibility that the overworked wife will withdraw older daughters from school to help her. A woman's other activities (educational, political) may enhance her overall power if these activities involve control of self, others, or valued resources.

Women's Educational Activities. Blumberg (1991b, 135–36) hypothesizes that women's domestic "drudgework" saps the time and energy of both women and girls, interfering with women's economic activities and girls' education. Relief from some household maintenance activities, either through help from male household members or improved technology, enables women and girls to engage in more economically productive activities and to continue their education.

Illiteracy hopelessly marginalizes women in a changing world where tra-ditional knowledge is losing its usefulness. Rural women's knowledge of how to generate subsistence and surplus is rendered obsolete as farming-for-profit replaces farming-for-subsistence, as forest logging destroys the resource base for gathering and hunting, as factory-made goods displace locally made goods in many markets, and as urban migration renders nearly all rural survival knowledge useless. Access to modern public education is of vital importance to women's empowerment in this changing world.

More girls *are* entering school in most Third World countries. Most governments have removed formal barriers to girls' school entry, while laws requiring compulsory school attendance are widespread. Girls' school enrollment worldwide quadrupled between 1950 and 1985, outpacing the large increase in school-age population (Sivard 1985, 18). Sivard suggests that these increases foreshadow a major change in women's ability to wrest opportunity from obsolescence. Young women's illiteracy rates are dropping but are still much higher than those of young men. The percentage of illiterate women aged twenty to twenty-four in East and Southeast Asia has declined from 38 to 13 percent between 1970 and 1990 (United Nations 1991, 46). However, lack of schooling in rural areas maintains high rural illiteracy rates. Nearly one-fourth of all women (ages fifteen and above) in East and Southeast Asia and Oceania were illiterate in 1995 (United Nations 1995, 90) and nearly one-half of women over age twenty-five in East and Southeast Asia were illiterate in 1990 (United Nations 1991, 46). Some non-governmental and women's organizations sponsor programs for women that integrate education for women's reproductive *and* productive activities, which are committed to improving women's conditions. These programs are small and relatively few but provide models for the educational empowerment of women (Stromquist 1989, 103).

Women's Political Activities. The political arena is the nearly exclusive preserve of men worldwide. For example, "women's representation in the highest councils of government rarely exceeds 10 percent" (Population Crisis Committee 1988, 8-9). In 1987 only 3.3 percent of the world's cabinet ministers were women, though by 1994 the figure had risen to 5.7 percent (United Nations 1991; 1995, 151). In African precolonial societies, women sometimes held public office and wielded direct and considerable political power (Hoffer 1974). In some traditional societies, women governed as chiefs, advised as king's councilors, or directed community women's affairs equally with the male director (Moore 1988, 133). In a few of these groups, women still retain some political power, but colonialism and the rise of the modern state have generally deprived women of these sources of power.[6] Reports of women's exclusion from politics are common in the ethnographic literature,[7] as well as in national statistics. Women, though, often exert political influence indirectly through family and kin-related activities (see, for example, Bacdayan 1977, 276-79; Collins 1974, 94-95). Sen and Grown (1987, Ch. 3), reviewing a variety of successful grassroots women's organizations, recommend that women empower themselves by organizing around important economic, political, legal, and cultural issues. Moser (1987, 1993) documents the effects of such empowerment.

In summary, women's economic power and activities affect and are affected by their domestic power and activities. Women's other activities and sources of power (educational, political) may also be influenced by their economic power and activities. Although women are generally less educated and much less politically active than men, certain categories of women may benefit from their activities in these arenas.

Micro-level Activities and Macro-level Policies and Structures

Changes impacting women's lives are often large-scale or macro-level changes. During European and North American industrialization macro-level changes, as demonstrated by Huber (1991, 17–19), affected individuals in several major ways: infant mortality and fertility declined, mass education expanded, economies grew, and safe artificial feeding methods reduced women's extensive reproductive responsibilities. Women in these industrializing economies then responded to increased demands for women workers by entering the labor force in record numbers. These major social changes called forth changes in values, aspirations, and expectations for marital behavior.

Blumberg (1991b, 123) postulates that macro-level impacts on women's daily exercise of economic power can be considerable. Women's micro-level economic power, she posits, is diminished by "economic, political, legal, religious, and ideological policies" and practices that disadvantage women. A strong male-dominated state, perhaps in concert with a well-organized male-dominated religious structure, is likely to diminish the value of whatever economic power women may develop in their own lives by enforcing policies and practices that limit women's options.

A national economy, its links to the global economy, and the economy of local regions affect women's economic power by providing the arena in which such power is shaped and exercised. Important elements of the local economy include the organization of household production, the availability to women of local resources for their production (e.g., forest products, farmland, credit), local cooperatives, and local markets for their products.

Food, Fuel, and Water. Blumberg (1991b, 131–33) uses the African food crisis to illustrate how macro-level structures and policies have negatively affected local economies and the food production decisions of individual African farmers. In much of sub-Saharan Africa, women are the primary food producers. Husbands and wives in most sub-Saharan groups maintain separate "purses" and women have obligations to provide for their needs and those of their children, in addition to maintaining obligatory exchanges with their own extended kin. Technical agricultural resources like training and credit are extended mainly to male "household heads," and cooperative schemes often direct the returns from women's agricultural labor to those same "household heads" who are registered cooperative members. National policies and local structures unresponsive to the interests of women farmers have precipitated production declines and, sometimes, outright sabotage by angry women farmers.[8]

The macro-level development patterns that Sen and Grown criticize have produced crises in both the global economic system (the macro-level) and the ability of many people to meet their survival needs (the micro-level). Sen and Grown go beyond Blumberg's analysis of the African food crisis by linking Third World crises in food, fuel, and water. On the macro-level, overemphasis on aggregate food production based on comparative cost advantage, while funneling assistance to export crop production and the most promising commercial food producers, has been coupled with near disregard for individual producers and the staple crops of poorer groups like pulses or millet. Commercial logging and poor agricultural practices sometimes result in deforestation. Deforestation, coupled with the privatization of uncultivated land, creates a shortage of fuel. Deforestation may also affect water availability by its effect on seasonal runoff and aquifer levels. Water is essential for household use and agricultural production, yet national governments and international organizations do not link water, logging, and agricultural policies or programs (Sen and Grown 1987, 50–59).[9]

Many ordinary people throughout the Third World are drastically affected by the food, fuel, and water crises analyzed by Blumberg and by Sen and Grown. It is, for the most part, poor women who must deal with the worst effects of these crises. Many women must travel farther for fuel and water and spend more time growing subsistence crops on fields with declining fertility.[10] These women must decide which basic needs are met and who in the family will most benefit from these scarce resources. Often women's work hours lengthen, they change to less nutritious but less labor- and fuel-intensive foods, and they allocate less food to themselves and, perhaps, to their daughters. With less food, a heavier workload, and fewer public services, it is no wonder that women's nutritional and health status declines (Sen and Grown 1987, 50–59).

Political Impacts on Women's Power. The United Nations Decade for Women (1975–85), with its emphasis on women's productive work and the integration of women into economic development, saw women's situation deteriorate in many countries (Sen and Grown 1987, 16; see Sivard 1985 for a more hopeful interpretation). Some development workers and Third World women now recognize the importance of women's self-reliance and political empowerment (Moser 1993; Charlton 1984). Tinker (1990, 53), in describing the international networks of Third World women that have developed as a result of United Nations Decade for Women conferences, notes that there is widespread agreement among these women that "only through connecting women's views of human priorities to national and global issues can women gain access to meaningful resources."

Women utilizing this "empowerment" approach to development seek to organize women around their practical needs to increase their own capabilities and self-reliance. Since many of these practical needs are the result of women's subordinate position, and since these groups sometimes work together to bring these practical needs into national politics where women's interests are otherwise poorly represented, this approach can challenge the gender stratification system itself (Sen and Grown 1987; Moser 1993).

In sum, Sen and Grown, Blumberg, Moser, and others have delineated the links between women's own productive and reproductive activities, and the macro-level economic and political structures, policies, and programs that shape these activities. Further, Blumberg and Sen and Grown have specified how a decline in women's economic power and concomitant negative impact on women's domestic activities (caused by changing economic policies and structures and by political decisions) may be at least partly responsible for the African food crisis or, more broadly, for the linked crises of food, fuel, and water.

Culture and Society

Cultural Gender Role Patterns. Cultural gender role patterns, including both division of labor by gender and gender images and ideologies, shape women's experiences and their perceptions of those experiences. Sanday (1981, 86; 1990) identifies three types of cultural sex role patterns. One pattern emphasizes competition and maleness, another cooperation and femaleness, and a third "joins the male and female in a relationship of complementarity and duality in symbolism and behavior." There may be more than one set of gender role patterns in a culture. Ideas about women may vary by life cycle stage or may be contested, with men and women holding differing ideas or with groups of men and women disagreeing about gender images (for examples, see Miegs 1990 and Lederman 1990).

Enculturation into prevailing gender role patterns creates particular expectations for female and male behavior. For example, an expectation may be shared by husbands and wives that men should be the family providers. This shared expectation may enhance his power in the household if he is an adequate provider or enhance her relative power if she must also be a provider

(Blumberg 1991b, 23). Women's socialization to accept male exercise of power in their families may impede women's exercise of their potential economic power. On the other hand, husbands' *felt* economic dependence on wives' economic contributions may increase wives' ability to exercise power in their families (Blumberg 1991b, 23–24). So, cultural gender patterns and socialization into these patterns may affect women's exercise of power and their experiences of male dominance.

Religion. Most religious systems deny women full spiritual equality and circumscribe their religious activities (Smock 1977, 386–91). Religious traditions, even when no longer central to people's everyday lives in secular societies, may still provide the values and ideology that deny women full equality (Smock 1977). Fundamentalist religious ideologies, often used to justify macro-level policies, structures, or programs, can also affect women's everyday experiences; for example, women going to work alone or attempting to enter a clinic for a safe abortion may become targets for violence. Women's exercise of power and autonomy in their daily lives may clearly be influenced by religious considerations. For example, Muslim and non-Muslim Hausa women from the same Nigerian village carry out different economic activities. Muslim women produce crafts while non-Muslim women in the village engage in agricultural production. The Muslim women do not control the income from their crafts, while the non-Muslim women are more likely to market their own products and control the resulting income (Barkow 1972; Longhurst 1982).

However, progressive religious movements may actually empower women. In the Spanish-speaking Caribbean, much of the grassroots organizing for social justice, including demands for gender equality, grows from religious groups inspired by liberation theology within the Catholic Church (Deere et al. 1990, 104–5). The Caribbean Conference of Churches links Protestant and Catholic, Spanish- and English-speaking activists in regional development, peace work, and political empowerment. The work of these progressive activists, however, is often hampered by conservatives within the Catholic Church and Protestant bodies.

Religion alone is often not sufficient explanation for women's subordination or empowerment. Whyte and Whyte (1982, 28) note that the great religious traditions do not necessarily dictate women's power, since these religions have merged with older local traditions and belief systems. They contrast two stereotypic Islamic women—one of Indonesia and one of Bangladesh. The Kelantanese (Indonesia) market woman, "overseeing her stall, telling her husband (if he is visible at all) what to do, driving a shrewd bargain while cracking jokes with all comers with complete self-possession" differs remarkably from the stereotypic Bangladeshi woman "who retires from view the moment a stranger appears at the entry to her compound, never goes to market and is reluctant to express an opinion." Yet both are Muslim. Religious traditions, like cultural gender patterns, provide part of the cultural context that influences both policy makers and ordinary women.

Kinship Organization. Kin groups or the household may provide some women with the base or the resources they need to improve their lives, though in some societies such groups may oppress rather than support women. Headship of a kin-based unit, descent and residence patterns enabling women to inherit and to live near their own relatives, and full membership in a corporate kin group make it possible for women to exercise control over themselves, others, or valued resources.

For example, through trade, contracting, producing valued commodities, or owning a shop or income property a Yoruba woman of Lagos may make enough money to become independent of her husband, attract dependents to her, and establish her own household. A house owner, whether male or female, is the senior authority figure in the domestic context (Barnes 1990, 268–73).

Residing after marriage near a woman's kinfolk is likely to enhance her economic power, both because of possible shared economic activities and because of support for exercise of her actual economic power in relation to her husband and his kin. Women who live matrilocally may also be more likely to inherit land or other wealth that directly contributes to their economic power. Nearby kinfolk may also assist with child care and other domestic tasks (Lepowsky 1990; Potter 1977). In pre-class societies Sacks (1979) found gender equality when women were members, with their brothers, of corporate kin groups that owned their own means of production. In societies stressing wives' relationships with their husbands, however, gender subordination was common.

Thus the nature of a society's kinship system and its relation to production may determine whether the domestic arena traditionally provided a source of power for as least some women. Kin-based networks may still provide resources important to rural women's power. With male migration to cities, children's school attendance, and other dramatic changes in traditional families and household production patterns, however, a woman without her traditional helpers must often struggle to provide domestic needs (Sen and Grown 1987).

In sum, cultural patterns like gender role patterns and expectations, religion, and kinship organization may affect women's power. Cultural gender role patterns articulate culturally accepted relations between the sexes. Religious practices, organizations, and laws may limit or enhance women's level of economic and other power. Both religious and cultural ideas and norms may contribute to the prevailing gender role ideology, which also affects women's everyday activities. Aspects of kinship systems, particularly ownership, residence, inheritance, and corporate kin patterns, may empower women by providing them with resources, allies, and economic arenas for action and support them by assisting with domestic responsibilities.

Women and Development

Gendered relations of power and subordination change in response to changes in production, reproduction, education, politics and policies, and culture. Recent historical changes integrating the economies of post-colonial Third World states with the global economy, often called "development," frequently exacerbate women's subordinate position. Ester Boserup (1970) first identified the negative effects of development on women. Women are hurt, she said, because development deprives women of some of their economically productive functions without enabling them to develop new and valued activities.

Other reports confirm this finding: that some of women's economic activities are displaced or fall under male control with the advent of more "modern" technologies, techniques, or factory-produced goods, usually owned, practiced, or produced by men. Moreover, women often lose their rights to land as traditional ownership and use rights are superseded by formal land titles or cooperative landownership granted to male "household heads" (Sen and Grown 1987). For example, the hand-crafted textiles traditionally woven and stitched by the women of one Guatemalan locality have been displaced by cheaper garments as women are forced into casual wage labor or unpaid labor in their husbands' enterprises (Ehlers 1990).

Modern high-yielding rice varieties, compared to traditional varieties, require more female labor overall, including labor in the nearly invisible and unpaid tasks of collecting and applying manure, transplanting, weeding, and harvesting (Ghosh and Mukhopadhyay 1988). These new varieties have no similar requirement for male labor in increased clearing, plowing, or planting. To contribute this additional labor, women must withdraw from other productive activities that they *do* control. As a result, their control over the production process and the products of their labor is eroded.

Agrarian reform has often similarly disenfranchised women peasants and wage laborers. In a comparison of agrarian reform in Peru, Chile, and Cuba, Deere (1988) found that nearly all landless Peruvian and Chilean women peasants and agricultural wage laborers were excluded from the benefits of agrarian reform since only "household heads" had access to land and were entitled to membership in production, credit, or service cooperatives that constituted the reformed sector. Cuban land reform, however, did a much better job of involving women as beneficiaries.

Economic opportunities for some groups of women do arise with "development." These opportunities most commonly include domestic work, prostitution, petty trade, and factory work, though women from higher social classes sometimes enter professional careers. For most women the opportunities entail migration to urban areas where they eke out marginal livelihoods in the "informal" economy, or in factory work. For example, in Lima, Peru, "sellers and servants" account for nearly one-half of all economically active women, and nearly all of these women were born outside Lima (Bunster and Chaney 1985, 5). Most Bangkok masseuses interviewed in another study were migrants from the poorest areas of Thailand (Phongpaichit 1982). While some young women migrate to urban areas to work in garment or electronics factories, others are employed by factories near their family homes (Lim 1982; Ong 1987; Fuentes and Ehrenreich 1983; Fernández-Kelly 1982; Wolf 1992).

In short, "development" seems to strike at the heart of women's power, undermining women's economic power (Boserup), redefining customary law and political relationships to women's detriment (Sen and Grown example), and altering economic systems so women have less control over their own labor and production (examples from Ehlers, Ghosh and Mukhopadhyay, and land reform and informal sector examples). These examples illustrate some of the variables and relationships already discussed.

Before proposing these relationships as the theoretical framework of this study of changes in rural Laotian women's work and power, I discuss the applicability of these relationships in Third World socialist settings, and I consider the situation of women in other parts of Southeast Asia.

Third World Women's Experiences
with Socialist Development

Socialist development has several common effects on Third World women. Examples from Third World socialist countries in Africa, Latin America, and Asia illustrate these common patterns. Declaration of or legal enactment of gender equality often occurs during the initial enthusiasm of establishing a socialist regime, as part of the transformation of past oppressive social relations and mobilization of the population to build a new society. Socialist societies also tend to draw women into economic production outside the home. Socialist governments are less effective in recruiting women to economic or political leadership positions, however. Such governments usually acknowledge the importance of women's dual roles in production and reproduction. Some have collectivized some aspects of women's domestic work in order to free women for greater public participation, and most at least promise to do so at some future time. In the meantime, they exhort husbands to "help" their wives with domestic work. These governments usually establish an official women's organization to mobilize and advocate for women.

In all socialist societies, gender equality is official policy and may be codified into law. In the southern African nations of Zimbabwe, Angola, and

Mozambique, for example, the ruling socialist parties all adopted gender policies like those of Eastern Europe and the former Soviet Union. Mozambique, more than any other African nation, is committed to gender equality and has created policies (gender equality), structures (a national women's organization with actual decision-making access within the party), and projects (cooperatives, irrigated agricultural projects) that aim to create gender equality (Davison 1988). In Zimbabwe and Guinea-Bissau, similar policies emphasize women's legal equality with men and women's importance as producers, but these governments are not creating structures and projects to ensure gender equality with predictable lack of change in actual gender inequality (Jacobs and Howard 1987; Funk 1988). One outcome of this official ideology that has benefited women is educational: school is extended to girls as well as boys, and women are included in the literacy campaigns mounted by most Third World societies in transition to socialism. Women have benefited more than men from these educational initiatives since women are much less likely than men to be literate. These educational benefits have accrued to women in China, Cuba, Laos, Nicaragua, Tanzania, and Vietnam (Croll 1986; Pelzer-White 1987; Chinchilla 1990; Curtin 1975).

Involvement of women in formal economic production is a central tenet of all Marxist regimes and characterizes other socialist governments as well. This is not so difficult among groups whose women traditionally are economic producers, as in sub-Saharan Africa and Southeast Asia. However, in China and Cuba, for example, it required considerable organization (Croll 1986; Curtin 1975). The peak of women's entry into the agricultural labor force in China coincided with the peak of collectivization. With collectivization, women, as members of a collective, received their own work points and were often supported by one or more social services like child care, health care, collective dining facilities, or other domestic labor-saving services (Croll 1986, 230-33). In Cuba, however, women's involvement in nonhousehold production continues to be low due to a strong traditional ideology about the "natural" division of labor and women's continuing domestic labor burden (Croll 1986, 234-38). As an old order changes, sometimes rapidly under the pressure of war or socialist revolution, opportunities for women often arise. During the wars in Vietnam, for example, schoolteachers became new authority figures responsible for conveying socialist ideals and behaviors to children and, through them, to parents. Many schoolteachers were women. The authority role of teacher was new for Vietnamese women (Pelzer-White 1987, 228, 230-31).

The record of socialist regimes in recruiting and promoting women leaders and decision makers appears to be no better than in other regimes, partly because of strongly entrenched male resistance and partly because women are still responsible for nearly all remaining domestic tasks, in addition to being full-time workers outside the home. Most political and management roles require additional training, travel, and meetings at lunch or during the evening when women's domestic responsibilities are most compelling. Only during war and then generally in the civilian economy are women encouraged to take leadership roles. This theme runs throughout all analyses of women's status in socialist countries (e.g., Croll 1986; Kruks, Rapp, and Young 1989; Charlton 1984, 186–88). Even in a country strongly committed to restructuring gender relations like Mozambique, women have gained more access to productive land but do not control agricultural technology and are much less likely than men to govern cooperatives or direct irrigation schemes (Davison 1988).

Even though most socialist governments pledge to socialize at least some components of women's domestic workload, few make the commitment of resources necessary to do this effectively. As noted earlier, this results in women's "double burden" and women's unwillingness or inability to undertake additional commitments to Party or state, or sometimes even to their own training. Of all Third World socialist governments, perhaps China made the most thoroughgoing effort to socialize domestic work during the Great Leap Forward in the late 1950s. Most of the newly established rural communes provided a range of services to free women's time for economic production. These services often included child-care facilities, dining rooms, laundries, grain-processing mills, and sewing rooms. Croll reports the example of one collective that calculated it had replaced the cooking labor of 105 people in as many households with just 8 people who prepared meals for all member households, thus saving more than 6,000 labor hours per year.[11] Yet many of these services ceased operation as suddenly as they had begun. The 8 cooks were paid, while the 105 private cooks had labored without cost to the collective (Croll 1986, 233).

Vietnam, China, and Cuba have all attempted to persuade and encourage male domestic labor. The Family Code of Cuba (1975) actually requires husbands to share child-care and household tasks equally with their wives when wives study or work outside the home (King 1979). China and Vietnam stop short of requiring 50 percent male responsibility for domestic tasks; instead, men are encouraged to "help" their wives (Croll 1986; Pelzer-White 1987). In the African cases reported, governments may rhetorically acknowledge the need for domestic support services, while providing no resources or incentives to local collective bodies for such services. Persisting attitudes of male superiority vitiate attempts to change the division of household labor (Croll 1986, 233, 243; Pelzer-White 1987, 226–33).

Nearly all Third World socialist countries establish a mass women's organization. This organization is almost always founded by the party or government to serve its purposes, which usually include mobilizing women's labor and support for the postrevolution (or postwar) reconstruction and development under Party or government direction. Secondarily, and often less effectively, the women's organization is to "advocate" for female emancipation.[12] Croll (1986, 250) notes the impressive and active role of women's organizations in Cuba and China in "explaining and implementing government policies to women's benefit." However, at least one Chinese feminist bemoans the "burial" of activist feminists in these politically powerless women's organizations (Wu Qing, personal communication, 1994).

Women's organizations, however, can be a conduit for issues, ideas, and problems from their grassroots in villages and neighborhoods to the national level where they might affect policy. At a national congress of the Federation of Cuban Women, nearly two thousand delegates from all parts of Cuba brought examples, suggestions for change, and criticisms from their own local women's groups and intensely examined, debated, and modified policy recommendations formulated by federation leadership, presenting their conclusions at plenary sessions before the entire congress and a listening and note-taking Fidel Castro (Randall 1979). In spite of Castro's attentiveness, women's secondary position in Cuba has changed slowly.

In short, while the gap between legal or declared gender equality and actual equality is often great, Third World women benefit when socialist development policies specifically address gender as an issue. Insofar as women are drawn into the labor force but their domestic workload is not relieved, female labor is being used to subsidize national economic development though women may also be viewed with more respect. A woman's power in the household may also increase because of her outside salary, and her social power may increase if "her" women's organization is able to actively advocate for women both locally and nationally. It is clear, though, that the proportion of women in leadership positions does not improve significantly with socialist development. The extent to which rural households must continue to produce their own subsistence, as well as participate in additional economic production, limits the time and extent of rural women's increased involvements outside the household, though socialist development often gives these women a basis for producing and earning in their own right.

This evaluation of the effects of Third World socialist development on women confirms the usefulness of the theoretical model of gender stratification and development presented throughout this chapter. Economic, political, and domestic arenas of power relations are central to the socialist approach to women's position, while culture and education are important in attempts to mobilize women. The relationship between production and reproduction provides an acknowledged dilemma for every socialist regime, while socialist governments often explicitly use macro-level policies, activities, and structures to influence women's activities. In Laos, socialist changes liberated rural women to work harder in agricultural and textile production and community activities while enhancing women's power in some ways and limiting women's power in others.

Women in Southeast Asia

Rural women in Laos are part of a larger cultural area containing numerous ethnic groups making their livelihood under a variety of cultural, economic, political, and geographical conditions. Yet some similarities between the situations of rural Laotian women and women in other parts of Southeast Asia may provide a useful context for analysis of the Lao case.

Unlike their counterparts in many other societies, women's social position is relatively high in much of Southeast Asia. Most Southeast Asian women are not secluded, treated with contempt or chivalry, or excluded from the agricultural or commercial economy. Women's relatively high status is based on social structural patterns commonly found in the region, such as the cultural valuation of gender complementarity, bilateral or matrifocal family organization, relatively weak state control, and the major contribution of women to family subsistence, surplus production, and the marketing of surplus and other goods (Ebihara 1974; Ebihara, Mortland, and Ledgerwood 1994; Geertz 1961; Potter 1977; Tanner 1974; Whyte and Whyte 1982; Winzeler 1982).

Both the cultural valuation of gender complementarity, rather than gender opposition, and cultural emphases basing authority on rank, rather than on sex, support and maintain women's relatively high social and economic position. Unity and complementarity is an underlying theme in many local Southeast Asian worldviews (Ong 1989; Errington 1991). Many Southeast Asians experience female and male arenas and activities as complementary, each a necessary and valued part of the larger whole, although male activities may be valued more highly than female activities. Ilongot and Wana women of New Guinea, for example, maintain the family domestic and agricultural homestead while men venture farther afield. Both women and men contribute to the household and community (Rosaldo 1980; Atkinson 1991). In spite of gender complementarity, however, "muted gender distinctions are inveigled into a prestige structure that values male activities" away from the homestead more than female activities on the homestead (Ong 1989, 297; Atkinson 1991; Ortner and Whitehead 1981). Male authority in these two cases derives from having access to distant realms (through Wana head-hunting among other tribes) or moral power (through Ilongot religious, legal, and political leadership).

Commonly occurring patterns of bilateral and especially matrifocal family organization often lead to residence clusters of kinswomen. Productive and reproductive work often occurs together in these clusters, so that the kin-based household economy is the entire local economy. This increases the power of these women in their individual lives and in their communities. Potter (1977), for example, demonstrates the influence of a married daughter, resident in her natal compound. The daughter is the communication channel between her husband and her father, who must avoid direct contact. Khmer women, in happier pre-Pol Pot times, combined work in fields, on their looms, and in commerce with domestic responsibilities toward their immediate and extended families. Kin neighbors exchanged labor, strengthening kin bonds while supporting household economies. Similarly, small home-based shops combined commerce and child care (Ebihara 1974). Relatively weak state control leaves power and authority over everyday life in the hands of the household and community, an area where many women exercise regular control (Winzeler 1982). Winzeler's analysis is supported by Blumberg's work (1988, 1991a) demonstrating how macro-level impacts on women's lives may "discount" her local and familial sources of power and prestige.

Women in many Southeast Asian groups are active contributors to family subsistence and cash crop production. Moreover, they often market their own surplus or engage in extensive commercial activities, keeping their profits for family expenditures or their own use. Blumberg and others indicate that surplus production and control over its distribution/disposal are central components of female power wherever it occurs (as previously discussed). Although these patterns tend to support both objective measures and subjective experience of female power in many Southeast Asian societies, the ideology of male superiority is evident in prevailing Buddhist and Islamic views of women and may limit women's power and authority (Keyes 1984; Khin Thitsa 1980; Kirsch 1985; Ong 1987, 1989; Van Esterik 1982; Kabilsingh 1991).

Numerous authors suggest that indigenous values and patterns determining women's economic and social rights and bases of power are currently being overtaken by larger systems of inequality as explosive growth of industrialization, natural resource exploitation, and international tourism change the gendered face of many countries of the region (Heyzer 1986; Khin Thitsa 1980; Lim 1981; Mather 1982; Ong 1985, 1987; Phongpaichit 1982; Sirisambhand 1991). In contrast, war, dramatic political changes, and recent socioeconomic transition are the main forces affecting structural patterns and cultural ideas supporting women's positions in Vietnam, Cambodia, and Laos (Pelzer-White 1987; Ebihara, Mortland, and Ledgerwood 1994; Boua 1981, 1982; Boua and Kiernan 1987; Sonnois 1990; Ebihara 1990; Brownmiller 1994; Hoang 1994; Le 1994; Pelzer 1994; Cheng and Praney 1994; Bouavonh and Latmani 1994; Vongsay 1994).

In sum, Laotian women are part of a region in which many women traditionally enjoyed moderately high status relative to men. Women in a number of Southeast Asian groups have experienced autonomy in implementing at least some of their economic ventures and had access to resources enabling them to be successful in these activities. Family and quasi-family patterns and networks have often enabled women to share labor, inherit land, attend school in towns, and mediate (at least informally) local community issues. The two major religious traditions have been interpreted in ways that have maintained women's economic bases, while providing the justification for women's lack of political and religious leadership.

Extraordinary changes have engulfed the region in the last several decades. Not surprisingly, women's lives have changed. Laotian women have been greatly affected by war and political change, as have the women of other socialist Southeast Asian countries, and are now beginning to reconnect with the active market networks of provincial Thailand. Industrialization, tourism, and exploitation of natural resources that have so strongly affected women of capitalist-oriented Southeast Asia are beginning to enter Laos as well. Even rural Laotian women in remote villages are encountering harbingers of such changes.

The approach to women's power developed throughout this chapter and summarized in Figure 1.1 *does* appear to be applicable to the changing situation of rural Laotian women. I use this framework to explore changes in rural Laotian women's work and power for three recent time periods—the traditional period (before 1975), the socialist period (1975–88), and the period of economic liberalization (1988–present). Rural women's control over people and resources is strongly affected by the relationship between their own productive and domestic activities, and by the macro-level structures, policies, and programs that shape these activities. Ethnicity is particularly important in conditioning responses to change, so I also explore how this framework applies to rural women of three different ethnic groups—the ethnic Lao, the Khmu, and the Hmong.

Striking changes in politics and government and in economic systems have occurred in Laos with the transition to socialism beginning in 1975, followed by gradual economic liberalization, first noticeable in rural areas in approximately 1988. These changes have affected rural women's sources of power by influencing their work and their involvement in the larger community. On the other hand, religious and kinship influences on women's power have stayed relatively constant through the three periods, though varying by ethnic group. Cultural gender role ideologies have, at least superficially, been modified by socialist political ideology. These changes, in a context of some continuity with the past, have affected rural women's activities and control over economic resources. Changes in women's power have implications for their own lives, for the well-being of their families, and for the further course of local and national development.

Information about rural Laotian women's economic power enables me to illustrate, in the following chapters, some of the relationships identified in Figure 1.1. These relationships include (1) relationships between women's domestic and other activities and sources of power, and women's economic power; (2) relationships between macro-level political, governmental, and economic changes and subsequent changes in women's activities and resources

FIGURE 1.1 Influences of Culture, Society, Economy, and Politics on Women's Power

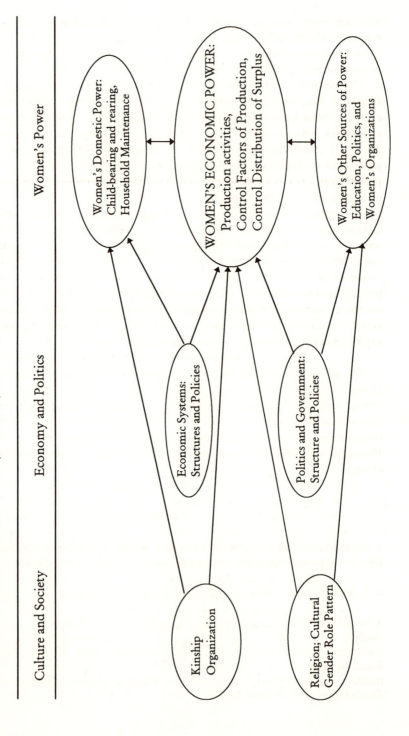

affecting their economic power; (3) the relationship of ethnic variation in religion, culture, and kinship to women's economic power; and (4) changes in these relationships over time from the pre-1975 "traditional" period through periods of socialism and economic liberalization.

The content of each oval in Figure 1.1 varies by both ethnic group and historical time period. Elements of Laotian women's economic power, for example, have been markedly affected by changes in national and regional economies, politics, and government. A major traditional source of economic power for ethnic Lao women before 1975 was the ability to produce and sell goods and to distribute the resulting income or goods. During the socialist period from 1975 to 1988, governmental policies suppressed private commerce and attempted to construct public commercial networks based on village buying and selling cooperatives and state stores. These political and economic changes negatively affected ethnic Lao women's economic power. Some Khmu women, on the other hand, began to benefit from socialist commitment to rural development, including rural education, local women's unions, and provision of drinking water systems. These changes, begun during the socialist period, lightened the very heavy work load of some Khmu women and connected a number of isolated Khmu women to regional governments, economies, and society. These ethnic Lao and Khmu examples briefly preview my exploration of rural women's changing economic power.

The next chapter introduces Laos. Recent events in Laos include dramatic changes in government, in economic policies, in foreign relations, and in official ideology. Traditional village Laos has also changed in response to these national and, in some cases, international changes. Cultural differences between three major Laotian ethnic groups—the ethnic Lao, the Khmu, and the Hmong—have shaped the responses of women in these three groups to these changes.

Notes

1. Sen and Grown write on behalf of the Development Alternatives for Women for a New Era network of activists, researchers, and policy makers, also called DAWN.

2. Women, however, often earn considerably less than their husbands.

3. Rosaldo (1974, 23) associates women's subordination with child-rearing. Sacks (1974) similarly locates women's lack of control over themselves, others, and economic resources in women's isolation in household or domestic labor. Blumberg (1978) also noted the constraints of breast-feeding on the activities of high parity women who, in traditional nonbirth-control-using conditions, are either pregnant or breast-feeding for most of their adult working lives.

4. Sen and Grown (1987, 50) define "reproduction" as "the process by which human beings meet their basic needs and survive from one day to the next." See Benería and Sen (1986, 150–56 and n. 5) for a fuller treatment of this concept.

5. While the domestic/public model of female subordination is still a powerful model in social anthropology, it has come under attack. In particular, it has been attacked for the assumed "naturalness" and universality of the mother-child unit, and for the arbitrary division between domestic or private and public that may be easy to see in Western societies but which may not exist in other societies (Moore 1988, 21–24, 31–35)

6. Carol Hoffer (1974) describes the interesting case of Madame Yoko, a ruler of the Kpa Mende Confederacy in Sierra Leone in the latter part of the nineteenth century during British colonial rule.

7. These reports may reflect the political reality or the male bias of earlier Western observers and ethnographers, rather than women's actual exclusion from power (Moore 1988, 133).

8. Blumberg (1991a) successfully demonstrates several macro- to micro-level links.

9. Reviews by Joan McFarland (1988) and Deniz Kandiyoti (1989) have been helpful in formulating my application of Sen and Grown's analysis to the Lao case.

10. In addition, "structural adjustment" policies of the International Monetary Fund and the World Bank have supported "open" economies in their lending programs to Third World countries, while requiring the elimination of many internal subsidies of basic goods and social services. Thus, women's increased work to obtain the food, fuel, and water necessary for family survival occurs in a context with fewer available health and social services and higher costs for previously subsidized basic goods. The World Bank (1990), though, claims that it has initiated a stronger effort to increase women's economic productivity in its programs in recent years.

11. These figures were quoted by Croll (1986, 232) from a newspaper article in *Renmin Ribao*, 2 June 1958; Curtin (1975, 40–41) includes laundries in her list of services provided by rural communes during this period.

12. Charlton (1984) comments that since most of these organization have no independent power base they are usually ineffective in advocating for women's issues within the Party or government.

2

Laos: History, Society,
and the Situation of Women

Home to numerous ethnic groups living in terrain as varied as high mountain ridges or wide river valleys, the Lao People's Democratic Republic (Lao PDR, or Laos) is just beginning to urbanize, industrialize, and commercially develop its natural resources (Lao PDR 1987; World Bank 1988; Bourdet 1990; Chi Do Pham 1992; Lao PDR 1995; Evans 1995; Far Eastern Economic Review—FEER 1996). This transition offers us an exceptional opportunity to examine how two different political-economic systems have been affecting women's situation in traditional Laotian[1] social groups. While French colonization and war disrupted traditional social life during earlier decades of this century, more recent socialist revolution and economic liberalization have had marked effects on rural Laotian women's traditional activities and sources of power. Although these effects have parallels in events, structures, and ideologies affecting women's lives in other parts of Southeast Asia, some of these changes are unique to Laos.

Changes relevant to understanding rural women have occurred at all levels after the 1975 socialist revolution and, more recently, since the beginning of economic liberalization in the late 1980s. These recent changes have been shaped both by women's traditional positions in their social groups and by historical events preceding the 1975 revolution. I begin by characterizing the broader Laotian context that impinges on women's contemporary situation, focusing particularly on the historical, social, and political setting. I discuss in more detail the two most recent time periods of greatest interest: transition to socialism and economic liberalization. This discussion includes gender ideology and government policies affecting rural women during these time periods. Then, I consider village society and economy, which is the context for rural women's activities and the venue for the exercise of women's economic power. I first present a brief history of major ethnic groups before reviewing variations in village life by ethnic group.

Social Context and the Situation of Women

Laos is a small mainland Southeast Asian country located between China and Vietnam on the north and east, Cambodia and Thailand on the south and west, and Myanmar (Burma) on the northwest (see Map 2.1). The flat, wide river valleys of the mighty Mekong River and its tributaries give way in the north and east to rugged mountains and the steep limestone peaks reminiscent of classical Chinese landscape painting. Its small population of 4.6 million (Schenk-Sandbergen and Choulamany-Khamphoui 1995, 13) occupies an ample land area of 235,690 km². However, an estimated population growth rate of 2.9 percent per year and a crude birthrate of an estimated 38/1000 is one of the highest in the world (Stuart-Fox and Kooyman 1992, xlvi; UNICEF 1992, 5).

Only 12–15 percent of Laotian citizens live in towns or cities, including small and isolated district centers (Lao PDR 1985), but the availability of electricity, television, a market economy, and health and educational services ensure that townspeople lead lives different from those of their country cousins. Towns evidence a more complex division of labor than villages, with a variety of service, commercial, and industrial jobs being performed. In both village and town, most jobs are gender-linked. In towns both men and women may be store owners, teachers, office staff, and Party members. Most government functionaries and technicians are men. Men staff the lumber mills and brick factories, whereas women work in textile and garment factories. Urban women may watch television in the evening or work by the light of electric bulbs. Town girls can continue to attend secondary or technical schools, if they qualify, without leaving home. Salaried or wage jobs are available to some town dwellers. Marketing, a common women's activity, and the production of food or goods for sale are options for town women.

By government acclamation a "pluri-ethnic" nation, Laos is home to nearly forty different ethnic groups.[2] Many leaders of the communist resistance were ethnic minorities, and the avowed intent of the new government was to create a nation in which historic ethnic differences and prejudices would be erased. When this ideal confronted the practical realities of creating a nation-state where no unified government had existed before and where resources were virtually unavailable, it was perhaps inevitable that the "pluri-ethnic" ideal would take second place to the immediate needs of administrative consolidation and economic growth (R. Ireson 1988).

The Lao government after the revolution classified all ethnic groups residing within the boundaries of the Lao PDR into three general categories, named after traditional residential sites that reflected cultural similarities.[3] These groups are the lowland Lao ("Lao loum"), midland Lao ("Lao theung"), and highland Lao ("Lao sung"). While no single ethnic group forms a majority, lowland Lao ethnic groups are numerically and socially dominant, comprising

Map 2.1   Lao People's Democratic Republic

about 65 percent of the population (15 percent actually live in midland areas). Midland Lao groups make up about 25 percent of the population and highland Lao comprise an additional 10 percent (C. Ireson and R. Ireson 1991).

Social organization among certain ethnic groups in Laos reflects the gender complementarity that has traditionally enabled some groups of Southeast Asian women to enjoy relatively high status. Among these Laotian groups, Indian influences over the centuries may have negatively affected women's position (Ngaosyvathn 1993). Women from most other Laotian ethnic groups do not enjoy even the remnants of relatively high status. When the situation of Laotian females is compared to males in Laos and to females in other Southeast Asian countries, one can see the strengths and weaknesses in women's position.

Laotian women are active in the labor force, concentrated in the large, mainly subsistence, agricultural sector. Politically, women are as inactive as women in most other countries, though there are myths and histories of women leaders in the pre-Buddhist past. Educationally, women lag far behind men, though with secular education and the building of rural schools many girls now at least have an opportunity to attend school. Buddhism devalues women as more attached to the material world, perhaps legitimizing their involvement in commerce. Some local religious systems allow female practitioners. Health care in Laos is rudimentary, and the burden of childbearing and domestic work is heavy for women of all ethnic groups.

Women in the Economy

Women make up more than one-half the active labor force of the country. They comprise 53 and 52 percent of workers ages 15–44 and 18–60, respectively (UNICEF 1992, 100; NULW 1989, 19; Lao PDR 1995, 25). Women predominate in the following sectors: trade and material supply, 60 percent; health and social welfare, 57 percent; agriculture, 54 percent (UNICEF 1992, 100); handicrafts, 60 percent; and education, 50 percent (NULW 1989, 19). Since 89 percent of the total labor force is engaged in agriculture (UNICEF 1992, 19), by far the greatest number of women work in this sector. Other sectors employing relatively large numbers of women are commerce, education, health, industry, and government administration.

Women agriculturalists are involved in all stages of production, but activities involving "capital acquisition and maintenance" (such as landmarking and preparation, shelter construction and repair, buffalo and cattle rearing) tend to be male activities. Women, however, have control over a few sources of wealth (UNICEF 1992, 101). UNICEF also suggests that the division of labor by sex tends to be more rigid among midland and upland ethnic groups, perhaps reflecting the relatively lower status of women among these groups.

TABLE 2.1 Women's Economic Activity

Nation	Est. % Economic Activity Rate of Women Aged 15+		Women as % of Labor Force
	1970	1994	1994 (proj.)
Laos/Lao PDR	80	68	45
Cambodia	59	50	42
Vietnam	71	69	47
Thailand	75	65	44
Myanmar (Burma)	54	47	36
Nepal	47	42	32
Bhutan	48	42	32
Bangladesh	5	62	41
United States	42	50	41
Japan	51	50	40

Source: United Nations 1991, 106–7; United Nations 1995, 141–45.

While the principle of legal equality among male and female workers was instituted in 1975, it has not been adequately implemented (LWU and Boupha 1984, 19; Phomvihan 1984, 9–10). The National Union of Lao Women (1989, 30) estimates that, in rural areas, women work two hours per day more than men. Their work includes production tasks as well as household and child-care chores.

Comparative statistics available from the United Nations note that the estimated percentage of economically active women aged fifteen years and over decreased from 80 to 71 percent between 1970 and 1990, with women constituting 44 percent of the labor force in 1990.[4] Like neighboring Vietnamese and Thai women, Laotian women are more economically active than women in South Asia, Japan, or the United States (see Table 2.1).

Women in Politics and Law

In the past, women rarely wielded political power. Although royal princesses were generally not allowed to accede to the throne, they might be appointed as governors. Wives of kings sometimes ruled in the absence of their spouses, or in their own names, though this was not as likely in Buddhist kingdoms (Ngaosyvathn 1993, 22–26). Women were granted the right to vote in 1956, but only one woman, a Neo Lao Hak Sat (socialist) representative, was elected to the National Assembly in 1958. There have been no women ministers even under the socialist government, though the head of the Lao Women's Union is sometimes considered of ministerial rank. In 1984 there were four female members of the fifty-three-member Party Central Committee (Stuart-Fox 1986a, 90), whereas in 1993 there were four women members among fifty-five. Two of them, however, were alternates rather than full members (Vongsack, personal communication, 1993).

Laws followed customary ethnic Lao practice under French colonialism, with women having legal right to own, manage, and bequeath property without the consent of their husbands. Recently, however, large scale land surveys to determine individual land ownership in some districts have resulted in the registration of land in the name of the "head of household," nearly always a man. This reportedly happens even when the registered land parcels have been inherited by the wife from her parents (Schenk-Sandbergen and Choulamany-Khamphoui 1995, 20). The French colonial administration required that everyone have a last name, with wives and children taking the last names of their husbands and fathers. This practice was modified in the 1989 family law, which allows wives to keep their own names (Ngaosyvathn 1993, 28–29). In practice, however, husbands sometimes take their wives' last names.

Ethnic Lao villages were governed by a single headman in consultation with several other respected older men. Officials at the subdistrict and district levels were exclusively male before 1975, though they seldom had much power. The headman was responsible for all village contacts with higher levels of government and for contact with unrelated outsiders. In Buddhist villages, a small group of male lay leaders was responsible for organizing villagers in support of the local temple. With the establishment of rural secular schools in the 1950s, women were sometimes recruited to teach at the school, but their leadership did not seem to extend beyond this arena.

Laotian women did not seem to have the necessary authority to govern or to participate in decisions affecting the whole community. Respected "middle-aged" women were often the organizers of women's activities in support of the local temple, a local festival, or visitation of a dignitary, though a woman leader was not formally designated. Young unmarried women served as dancers, food stall attendants, or drink-servers. Government business involving women's issues was sometimes carried out by the wife of the village headman. In household or extended family-sponsored events like weddings, ordinations, or funerals, women took major organizational responsibility, though the ceremonies themselves were conducted by monks or male elders. In a village controversy or dispute, women might be involved in the informal communication often used to resolve such conflicts.

Girls, Women, and Education

Traditionally, ethnic Lao boys in Buddhist villages and in towns were educated by monks in the temple. Ethnic Lao girls and children of other ethnic groups learned life skills from their parents, siblings, and relatives. With the development of secular education in urban areas during the French colonial period, some girls began attending school. Education became available to the majority of children only with the more recent growth of schools in rural areas. Most villages have one to three grades of school, whereas 30 percent of villages have full primary schools. Secondary schools are located within 10 kilometers of more than one-half of all villages, usually in provincial capitals or district centers.

The quality of the educational system is poor, however. Government payment of rural teachers' salaries is so erratic that teachers often remain at their posting only if they are paid by villagers and only if they are able to obtain land locally to cultivate their own rice field. Although many children repeat first or second grade, most of these drop out of school. Less than one-half who enter first grade complete the five grades of primary school. UNESCO (1985, 52) indicates that only 14 percent complete primary school in five years, but the Asian Development Bank (1989, Vol. 2, 59) reports a 45 percent completion rate. These very different rates may reflect the marked differences in school attendance and dropout in different parts of the country. For example, Vientiane Province reports that 12 percent of first graders drop out, while Luang Prabang Province reports that 39 percent of first graders quit school (UNICEF 1992, 85). The situation is worse for ethnic minority children living in small or isolated villages. Most of these children must attend special ethnic minority boarding schools. These "special" schools have meager budgets and, like village schools, teach only in the Lao language. Because education is an important tool for national integration, extending literacy and education into rural villages was a high priority for the new government (Chagnon and Rumpf 1982).

The national literacy campaign beginning in 1977 reached more than one-half of all villages, educating illiterate adults in the rudiments of reading and writing in Lao. Twenty percent of villages continued their adult literacy program for five years or more (Lao PDR CPC 1993). In the few areas with continued access to classes and reading material, men and women have maintained their skills, while most others have forgotten what they learned. This campaign had the potential to be especially beneficial to women, since many more women than men are illiterate. Thirty-six percent of adults ages fifteen years and older still cannot read and write, however (Lao PDR CPC 1993).

Girls are much less likely to attend school than boys. Although many girls begin school, relatively few complete their primary education (M. Viravong

1995, 3). Usually only a few boys from rural schools are encouraged to continue their education in the district or provincial capital. Fewer girls are allowed to continue their schooling after completing the village school. Parents expect that girls will miss their family tremendously if they leave home. Furthermore, parents rely more on girls' daily labor than they do on the work of boys. So, the higher the level of education, the lower the percentage of female students, the lower the percentage of ethnic minority students, and the lower the female percentage within each of the three general ethnic categories (see Table 2.2). This is reflected in the lower ratio of female-to-male students in provinces with large populations of minority people like Luang Prabang, Xieng Khouang, and Oudomxay (see Table 2.3), although the situation may be improving (Lao PDR 1995, 27).

Similarly, more adult women than men are illiterate and minority group women are less likely than their husbands to speak and understand the Lao language. The number of illiterate women over thirty-five years of age is at least three times greater than the number of illiterate men over thirty-five. These results seem to be true whether comparing men and women in areas near Vientiane or in more remote provinces (Maroczy 1986, 1; Mukherjee and Jose 1982).

Women's Health

Women's life expectancy is slightly greater than men's, but both figures are quite low in comparison with other countries. Since women experience pregnancy and birth frequently throughout their reproductive years, women are at risk throughout this period. The national total fertility rate is 6.5 (Iinuma 1992, 15). Women typically give birth six to eight times and lose one or more children sometime during childhood, mainly to communicable diseases (UNICEF 1992, 98, 49–50; Lao PDR CPC 1993). Two sample surveys report that on average women over fifty had given birth eight to nine times with a birth interval of less than two years (UNICEF 1992, 98). Birth spacing programs have just begun (Lao PDR 1995, 35–36). Most women outside Vientiane give birth at home without the assistance of a trained birth attendant, and maternal deaths are not uncommon. Over a three-year period in Luang Prabang Hospital, the maternal mortality rate was 924/100,000 births (Perez 1989, 8), though the official estimate is lower at 656/100,000 births (Lao PDR CPC 1993).

Hard work and inadequate nutrition increase mothers' risk of death in childbirth. Iron-poor diets, frequent births, and endemic malaria combine to produce dramatically high rates of anemia in adult women. For example, the average hemoglobin for pregnant women examined in Vang Vieng Hospital (northern Vientiane Province) during six months of 1968 was 11.2. At that time in the United States, iron supplements were prescribed for a hemoglobin

TABLE 2.2 Proportion of Pupils by Ethnic Group and Sex

Educational Level	Ethnic Category (%)		% Female within Category
Primary	Lowland Lao	80	46
	Midland Lao	16	40
	Highland Lao	4	26
Lower secondary	Lowland Lao	93	42
(middle school)	Midland Lao	5	32
	Highland Lao	2	15
Upper secondary	Lowland Lao	96	40
(high school)	Midland Lao	2	27
	Highland Lao	1	10

Source: UNICEF 1992, 150.

TABLE 2.3 Ratio of Female-to-Male Primary and Secondary Students, Selected Provinces

Province	Number Female per 100 Male Students
Vientiane Prefecture	89
Vientiane	84
Savannakhet	84
Bolikhamsay	84
Luang Prabang	70
Xieng Khouang	67
Oudomxay	58

Source: UNICEF 1992, 151.

level below 13 or 14 (C. Ireson 1969, 13). The health and childbirth situation has changed little for Lao women in the intervening years. In Laos female infanticide or neglect is not evident, though infant mortality rates are among the highest in the region. Estimated infant and under-five mortality rates of

117/1000 and 170/1000, respectively, ensure a low life expectancy of only forty-nine years (UNICEF 1992, 49). Deaths of infants and children are much higher in rural and especially in ethnic minority areas. One study reported an infant mortality rate of 193/1000, whereas consultants for the World Health Organization estimated 350/1000 in some areas (UNICEF 1992, 50).

The entire population of Laos is exposed to a variety of common and endemic diseases including malaria, diarrhea, respiratory infections, measles, meningitis, and tuberculosis (Lao PDR CPC 1993; UNICEF 1992, 51). UNICEF characterizes Laos as having "one of the poorest health situations in the world," partly because "the construction of a nationwide primary health care system has totally failed" (1992, 135). As a result of this failure, the availability of health facilities for Laotian villagers depends on their proximity to a functioning urban hospital or to the Thai border. Health care, therefore, is nearly inaccessible to many mountain-dwelling minority groups unless they make extraordinary efforts to obtain it. Cross-national comparisons of selected health statistics illustrate the poor health of Lao people, a situation that is exacerbated, among women, by frequent pregnancies and births (see Table 2.4).

Women and Family

Family size averages six members (Lao PDR 1985). Most young women marry at eighteen to twenty years of age, though in rural areas, and especially among certain ethnic groups, the age is much lower—fourteen to fifteen years. (NULW 1989, 22). While a national sample survey indicates that only 66 percent of women ages fifteen to forty-nine are currently married, it is commonly understood that marriage is nearly universal for both men and women (Lao PDR CPC 1993; NULW 1989, 22). Sex ratios by province indicate that men are more likely than women to migrate to the Vientiane area, perhaps leaving rural households short of needed male labor (Lao PDR 1985). Recently established factories in Vientiane, which draw on the labor of young women, may be changing these patterns of migration (Lao PDR 1995, 7, 17). Most of the population live in rural households, but female-headed households may be more common in towns. A study by Rietmeyer (1988, 7, 23) of urban areas in Vientiane Prefecture found that 13 percent of households were female-headed while another study by C. Ireson (1989, 28) in neighboring Bolikham-say Province rural areas found that 7.5 percent of households were headed by women. To date, no information has been gathered on domestic violence.

Lao History and the Political Mobilization of Women

The current situation of Laotian women has its roots in the past and in the traditional cultures and societies of each Laotian ethnic group. Midland Lao are

TABLE 2.4   Health Indicators: Laos, Selected Asian Countries, and the United States

Nation	Life Expectancy at Birth (Yrs) 1990–95		Total Fertility Rate (Births per Woman)		Maternal Deaths (per 100,000 Live Births)	Infant Mortality (per 1,000 Births)
	f	m	1970	1990–95	1990	1990–95
Laos/Lao PDR	53	50	6.2	6.6 [a]	656 [a]	97
Cambodia	52	50	6.2	4.5	900	116
Vietnam	66	62	5.9	3.9	120	36
Thailand	72	67	6.1	2.2	20	26
Myanmar	59	56	5.7	4.2	90	81
Nepal	53	54	6.2	5.5	1500	99
Bhutan	49	48	5.9	5.9	1310	129
Bangladesh	53	53	6.9	4.7	480	108
United States	79	73	2.6	2.1	7	8
Japan	82	76	2.0	1.7	10	5

[a]Lao PDR Committee for Planning and Cooperation, 1992–93 information; United Nations 1990 figures are 6.7 total fertility rate and 300 maternal deaths.

Sources: Lao PDR Committee for Planning and Cooperation 1993; UNICEF 1992, 49; United Nations 1991, 67–70; United Nations 1995, 28–32, 84–88.

descendants of Mon-Khmer–speaking indigenous peoples who have inhabited the region for several thousand years. In a series of migrations beginning about a thousand years ago, Tai-Lao peoples began moving into Southeast Asia, probably from southern China. Most of these groups organized politically and militarily around a local leader; thus, they were able to defeat or displace the native people (Wyatt 1984, Ch. 3). Over the centuries the power of some of these local principalities expanded. The Lao kingdom of Lan Xang was established in the fourteenth century with its capital in Luang Prabang. Lan Xang fluctuated in size and power but endured for more than 350 years (Stuart-Fox and Kooyman 1992, 71–72), though parts of the country were at various times incorporated into larger empires based in Thailand, Cambodia, and Vietnam. After the demise of a unified kingdom of Lan Xang, Laos was characterized by small kingdoms, river towns, and isolated subsistence villages, some of which fell under the suzerainty of neighboring rulers. Laos was the last colony to be incorporated into French Indochina, though the French did little to develop Laos.

Throughout the centuries, Thai, Vietnamese, or Khmer suzerains, Lao kings, and French colonial administrators exercised only limited and sporadic control over village life, though traditional village life before 1940 was periodically disrupted by colonial demands for corvée labor and taxes (see Berval 1959; Dommen 1964; Steinberg 1987; M. S. Viravong 1964; and Wyatt 1984). After such a disturbance, most villagers returned to traditional village life, unless the disruption irrevocably breached the relative isolation and autonomy of the village. When the French attempted to reassert control over Indochina after World War II, several years of war ensued, culminating in defeat of the French in 1954 at Dien Bien Phu in the mountains of Vietnam near Laos. During this period, women nationalists and especially combatants' mothers formed groups to care for soldiers and to protect and help nationalists working underground against French domination. Women became soldiers, scouts, messengers, or organizers of campaigns for production, education, or hygiene to support Lao independence and self-sufficiency (LWU and Boupha 1984).

Independence and Civil War

After the French defeat, Laos became an independent country, united politically under a king and a civil government. The newly formed Lao People's Revolutionary Party, through the Lao Patriotic Front (Neo Lao Hak Sat), established the Lao Patriotic Women's Association (LPWA) in 1955 under the leadership of Khamla Vongsack, a Party Central Committee member. The Lao Patriotic Front, the communist political party, organized the Women's Association and designed its program of action. At least partly as a result of pressure from the Neo Lao Hak Sat, women were accorded the right to vote and to be elected to national office in the 1958 elections of the first coalition government. A member of the Neo Lao Hak Sat was the first woman delegate elected to the national assembly. Peace after independence lasted less than three years with the beginning of fighting between various Laotian factions. Less than a year after the 1958 election, a number of Party leaders were arrested, destroying the coalition and sending many Pathet Lao supporters back to the "liberated zones"[5] of Houa Phan and Phong Saly.

At that time the main tasks of the association were to rally women in these areas of Laos behind the Party-led struggle for control of the nation, mainly by carrying out support activities that included supporting soldiers, performing jobs vacated by men who left for the front lines, safeguarding community security, as well as by raising, feeding, and clothing their children. Founding members of the Lao Patriotic Women's Association were the wives of Party Central Committee members, reflecting the association's origins in the Party and the "women's auxiliary" character of its initial years. For example, Khamla Vongsack initially organized and presided over the LPWA; she was married to Souk Vongsack, Pathet Lao ambassador to the Royalist government in

Vientiane. Khampheng Boupha became LPWA president when Khamla was diagnosed with cancer; Boupha is the wife of Khamphay Boupha, who later became senior vice minister of foreign affairs (Stuart-Fox 1986a, 77, 89). The wife of Phoumi Vongvichit, an early Lao Issara leader and long-time Politburo member, taught school and was a member of the Central Committee of the LPWA. Committee members of the LPWA made international connections with other socialist women's organizations, and in 1962 joined the Women's International Democratic Federation.

In 1964 after the collapse of the second coalition government, American and Royalist bombing in Laos began, heralding the beginning of eleven years of bombing and renewed war in Laos (see Adams and McCoy 1970; Brown and Zasloff 1986; and Evans and Rowley 1984). During this period before the establishment of the Lao PDR, massive American bombing devastated productive farmland and villages, and destroyed provincial and district population centers. The population in these areas were reduced to refugees or to cave and forest-dwelling farmers barely eking out their livelihoods. During this period the Pathet Lao, heavily subsidized by the governments of the former Soviet Union, China, and North Vietnam, governed a limited number of people engaged in subsistence production.

As this war, now part of the second Indochina conflict, expanded and intensified in Laos, the Party called on one of its Central Committee members and president of the LPWA, Khampheng Boupha, to reorient the activities of the women's association. The more activist association began organizing local women's associations throughout Laos wherever the Neo Lao Hak Sat and the People's Army were actively engaged, educating, mobilizing, and uniting women for the struggle. The messages were those of national liberation, collective solidarity across ethnic groups, and equality. During this period, women became more involved in the revolution as heads of governmental departments and schools, and served as messengers, transporters of war supplies, and soldiers. One group of women, workers in the October 12 Textile Mill, converted a cave into a textile factory, excavating "rooms," hauling and installing heavy equipment, and patrolling the immediate area to ensure continued production (LWU and Boupha 1984, 5). Many village women took over men's tasks in the field and community. These women plowed and harrowed the paddies, rebuilt houses destroyed by bombing, and repaired damaged roads. They also performed chores on their own farms, gathered food, and maintained their homes and families. Women were often forced to work at night when B–52 bomber crew members were less likely to see them.

Association activities included organizing women's associations in villages and women's sections in governmental units and advocating for the needs of women and children. Individual women's groups often carried out support activities for the revolution, for example, by sending gifts and letters to soldiers, helping war widows, or cooking for important occasions. At individual association meetings, LPWA officers or visiting guests most often educated members about the Party program for liberation, while urging women to give up traditional beliefs and customs that maintained the low status of women and minority group members. Women were particularly encouraged to abandon "backward ideas handed down from the previous regime [such] as: inferiority complex, dependence upon men, disheartenment, selfishness, narrow-mindedness, superstition" (LWU and Boupha 1984, 16). Women in more advanced women's units shared experiences and critiqued their own and others' efforts to support socialist liberation.[6]

People in the Royalist-held areas during the same period had a somewhat different experience. Many were visibly prosperous, displaying their wealth in fancy cars and large villas. Massive infusions of American aid to the Royalists fed war refugees, financed the Royalist military, supported the flamboyant lifestyle of government bureaucrats and enterprising private businesspeople, while poor girls and women were enticed into a thriving sex trade. Royalist women were not organized in defense of the kingdom, unlike Pathet Lao women, and government programs for women emphasized only their domestic activities and other "backward ideas" (in Pathet Lao terms). Like those in Pathet Lao areas, however, many were displaced by war, and many women were obliged to take full responsibility for family survival, with little help from soldier-husbands.

Women's Lives with the Pathet Lao

During the extended periods of war against the French and later against the Americans and the Royalist government, living conditions for women, and indeed for the entire citizenry, were difficult. Families were often separated, work was often carried out in caves or at night, basic services such as education and health were rudimentary or unavailable in the countryside, and bombing destroyed homes, fields, and lives. Children of Pathet Lao officials were often sent to the perceived safety of Vietnam or other countries to study. They then returned to the Pathet Lao-controlled zones where their skills were immediately put to work for the revolution. Family members were often separated as they worked in their own ways for revolutionary goals. Portraits of specific women help us see how they arrived at positions of power and how they survived the wars.

Davone Vongsack, daughter of the first Women's Association president, rarely lived with her parents. As a young child during the French war period, her parents sent her to Thailand for primary school while they continued working in Laos. Completing five grades of school by the age of nine, she joined her mother in Houa Phan, where her mother taught her to read and write Lao. She then journeyed to Vietnam for secondary education, attending a Vietnamese middle school in southern China since northern Vietnam was unsafe. She completed her high school education in Hanoi and then graduated from five years of medical training. She returned to Houa Phan in 1964 and was initially assigned as a physician at the Party's central headquarters. The following year she began teaching basic medical skills to aspiring nurses, establishing a school for mid-level nurses in 1967. Since there were no Lao medical texts, she translated her Vietnamese textbooks and notes into Lao, aided by the careful editorial assistance of Prince Souphannavong, one of the major Pathet Lao leaders. From 1967 to 1975, with bombs regularly falling outside the cave sheltering the school, she directed the nursing school. Graduates from this school formed a network of health workers throughout Pathet Lao-controlled zones. Even today, Dr. Davone frequently meets her former students as she visits clinics and hospitals in the provinces (personal communication 1985–86, 1993).

Outhaki Choulamany completed medical school at an eastern European university before returning to head a department in the central hospital for government workers in Houa Phan. The fifty-bed hospital covered all major medical specialties and trained basic-level nurses. The hospital, classrooms, student dormitories, and apartments for workers and their families were located in a single cave. Fortunately the hospital cave was near Dr. Davone's nursing school cave, so Dr. Outhaki sometimes taught at the nursing school. All workers received a rice ration and canned food. Cave-dwelling families tried to raise animals, grow fruit trees and plant vegetables, but only the vegetables survived frequent bomb attacks. Sometimes family members risked the bombing to gather fresh leaves, shoots, and fruits from the forest. Doctors did not see the sun except during their lunch break. Unfortunately, U.S. planes often bombed during that brief time. Outhaki's husband lived in another cave 12 kilometers away. Every few weeks he would risk the 12-kilometer walk to see his family. Women raised their children alone, as well as capably carrying out their jobs. Dr. Outhaki remembers this as a difficult time, although, for women with ability, it was a time of equality between women and men. Few people had solid technical training, and the skills of both men and women were desperately needed (personal communication, 1993).

By the time Soumountha Yutitham was old enough to attend school, Lao study in Vietnam was well organized. Hundreds of children of Pathet Lao cadre studied at Soumountha's school in Hanoi. The school was bombed in 1972. Soumountha says she was nearly killed along with forty of her classmates. The school, with several hundred surviving children, subsequently moved into the Vietnamese hinterland. Soumountha stayed in Vietnam after the war, graduating from high school and earning a seven-year medical school degree before returning to manage and practice obstetric, gynecological, and pediatric services in the main hospital of her northern home province of Oudomxay. Soumountha is unique because few Khmu children, and hardly any girls, attended school at that time. Soumountha's father, though, was a Khmu leader and valued education for all of his children. Today Soumountha is one of the best educated Khmu women in all of Laos (personal communication, 1993).

Daughters of civil servants were not the only active participants in revolutionary activities. One young woman of northern Luang Prabang Province joined her brothers in the forest carrying out guerrilla activities. Her guerrilla band was constantly on the move, often battling diseases such as malaria and dysentery as well as the opposing army. After several years she married a fellow guerrilla, returning to her village to raise their children. As a high school student in a contested area, another girl aspired to be a soldier, supplementing her academic subjects with military studies. In one engagement she was shot in the leg, but recovered in only two weeks. After further study in Xieng Khouang and Vietnam, she spent ten years teaching primary and middle school in several districts in Xieng Khouang. During part of her teaching career, Americans dropped a record number of bombs on her home province (Khamphone, LWU staff, personal communication, 1993).

Ordinary village women with no ideological commitment to either side of the conflict also suffered from the war, even in noncombat zones. Kiang remembers that one day the Vientiane (Royalist) army parachuted into her village and occupied it. The village head recommended that all of the unmarried young women hide in the forest. Six families with young women and several other villagers as well, including Kiang, hid for eight months. They traveled from mountain to mountain, building temporary shelters for a few days and then moving on so they would not be found. Her mother sent her word via a prearranged messenger when it was safe to return. Even then, her mother rarely let her leave the sleeping area of the house. The same army unit returned to the village one day and a soldier wanted to "marry" her. She was only seventeen and not interested in being coerced into marriage as the second wife of a soldier and stranger. She refused, though other village girls had been coerced into such marriages (Kiang McIntosh, personal communication, 1993).

Socialist ideology touted collective work and equality between the sexes, so the Party attempted to promote the collectivization of child care in order to lessen the conflict between household maintenance and economic production. Other contributions to women's equality and well-being were the establishment of kindergartens and day-care centers, the provision of free schooling in Vietnam for the children of civil servants, and the support of women's reproductive responsibilities through policies of paid maternity leaves, special baby-nursing breaks during the workday, and shorter work hours for women with many children. These contributions, however, were available only to women government workers (LWU and Boupha 1984,

17–18); women often raised children alone in administrative centers and in villages during the war years. A few village cooperatives established day-care centers or kindergartens.

Throughout their careers as government employees, Drs. Davone and Outhaki and other women cadre regularly worked for women's issues. Dr. Davone, for example, established a women's group within her school and also was a founding member of the unit that eventually became the Ministry of Health. At the same time, Davone says, two other women who today are members of the executive committee for the Lao Women's Union were also doing women's association work in Houa Phan. As the long fight for socialist/nationalist control of Laos began to subside in 1973 with the cessation of U.S. bombing, cave-dwelling cadre and villagers moved their dwellings into the fields near their former homes, in preparation for a bigger move.

A Royalist-communist coalition government in 1973 gave way relatively calmly to communist control in late 1975 with the founding of the Lao People's Democratic Republic, a socialist nation whose leaders proclaimed their support for female mobilization and emancipation. The Royalist economy collapsed along with the government, and the Pathet Lao were called on to manage their bankrupt remnants as the victorious communists moved from their mountain redoubts in the north and northeast to the capital city. The collapse of the war-driven economy and the ensuing period of revolutionary enthusiasm and consolidation ushered in a time of scarcity and a return to subsistence concerns, even in urban areas.

Transition to Socialism

In this political and economic context, the new government attempted to deal with economic crisis, consolidate its administrative control, and implement its Marxist-Leninist ideology. The first ten years were oriented toward central economic planning and internal development, while the next few years saw decentralized economic development with greater orientation toward external markets and sources of capital (Bourdet 1990; UNIDO 1992). Throughout this period Laos "exhibited a poor macroeconomic performance. The rate of growth of the Gross Domestic Product has been low compared with that of neighbouring countries (or comparable developing countries)" (Bourdet 1990, 3). Official government plans, resolutions, and decrees provide a broad outline of the policy directions that have affected the course of Lao development and the lives of rural women since 1975.

The mainly subsistence, rice-based economy of the Lao village continued after 1975, but with incentives to establish collective work groups and village-wide agricultural and marketing cooperatives. From the beginning, socialist leaders were committed to a gradual transition to socialism, rather than a rapid and radical transformation, but even before the Lao PDR was declared, many

Vientiane businesspeople and government officials fled. With the cessation of Western aid in May 1975, and a blockade imposed by Thailand later that year, urban dwellers experienced severe shortages of food and goods, while prices skyrocketed. The immediate reaction of the new socialist government was to clamp down on private enterprise, restricting and sometimes completely prohibiting private businesses, nationalizing industries, and appropriating properties of those who fled (Chanda 1982, 117–18). The government strictly controlled imports while prohibiting domestic marketing and the interprovincial movement of trade goods. By the end of 1976, Chanda (1982, 118) reports, the government had established 92 state-run stores and 138 marketing cooperatives. State stores provided an unpredictable variety of goods at relatively low prices and erratically bought and sold in bulk from the village cooperative. Prices in state and cooperative stores were often listed in rice as well as currency, reflecting the limited scope of the monetary economy.

The government urged self-sufficiency, counseling everyone to grow their own vegetables, raise poultry and livestock, and weave their own cloth. Students, teachers, and government workers planted vegetables in beds around their schools and office buildings. Women reassembled stored looms, again teaching their daughters how to weave. Government propaganda encouraged farmers to participate in "solidarity and labor exchange units" in a preliminary move toward the organization of cooperatives (Evans 1990, 44). The fledgling government instituted an agricultural tax as it had in the old Pathet Lao zones. Reaction against the tax was swift in some areas, as farmers destroyed their orchards or livestock, or decreased production to avoid paying the tax (Chanda 1982, 119-21).

Other goals of the new government included the eradication of decadent Western and Thai influences, equal development of rural and urban areas, education (including political education) for all, and widely available health care. This led to regulation of clothing, hairstyles, music, social behavior, and religious expression. The Lao language was purged of its foreign influences and spelling became completely phonetic. A widespread literacy campaign successfully taught the rudiments of reading and writing to many illiterate peasants, while one or two grades of school became available in many villages. Population growth was encouraged in order to build the labor force, and birth control was prohibited. Health care continued to be unavailable to most villagers, however.

Socialist rhetoric valuing women's contributions in war and reconstruction and emphasizing collectivized work was based on a firm foundation of women's traditional engagement in economic activities. Although rural women's work burden continued to be heavy, Laotian women were able to maintain their importance in the rural economy.

To support an ambitious leap from the existing system of widely dispersed household and individual enterprises toward fully socialist production, Kaysone

Phomvihan, general secretary of the Party and prime minister until shortly before his death in 1992, announced three simultaneous revolutions: in the relations of production, in science and technology, and in ideology and culture (Doré 1982). Party and government attempted to establish large-scale production enterprises responsive to government production targets in all economic sectors, including agriculture, industry, and trade, by mandating the creation of agricultural cooperatives, establishing and then consolidating state farms and other state enterprises, and developing a national trade network (Lao PDR 1986, 38–39).

Laos' dual political structure after 1975 consists of governmental administration and the Communist Party. Women are not well represented in either structure. No ministers are women, though occasionally a ministerial department or a ministry's provincial office may be headed by a woman. Provincial governors are exclusively male. I have never met or heard of a woman district chief, subdistrict leader, or village head, though a few may exist. Some women are Party members, though Party membership is only 9 percent female (KPL 21 July 1990, 2; UNICEF 1992, 94). The upper reaches of the Party are dominated by men, and the Politburo is entirely male. Party leadership is responsible for initiating major policy changes.

Food self-sufficiency was an official goal during the late 1970s. Collectivization of agriculture was the main method envisioned to achieve this goal. In May 1978, following a governmental decree on the management of agricultural cooperatives, the government launched an intensive campaign to persuade farmers to join cooperatives (Chanda 1982). Agricultural cooperatives would, according to the Politburo resolution, "turn private relations of production into collective relations of production . . . so as to serve the people's lives and the socialist industrialization of our country better" (Evans 1990, 49–50). Cooperatives, it was thought, would enable farmers to more efficiently use their labor, farming inputs, and technology. In addition, communist leaders expected cooperatives to rapidly demonstrate the superiority of collective over individual production, to raise socialist consciousness among the populace, and to increase governmental control over the countryside (Stuart-Fox 1986a, 100). Other aspects of government policy during this period included the promotion of exports, expansion of the state trading network, development of transportation, and training of government cadre in collective socialist economic management (Chanda 1982, 122). Floods and peasant resistance to pooling their means of production led to poor harvests in 1978 and 1979 and to an increasing flow of refugees into Thailand. The suspension of the intensive cooperativization campaign in 1979 signaled a more pragmatic approach to economic reorganization, though encouragement continued for voluntary cooperatives and collective work groups.

The Party Central Committee announced sweeping economic reforms in 1979. Individual business and commerce were no longer prohibited, prices on controlled items were adjusted so they were more in line with actual market prices, and profit became the central criterion for judging state enterprise performance. Agricultural taxes were based on land farmed, rather than on production (Stuart-Fox 1986a, 100–2). Near-market prices for produce and modified taxes provided incentives for increased farm production. These changes led to the reemergence of trade and industry in towns and to the reappearance of food and other agricultural goods in markets (Chanda 1982, 126). By the early 1980s the hardships of war and rapid revolutionary transformation diminished, returning village life to approximately the same level and style of living enjoyed by villagers in the early 1960s.

Government policy in the first half of the 1980s continued to rely on central economic planning and some restrictions on trade. The main accomplishments of this period were increases in rice and cash crop production, with the achievement of near self-sufficiency, and an increase in timber harvest and export (Lao PDR 1987, 9). Self-sufficiency in rice production was first achieved in 1984 (World Bank 1988). In 1985, at the end of a disappointing economic performance in all other sectors, more conventionally socialist members of the Party Central Committee prevailed, at least for a short time, with government attempts to revitalize agricultural cooperatives, increase taxation, and contain private business (Stuart-Fox 1986a, 103–4). This orthodox communist response, however, was short-lived.

With *glasnost* and *perestroika* in the former Soviet Union, Soviet-allied Laos began its own careful process of economic opening to the West, beginning with the adoption of extensive economic changes called the New Economic Mechanism (NEM) approved at the Fourth Party Congress in 1986. However, little change was visible at first.

Economic Liberalization

The policies associated with the NEM overhauled the structure of incentives so that market mechanisms and the private sector became more prominent, in order to encourage private and foreign investment and to further economic growth. Changes also include "a more liberal trade policy, a floating exchange rate policy, an increased monetization of the Lao economy, a liberalization of the banking sector, and a more restrictive fiscal policy" (Bourdet 1990, 25). These changes were instituted gradually, and by 1988 they began to have visible effects in rural areas.

Agricultural producers were allowed to market their crops through private as well as state channels, cooperatives were deemphasized and land was assigned to households, and cash payment of taxes was required[7] (Bourdet 1990, 25–26). Most trade restrictions and tariffs were removed or lowered to stimulate trade. In attempts to control extensive and lucrative legal and illegal logging and log export, taxes on exported logs and wood products were first increased. Then logging and finally the export of unprocessed logs were banned by decree, at least temporarily. Most state-owned enterprises were given autonomy, sold, or leased, a process largely completed by 1994 (Evans 1995, xv–xvi). Beginning in 1988 with an investment code allowing foreign investment with repatriation of profits after payment of investment taxes (Bourdet 1990, 28), the Supreme People's Assembly began to implement the New Economic Mechanism by drafting and adopting economic laws similar to the 1990s laws regulating contracts, inheritance, and property rights.

Policies associated with the New Economic Mechanism, especially the investment code and limited market exchanges with Thailand in 1988, led, by 1990, to widespread availability of consumer goods from capitalist countries, some marketing possibilities for Lao goods, and increased business opportunities both for international businesspeople and for the Lao themselves. A constitution was promulgated in 1991 and adopted by the National Assembly, the renamed Supreme People's Assembly. While the Party is named as the "leading organ" of the Lao political system, the constitution seems designed to make the exercise of Party power "less arbitrary and more predictable" (Johnson 1992, 84), though leading advocates of free speech or a multiparty system have been jailed. The lack of a legal framework has been one of the barriers to foreign investment.[8]

The collapse of major sources of foreign aid from the former Soviet Union and eastern Europe accelerated the growth of foreign assistance to Laos by multilateral, bilateral, and private donors and loan agencies. In addition, foreign investment increased dramatically, with garment and textile exports displacing timber and electricity as the top foreign exchange earners in 1992 (*Far Eastern Economic Review* 1994, 159). In the early 1990s small-scale manufacturing, mining, and forestry attracted most foreign investment money. Since 1994, however, the energy sector, especially numerous hydroelectric projects, has captured the most outside investment funding (FEER 1996, 159). In nearly every year since 1988, the gross domestic product of Laos has grown at a rate of more than 7 percent per year (FEER 1993, 154; FEER 1994, 159; FEER 1996, 160; M. Viravong 1995, 2).

Laos' economic opening to the global capitalist economy is starting to have notable effects on the economic power of rural women, though the economic growth common to many other Southeast Asian countries is just beginning. Industrialization, natural resource development, and tourism are hampered by the poorly developed physical infrastructure. The few existing roads are sometimes passable only part of the year. Internal communication by telegraph or radio-telephone is unreliable. However, air travel to most parts of the country is possible most of the year, and the Mekong River and its tributaries are also important for domestic transportation and communication. Communication satellites connect Lao telephones to the world beyond Southeast Asia. Relatively dependable electricity is available in parts of the

Vientiane Plain and in selected Mekong River towns. The economy is only partly monetized, with the division of labor in villages of all ethnic groups mostly determined by age and sex. With economic liberalization, more wage jobs are available to both women and men in manufacturing and tourism. These economic changes are most apparent in towns along the Thai-Lao border, but are also beginning to reach far into the hinterland.

Socialism had shallow roots in Laos, one longtime observer notes, and it was easily uprooted. Less than a generation was educated in socialist schools or participated in other socialist institutions (Evans 1995). The daughters and sons of communist and Royalist elites are creating a new elite committed to capitalist modernization (Evans 1995, xix). Critical for the lives and well-being of Laotian women are the decisions made by the modernizing elite. Surrounded by prospering capitalist economies in southern China and Thailand and a swiftly developing capitalism in Vietnam, Laos is being pulled into the regional capitalist economy. If Laotian decision-makers can maintain control of Laotian development, avoid some of the excesses of capitalism, and make political and economic policy decisions that support and modernize women's work in rural households and communities, then rural Laotian women may also benefit from the dramatic changes now under way in Laos.

Equality and Policy During Socialism
and Economic Liberalization

"Women have been liberated to work harder," claims one woman of Houa Phan. The billboards of the provincial capital support her claim. Stalwart women wield variously a weapon, a pick, a hoe, a broom, a teapot of boiled water, and a pan of animal feed. "Work to construct reliable irrigation systems to grow and raise enough food," enjoins the billboard in front of the province party secretary's house, as the billboard women help build an irrigation canal (see Photo 2.1). The billboard accurately reflects official Lao socialist ideology about women's roles.

Socialist ideology recognizes the importance of women's roles and influence in the reconstruction of the country and in the transition to socialism. General Secretary (of the Party's Central Committee) Kaysone Phomvihan, for example, has said that

> In the new revolutionary stage, work among women is aimed at achieving equality between men and women, real liberation for women, thus enabling them to contribute to the building of socialism. We should assist our women through education work, to enhance their political consciousness, their knowledge in all fields, promote their role of mastery, participate in social activities and in the management of the affairs of the country, especially in jobs suitable to women such as those in health services, education, and so on. (Phomvihan 1982)

PHOTO 2.1 Billboards in Lao towns advertise socialist ideals, like this billboard in Sam Neua portraying women and men working together for national development.

After liberation, women were directed by the Party and the Lao Patriotic Women's Association[9] to practice the Three Goods and the Two Duties (i.e., to be a good citizen, a good mother, and a good wife, and to participate in activities for national defense and construction, and women's emancipation). The national women's organization is a "mass" organization to which, ideally, most women belong, in their village, in their neighborhood, or at their place of work. Besides being the channel for Party and governmental directives to ordinary women at the "grassroots," the Women's Union has the potential to be both an advocate for the rights and power of various major groups of women, including rural women and ethnic women, and a development agency. Under socialism, then, women were expected to labor in the public sphere as well as in the domestic sphere to "build socialism" (i.e., to participate in activities for community betterment, to increase production of needed goods, to continue maintaining their families, and to support the new state). But Comrade Kaysone's remarks and the Three Goods and Two Duties slogan of the Lao Women's Union demonstrate some of the common barriers to women. The exemplary socialist leader was quick to rhetorically encourage women's emancipation, yet his 1982 speech made it clear that women and men are different, with women "appropriately" excelling in education and health fields, rather than in industry, agriculture, economic planning, or other fields.

This stereotyping extends women's household-caring activities into the public sphere, while ignoring women's traditional experience in other areas such as in cottage industry, agriculture, marketing, and the administration of at least part of the household economy. Perhaps also, the notion of gender complementarity, common throughout Southeast Asia (see Chapter 1), still shaped his ideas of gender equality. Similarly, the Three Goods and Two Duties slogan of the Lao Patriotic Women's Association and its successor, the Lao Women's Union, is hardly a clarion call for women's liberation. Instead, it reinforces women's traditional domestic responsibilities, while, as the Houa Phan woman said, liberating women to work harder outside the domestic sphere.[10] Strident Marxist-Leninist ideological pronouncements of the young government, though, have waned as policies have become more pragmatic.

Since 1986, the socialist ideal of gender equality has been included in the constitution, and the Lao Women's Union has grown in capability, budget, and respect. While the equality of men and women had been a constant feature of Lao socialist ideology, only in 1991 was it guaranteed by law. Article 22 of the constitution, circulated in 1990 and ratified by the Supreme People's Assembly in 1991, states that "men and women are equal in all aspects, namely politics, economy, culture, and social and family affairs" (FBIS 1990, 43). In a few provinces and districts with gender-inclusive village development programs, nearly always administered by the local women's union, women are more likely than before to be recognized as competent farmers and village leaders. Socialist ideology of gender equality, its recent institutionalization in the constitution, and the women's organization (an official government body) are important elements of the political context affecting the work and power of rural Laotian women.

Despite these official mechanisms to protect women's rights, some past and current national policies have actually hindered women's liberation, while other policies have positive or mixed effects on women. In any case, changing national policies since 1975 have clearly impacted rural women's productive activities and power. Economic policies targeting agriculture, forests, textiles, commerce, foreign aid, and investment have directly affected rural women's work and power by prohibiting or encouraging certain activities and by providing structures (e.g., organizations, licensing requirements) that affected women's control over themselves, others, and other resources. In addition, social policies in health and education have indirectly affected women's economic productivity.

Women members of paddy-cultivating households, for example, were necessarily involved in some level of agricultural cooperativization during the socialist period. Paddy farmers were strongly encouraged, or even compelled by Party or state, to create village agricultural cooperatives. The mechanization provided by the government to some cooperatives benefited mainly men, since it replaced male labor. However, women received work points in their own names for their cooperative labor. Their paddy work was no longer controlled by their husbands or fathers or hidden as "unpaid family labor." Cooperatives, though directed by a few village men, made women's work more visible by paying for it in work points. Government policy on cooperatives, then, had a direct effect on women's agricultural work.

The effect of government policy toward private enterprise since 1975 also illustrates the effect of policy on women's work and power, especially on women who traditionally relied on marketing to produce some of their income. The new government suppressed private enterprise after 1975 and created an ineffective state marketing network to replace it. Private business was viewed with suspicion until the late 1980s. These policies had the potential for destroying one of rural women's most important sources of power and autonomy since nearly all petty and local traders were lowland Lao women. Ultimately, though, the government was not able to develop viable alternatives to private trade, and the Fourth Party Congress of 1986 initially announced the New Economic Mechanism. At about the same time cooperatives were de-emphasized, removing possible local pressure to support the village buying and selling cooperative. As a result of these policy changes, many women resumed their entrepreneurial activities.

Capitalist development in other Southeast Asian countries has had strongly negative effects on some disadvantaged groups of women while enabling other groups of women to achieve important roles in business or the professions, though not in the political arena. With the implementation of the New Economic Mechanism, a similar mixture of effects is beginning to occur in Laos. Women traders have been instrumental in expanding rural markets, increasing the potential for cash income in rural villages. In Vientiane and nearby towns about 2000 women manage small businesses (Lao PDR 1995, 31) and more light industry and handicraft opportunities are available in urban areas. However, some undesirable changes are already visible in urban areas and may also be affecting rural areas. Cash for labor is replacing labor exchange among relatives and neighbors. Women, disproportionately laid off during the privatization of state enterprises, search for or create new income opportunities, even those with low or unstable incomes. Child-care services have been discontinued. Urban work opportunities for women, such as garment factory work and prostitution, offer low wages and exploitative working conditions (M. Viravong 1995), while few technical and professional positions are available for educated women (Lao PDR 1995, 26, 30–31).

Even noneconomic government policies have indirectly affected women's work and power. An intensive literacy campaign conducted during the early years of the new government enabled many women to learn basic reading and writing skills, while governmental commitment to rural education to facilitate political and social integration made schooling available to many rural girls. More recently, a birth-spacing policy and the cancellation of a ban on birth control have enabled a few women to begin controlling the number and spacing of their children. Education and birth control are important resources now available to some girls and women as a result of government policies.

Summary

Laos is a small "least developed" and land-locked country in Southeast Asia. Subjected to two wars of national liberation during this century, village and national life was often disrupted. Laos is home to a number of different ethnic groups including the ethnic Lao, the Khmu, and the Hmong. The events of recent years, especially the transition to socialism after 1975 and the current economic liberalization, have led to a number of changes in Laotian village life, including changes among all three of these ethnic groups.

This chapter has provided the background for a more detailed look at rural women's traditional sources of power and subordination among all three groups. In Chapter 3 we will discover that ethnic Lao women enjoy several (though limited) traditional arenas of power and have several sources of economic power, whereas Hmong women customarily exercise very little power in any arena except through persuasion and the threat of suicide. Khmu women traditionally fall somewhere in between, exercising a little power in a few arenas and having a few potential sources of economic power.

Notes

1. I will use the term "Laotian" to refer to the country or to the entire population of the country, and the terms "Lao" or "ethnic Lao" to refer to people of lowland Lao ethnic groups.

2. A list of 68 groups has been generally accepted, but the Institute of Ethnology of the Lao Committee for Social Sciences recognized a working classification of 38 groups in 1989 (Khambai Gnundalath, Institute Director, personal communication, 1990).

3. Chinese, Vietnamese, and south Asians emigrated to Laos mainly during this century to engage primarily in commerce, various trades, and colonial administration. Today some continue to live and work in urban areas, but they are without great economic or political influence. I therefore exclude members of these groups from this discussion.

4. These U.N. statistics indicate a lower rate of economic participation than the government statistics quoted earlier.

5. The Geneva Accords of 1954 formalized Lao independence from French colonial rule and designated two provinces, Phong Saly and Houa Phan in the far north and east of the country, as "regroupment areas" for supporters of the Lao resistance, generally

called the Pathet Lao. Houa Phan, the more accessible and less mountainous of the two, became the center of communist administration during the ensuing twenty years of liberation struggle.

6. The more recent history of the Lao Patriotic Women's Association and the Lao Women's Union is discussed in Chapter 8.

7. In the past, taxes were commonly paid in rice.

8. A list of major reforms under the NEM and further economic developments in 1991–1992 were provided by the Resident Representative for the International Monetary Fund in Vientiane (Chi Do Pham 1992).

9. The name was changed to the Lao Women's Union in 1985.

10. In more recent versions of the slogan, men are rhetorically encouraged to "help" their wives with domestic tasks.

3

Traditional Sources of Power in Rural Women's Lives

Cultural ideas and organizational patterns common throughout Southeast Asia support the relatively high status of some groups of Laotian women, but women of other groups do not share most of these ideas and patterns and are more subordinate. To adequately explore the effects on rural women of macro-level changes during the socialist transition and economic liberalization periods, it seems necessary to understand changes in the work and power of women from more than one ethnic group. Three groups, representative of the three ethnic group categories commonly in use among Laotians themselves, have been selected: the ethnic Lao (the major lowland group), the Khmu (the most numerous midland group), and the Hmong (a major highland group). Women's traditional social position, work, and power are somewhat different in each group, so women of different groups react differently to change.

In later chapters I will explore how changes in the variables presented in Figure 1.1 influence women's power with socialism (1975–88) and then economic liberalization (1988–present) for women in each of the representative ethnic groups. But first, this chapter discusses women's traditional activities and power in each of these ethnic groups and the village context that shaped the lives of women in each group before 1975.

The vast majority of Laotians live and work in rural areas. People of all ethnic groups reside in villages, though they may spend up to several months at a time living in a field hut during the growing season. Village services, which were rudimentary before 1975, are still very basic: a few grades of school, a health post, wells or water system, a rice mill, or access to a road. Schools in many villages are temporary structures with dirt floors that must be rebuilt every year. Government efforts both before and after 1975 resulted in health posts in a few villages, but they were seldom in operation or supplied with medicine. A few villages, mainly ethnic Lao villages that benefited from aid programs in the decades before 1975, have drilled wells. Some wells that were dug are lined with cement rings for sanitation. Villagers near mountains may pipe their water from mountain springs using either bamboo lengths, wooden troughs, or plastic pipes. Less-remote villages are often connected to the district center or the provincial capital by regular truck or boat taxi service. Small rice mills operate in many villages which normally produce enough or nearly enough rice for their annual needs. Electricity was rarely available in villages before 1975; however, it is now available in a number of villages in the Vientiane Plain and in a few other accessible areas. Although rural dwellers of all groups devote most of their time and energy to meeting their own subsistence needs, village and family organization, and economies and practices vary significantly by ethnic group. All groups depend mainly on agriculture supplemented by domestic animals, wild food (animals, plants, fish), and crafts.

Village life provides the immediate context for most women's exercise of economic power. Women's activities, cultural meanings imputed to these activities, and women's economic resources form the basis for women's economic power in all ethnic groups. All rural residents, including women, are affected by changes in national or provincial structure and policy in the context of their lives and experiences as villagers.

Women's power in traditional Laos in all three ethnic groups was not formal or readily visible. Men were officially the household "heads," the village decision makers, the central actors in many religious and nonfamily rituals, and the heads of state, lineage, or clan. But during a village sojourn or a walk through any market or field, one could identify women at work in economy and family. Laotian women exercise power and experience autonomy in several arenas, though their sources of power and autonomy vary by stage in life cycle as well as by ethnic group. Rural women of all ethnic groups are involved in economic activities essential for the livelihood and well-being of their households and communities. Not all women, however, control economic resources or allocate products above those needed for subsistence. Rural women of all groups are also central to domestic and family life, but the degree to which they are solely responsible for household maintenance and limited to this sphere also varies by stage in family cycle in each ethnic group. Women's power or subordination in other arenas like politics, education, or religion differs from one ethnic group to another.

For each of the ethnic groups in turn, I examine rural women's traditional activities and control over resources and other valued goods in each potential arena of power or subordination (the economy, politics, education, religion, and family). I begin with a detailed presentation of ethnic Lao women's power, illustrated by two of my own research projects based on pre-1975 information, and then contrast this with the pre-1975 situation of Khmu and Hmong women. Finally, I summarize in tabular form women's traditional sources of power by ethnic group. For all groups I draw on the existing literature, limited though it is.[1]

Ethnic Lao Women and Traditional Village Life

Ethnic Lao villagers live mainly in the lowlands of Laos on the plains along the Mekong River and in other river valleys. The ethnic Lao of central and southern Laos share their cultural history with the Lao (Thai) Isan of northeast Thailand, and there are also some cultural links between the northern Thai and the ethnic Lao of northern Laos. There are several ethnic subgroups within the larger category of ethnic Lao. People in these groups are culturally very similar, though perhaps the Lue are the most distinctive.

The Village

In addition to the few village services that prosperous villages of all ethnic groups may enjoy, ethnic Lao villages may contain a Buddhist temple, often the most substantial building in the village. Also, even in smaller villages, one or more village women may transform part of her front porch or a space under her house into a small store or soup shop. Few villages have a daily food market, though a rotating market may regularly sell in a particular village one day during its rotation.

The village landscape in Ban Xa Phang Meuk on the plain north of Vientiane "includes lowland paddy fields, upland cleared and forested areas, all of which the villagers consider part of their village" (Branfman 1978, 2). Houses in Phone Sung, 50 kilometers north of Vientiane, are raised 5 to 7 feet above the ground by strong wooden posts and "consist of three units: a communal area for eating and receiving guests, a closed-off area in which the family sleeps and keeps its belongings, and a kitchen/washing area" (Barber 1979, 112). Variations on this style are numerous, even within Phone Sung. Poorer houses are lower and made entirely of bamboo and thatch, whereas richer families construct their houses of sawn wood and tin or tile roofing. Gardens are scattered around the perimeter of most ethnic Lao villages like Phone Sung (Barber 1979, 113). Besides the temple and the primary school, in Pha Khao, a village near Vientiane not far from Ban Xa Phang Meuk, residents use other public spaces between houses as a playground, a lumber yard, and a gambling venue (Ayabe 1961, 3).

Most rural Lao households are composed of a marital couple and their children, though a consistent percentage are extended, primarily including relatives of the wife. There is a tendency for young couples to live with the wife's parents, at least for a few years (Condominas 1970, 19). Of married Phone Sung couples with one member born outside the village, nearly three-quarters of the in-marrying spouses were men (Barber 1979, 117). The population is young, with one-half of the population twenty years old and under in Pha Khao and 58 percent under twenty in Phone Sung (Ayabe 1961, 50;

Barber 1979, 116). Boys and young men are more likely to leave the village for schooling, travel, army service, or work, so young women (between the ages of fifteen and twenty-five or thirty) outnumber young men in the village setting.

Traditional Village Economy and Women's Economic Power

Village and Household Economy. The rural household economy, which comprises the entire economy in most rural areas, is based on subsistence rice production often carried out in both paddy and dry hillside fields (swiddens). The fundamental economic task of a rural household is to grow enough rice to feed its members for the year. The growing season extends from about June through December, though clearing of dense brush and small trees from a fallow swidden begins in February or March. After the slash is dried, farmers burn it, build a fence, and, after a few early rain showers, plant rice seed with a dibble stick. In the meantime, interspersed with swidden work, the farming family is also repairing paddy dikes and preparing the seed bed for paddy rice cultivation. Depending on the weather, rice seed beds are planted in May or June. After the rains have begun and the soil is wet, one of the men in the farming family and his water buffalo plow and then harrow the fields to break the earthen clods into fine mud. Family groups often exchange labor for pulling, bundling, carrying, and transplanting rice seedlings.

Meanwhile, back in the swidden, rapidly growing weeds require the nearly constant attention of one of the women farmers, who may also plant other food crops like cucumbers, beans, root crops, corn, or peppers. Paddy rice, on the other hand, is rarely weeded, since standing water somewhat controls the weeds. Exchange labor groups often work together to harvest and to thresh at least some of the rice at the end of the rainy season (Ayabe 1961; Barber 1979, 133–35; Kaufman 1956; R. Ireson 1992). A few villages with irrigation systems grow a second rice crop during the dry season and farmers often cultivate gardens on river banks or other irrigable fields (near a well, stream, or irrigation system) during the dry season, hauling water to irrigate the vegetables.

Agriculture is the base of the village economy. However, urban employment for villagers near Vientiane grew between the 1950s and the 1970s as 84 percent of adults in Pha Khao in the 1950s and 76 percent of adults in neighboring Xa Phang Meuk in the 1970s were employed in nonagricultural activities (Branfman 1978, 7). However, in Xa Phang Meuk, a mere 9 kilometers from Vientiane, 85 percent of household heads considered themselves farmers, while over 90 percent engaged in farming activities (Branfman 1978, 6). War also affected this pattern of agricultural employment. One 1968 survey, including villages far from urban centers, reported that 42 percent of the households had at least one member who worked for wages; nearly one-half of these wage workers were soldiers (C. Ireson 1969, 7). In the 1980s, though, even villages near Vientiane resumed their agricultural focus. Two out of three surveyed villages of ethnic Lao near Vientiane, averaging nearly seven members per household, reported dependence on agricultural products (Maroczy 1987, Tables 1, 15 and 29).

Most rural families have livestock including water buffalo, Asian yellow cattle, pigs, and poultry. Buffalo are the main source of farm draft power. Families "bank" their savings by investing in both cattle and buffalo. Most families raise chickens and a few raise ducks. On the average, households own from 1.5 to more than 4 buffalo each. Xa Phang Meuk, Pha Khao, and Kaufman's sample are poorer in buffalo while Phone Sung villagers are richer in buffalo, on the average (Branfman 1978, 20; Ayabe 1961, 30; Kaufman 1956, 4–5; Barber 1979, 160).

"The wealth of the lowland Lao is in their rice fields and animals, while their welfare system is in the forest" (C. Ireson 1991, 23). This was true traditionally and is still true today. Forest gathering and hunting are part of the household economy (Branfman 1978; Condominas 1970; Maynard and Kraiboon 1969). Brush-covered upland fields, in fallow, as well as more mature forest, regularly provide food, fuel, medicinal plants, and fibers. In addition, villagers rely on the forest for food during poor crop years (Halpern 1958; Orr 1966). Household members also sell forest products like mushrooms, herbs, bamboo shoots, birds, and small animals (Kaufman 1956; Wulff 1972). Fish are the major source of dietary protein in addition to rice (Condominas 1970; C. Ireson 1969, Figure 5). Fishing is done with several different kinds of nets, baskets, and traps. Freshwater crabs and shrimp are also gathered in this way.

In the past, ethnic Lao women wove most of the cloth for their family's clothing. But manufactured clothing has steadily replaced all but the traditional woman's skirt, or *pha sin*. This process was well under way in the Vientiane Plain by the 1950s, though Kaufman (1956) found that 65 percent of the households he surveyed still had a loom that was used sporadically.

There is still a local market for woven goods traditionally made from grasses or bamboo. In a study of three Vientiane "suburb" villages, which are located near a swampy lake with an abundance of tough grasses, Maroczy (1987) found that 30 percent of the families surveyed weave mats, hats, and rice baskets for market. On the average, income from these products provides almost one-quarter of household income (Maroczy 1987, 10, Tables 28 and 33).

Larger, more prosperous villages may support one or two seamstresses or tailors who earn their living making shirts, blouses, trousers, sheets, and other items. Many villages have artisans or other specialists such as blacksmiths, carpenters, boatwrights, herb doctors, shamans, midwives, and barbers who depend on farming but practice their specialty when the need arises.

Villagers themselves, even those near urban areas, make many of their own baskets and tools. They make their own "fishing implements, ax handles, water buckets, and other bamboo and wooden objects" (Branfman 1978, 20). They repair their own oxcarts, replace their own thatch roofs, and weave bamboo walls for their houses. They construct components of their own simple wood and bamboo houses and with the help of neighbors "raise" and assemble the house frame.

Besides the small village stores operated by local women and the periodic market that may regularly appear in the village, trade is limited. However, the economy of most Lao villages has not constituted a completely closed subsistence system for decades, if ever. Silver and gold have been used as repositories of wealth and for substantial payments for several hundred years (Barber 1979, 150). Barter trade networks have functioned for decades, if not centuries, in the Vientiane Plain and other regions along the Mekong River where ethnic Lao are concentrated. Essential commodities like salt, cotton, and iron, which are not produced in all localities, were exchanged. Rural families can also sell small agricultural surpluses and forest products at district market towns (Branfman 1978, 23-24). Before 1975, Chinese often controlled much of the local commercial market in the larger villages. They often operated the largest store, purchased rice for district rice mills, and loaned money to villagers (Kaufman 1956, 7).

Research based on pre-1975 evidence finds that paddy landholdings are fairly equally distributed (Evans 1990, 68-69), with villagers holding, on the average, less than 2 hectares (ha)[2] of land (Kaufman 1956, 7; Branfman 1978). Few households in three surveyed Vientiane Plain villages held more than 5 ha, ranging from only 3 percent in two villages to 17 percent in one village (Taillard 1974, 144). Except in urban areas, almost all families have access to some farmland. Swidden fields are used temporarily by farmers who hold no permanent rights to these fields.

Unfortunately, most previous village studies ignore women's work. Ayabe's view (1961, 29) of occupations does not allow him to identify women as having an occupation, not even that of weaver or farmer. Branfman (1978, 21) does note that women engage in washing clothes and cooking and that they spend a great deal of time threshing and winnowing rice. Traditionally, however, ethnic Lao village women are important economic actors.

Women's Economic Power. The strength of ethnic Lao women centers in their key economic roles. Women control the production and distribution of some of the goods they produce, and women who care for their aging parents receive the major portion of the family inheritance. Women traditionally have held the family purse strings and, while not the sole financial decision makers, have shared this role with their husbands. In a multigenerational household, the middle-aged couple[3] is usually financially responsible for the family. The household makes a large purchase or sale only if both the husband and wife agree. Women keep the family money and are usually responsible for everyday financial management of the household. Economic activities that traditionally are controlled by Lao women include gardening, small animal raising, forest gathering, textile and other craft production, and marketing. Rice farming in both paddy and swidden (upland field) is traditionally carried out by the family as a unit, and sometimes by an entire extended family, and women are important contributors to family rice sufficiency.

Ethnic Lao women farm with their husbands and families. Some village roles and productive tasks, like transplanting rice seedlings, harvesting and carrying rice, and some ritual specialties, are traditionally open to both women and men. Most are gender-identified by custom, though the division of labor is not rigid and anyone can perform nearly any task without social disapproval. Women and girls are mainly responsible for cooking, household maintenance, water carrying, forest gathering, and care of small domestic animals. They also transplant rice and weed swidden fields. Men and older boys are mainly responsible for care of buffalo and oxen, hunting, and plowing the paddy or clearing the swidden fields. The oldest working man in the household directs household rice production and represents the family in temple rituals and village councils. Both sexes plant swiddens, harvest, thresh and carry rice, and work in the gardens. Most Lao petty traders have been women. In the following pages, Laotians who participated as adults in Lao village life before 1975 describe women's and men's activities.

Paddy Rice Farming. In traditional paddy rice farming, rice is grown in standing water. The field, called a paddy, is plowed and harrowed several times before rice seedlings are transplanted into it. Men nearly always plant the seed bed, plow and harrow the paddy, and attend to the water level in the paddy, though when there is no man in the family, women in some villages carry out any or all of these tasks. For example, one informant from southern Laos reports that

> I never plowed, . . . but my sister had to plow because there was a lack of males in the family. There was no male. There were only female children. Our father was old; when he was tired, my sister had to do it. When she plowed, I pulled the seedlings until my sister . . . married. My sister then quit plowing." (Interview #16)[4]

Another woman from central Laos agrees that "If there are no men, women also plow rice fields." When asked if she knew how to plow, she says, "Yes, but I cannot do heavy work like land clearing because it is too heavy" (Interview #10).

A man from southern Laos insists, though, that women never plow.

Informant: Plowing is men's work; the women never do it.
Interviewer: The women have never plowed once in your village?
Informant: No, never. (Interview #9)

PHOTO 3.1 Children sometimes accompany their mother as she works, like these children who play near their mother while she uproots seedlings.

A woman from central Laos confirms his report. Her mother was a widow and divorcee. "It is so hard to grow up without a father. Without a man, you can't grow rice and have a farm." When her only brother was old enough, he plowed the fields, so the family did produce their own rice, but when her brother was mistakenly drafted into the Royalist forces,[5] life was very hard. The informant, her sisters, and her mother worked for her uncle in the same village. They were unable to work their own land since they could not plow. In exchange for their work, the uncle gave them rice, but they still did not have enough food. They sold or traded for additional food. They even traded some of their buffalo, though some were killed by the army. The household of women could not properly take care of the buffalo anyway, since they could not go deep into the forest to look for them at the beginning of the cropping season.[6] Her brother was gone for two years before he was allowed to return to his family. When he returned, the fields were full of weeds, there was no buffalo, and most family possessions were gone. The household had to begin all over again. This hardship occurred mainly because, in her area, it was inconceivable that women would plow, harrow, or look for ranging buffalo in the forest. It was not until later in her life that she saw ethnic Lao women plowing in another district (Kiang McIntosh, personal communication, 1993).

While men or older boys (in most cases) were plowing, women and girls were often uprooting and transplanting seedlings (see Photo 3.1), though men and boys would sometimes help with transplanting. "Because women are not strong," according to one female informant, "women uproot seedlings and transplant, and men plow" (Interview #7). This is a time of steady work for all, as one man recounts.

Interviewer: What about transplanting seedlings? Women transplant more than men? or the same?
Informant: Women do more than men.
Interviewer: Why? They don't do it together, then?
Informant: No; generally, women do this. They hold that this is a woman's job. The men do more plowing and harrowing.
Interviewer: What do men do after plowing and harrowing? Do they just go and sit?
Informant: No, they go help transplant, too (laughs); or if they don't want to transplant they could go to take care of the paddy dikes and level of water of the paddies.
Interviewer: They don't just sit and have a smoke?
Informant: No! (laughs). (Interview #34)

Another man remembers the behavior of male workers less charitably. He reports that "boys plow and when they're done they go to eat, and girls transplant" (Interview #20). Yet another man reports that agricultural work in groups is great fun. He says, "one guy harrows, one plows, others just transplant, some uproot seedlings, carrying seedlings. We talk with the girls (laugh). . . . After working we have something to eat plus drinks, a smoke. It's fun, right? We make jokes with friends, girls and boys enjoy talking to each other. We forget being tired. We don't feel tired, instead we enjoy" (Interview #40).

Not one informant reported weeding the growing rice, or applying fertilizer or insecticide during the growing period. Traditionally, few households carry out these activities. Harvesting (i.e., cutting the rice stalk and laying it on the field to dry) is often done in groups with more women than men. If one household has a large field to harvest and insufficient labor, they often invite others to work with them for a day (called *vaan* in central and southern Laos). One man reports that "working this way is not tiring; working is enjoyable because there are many people: men and women, boys and girls. If we *vaan* many, we enjoy working the whole day. . . . We continue harvesting until dusk, the sun goes down, and we are still harvesting, until we can't see any more. . . . Then we have dinner together" (Interview #39).

One male informant says that in his village "the work is divided up into tasks. There's harvesting. . . . Women must harvest, the men tie and carry the sheaves, carry to the shed. Children watch the buffalo, keep them from eating the rice" (Interview #6). Another says that "if there are two men in the family, the women can just do the harvesting; the men can tie the rice stalks and carry them to the barn. Tying is not simple! One day, you tie between 3-4 rice paddies. Sometimes, you can do about 700–800 ties" (Interview #18).

Both men and women may carry sheaves to the threshing floor or rice to the granary. Sheaves are positioned on either end of a bamboo pole, which is carried on one's shoulder. Unhusked rice grains from the threshing floor may be carried in baskets on either end of a pole or in a large bag on one's shoulders. Men are much more likely to carry bagged rice. Carrying is hard work. One experienced woman farmer says, "Oh yes, I have worked it all. I used to carry paddy unhusked rice if the villagers asked us to help. I carry paddy on my shoulder pole and it [shoulder] is swollen" (Interview #12).

Many informants report that threshing was the highlight of the agricultural season, especially during their adolescence. Both men and women report much labor exchange, helping other families and flirting in lively work groups late into the night. "We clear the ground and put a large bamboo mat on it.[7] Women shovel grain while men wave fans to winnow the grain. You have to know just how to do it" (Interview #32; man from northern Laos). Another informant says, "As it was done in our village the threshing was the last chore of the season. Those with . . . a smaller farm would get done sooner . . . so [they had] . . . the opportunity to see what others were up to. . . . We would hang out and enjoy the chicken soup . . . just take the opportunity to help out" (Interview #37). During threshing season, "young men and women would thresh . . . and socialize with a lot of fun under the moonlight" (Interview #19). Another says, "The boys come to help the girls. A house with girls, they [the boys] really like to go help. . . . And if the fields are near the village, the boys really go help a lot. You don't have to ask them. If they hear . . . the sound of threshing, TUM, TUM, they'll go" (Interview #34).

"Threshing like this is really fun!" agrees a woman informant. Just get young women to help you, and young men will be attracted. "Oh, that's fun! When you've finished the threshing, then you eat chicken" and flirt some more (Interview #35). Since the young people have come to flirt, sometimes they do not pay attention to the rice grains scattered all over as they thresh rice very energetically. So older people "have to come keep an eye on things" (Interview #34). Reporting on common events during this season in his southern village, a male informant says that

> Young men went out visiting the girls and on the way home late at night, . . .
> feeling hungry for chicken soup and finding nothing to do . . . would stop to
> help thresh rice. . . . Some owners might . . . be asleep . . . but the young men
> would sneak up and start threshing away. . . . As the owner woke up and saw
> them working, . . . it was only a courtesy to get up and butcher a chicken to
> make soup for them (laughter). (Interview #37)

Carrying rice and loading it into the granary are tasks done by men, women, or mixed groups, depending on the customs of the village, although men are traditionally responsible for hauling rice by oxcart. As with threshing, a number of people might help with these tasks, turning work into a social occasion. For example, one woman from southern Laos reports on her Uncle Lom's farm.

> He got a lot of rice paddy and his farm is far from the village; he used thirty buffalo and thirty carts. They loaded up and made a long line. One buffalo can carry thirty baskets of rice paddy but some buffalo can carry only twenty-one or twenty-two baskets. When they arrived home . . . five to six women . . . unloaded the rice paddy into the barn. The women were relatives from our village. . . . This is women's work. (Interview #8)

A man from central Laos remembers hauling rice by oxcart, saying, "This is the most fun of all! Our oxcarts follow one another. We sing all the way transporting rice to the village. . . . All the girls line up to help . . . carry rice to the barn. We mix boys and girls. . . . If you're slow, the girl will drop the basket over your head. We go help everyone" (Interview #18).

> *Interviewer*: The majority of people to drive the oxcarts, are they young men?
> *Informant*: Yes, young men.
> *Interviewer*: The . . . girls . . . help move the rice to the barn?
> *Informant*: The girls! The elderly will just watch. They watch us and supervise us. . . . According to our tradition, of course! (Interview #18)

In paddy farming villages, then, the senior working man in the household organizes paddy work. Women and girls traditionally uproot and transplant rice seedlings, harvest, thresh, and load rice into the granary. Men and boys often help with all of these tasks. In addition, women or girls sometimes plow, harrow, or carry out other male tasks, if there is a shortage of male labor. The senior household woman usually keeps the keys to the granary.

Swidden Farming. Swidden or slash-and-burn agriculturalists traditionally clear forest or brush covered land, burn slash for fertilizer, and seed the land without plowing or hoeing. Swidden fields are typically located on hillsides. Swidden farming season traditionally begins with the selection and clearing of farmland from forest or fallow fields. Experienced ethnic Lao swidden farmers leave the felled trees and cut underbrush to dry for several weeks before burning the new field, and then plant immediately after the first rains of the rainy season. One male farmer from the north describes the process like this:

> Fifteen or twenty people in all help clear the *hai* (upland field). Lots of different kinds of trees—women clear brush, then men fell trees. Felling big trees is the task of men. We have to know how to fall them and where to fall them. You have to be very careful—you have to know where the trees are going to fall; otherwise, they might hurt you. We start clearing fields in the third lunar

month [about February]. After drying, burn the slash—cooperate in cutting firebreaks just before burning in the fifth month [April] which is very hot. (Interview #32)

After the clearing and burning, the new field is seeded directly. Rice seedlings are not transplanted, and the hillside is generally not cultivated. One woman from central Laos explains that men jab holes in the soil with sharp sticks, while women put seeds in the holes using a long bamboo tube (Interview #29). In one southern village,

> Men make the holes for seeds and the women put in the rice seeds and cover the hole behind them. . . . Men, three, four, five of them, continue digging the holes and women put rice into the holes and cover them. If we don't cover the holes the rice will be eaten by insects, especially ants. We use our hand putting rice in the holes and cover them. The rice is in a basket; we seed it and cover it by hand. You should not put too many rice seeds . . . in the holes. If we put in three to four seeds for one hole, when they grow they tiller [grow shoots] well. (Interview #40)

After planting is finished, women are primarily responsible for keeping weeds under control and for planting and harvesting vegetables and fruits in the upland field. The process of harvesting, threshing, and hauling rice back to the village is carried out much as it is in paddy rice cultivation.

Gardening. Traditionally, lowland dwelling households plant dry season gardens on river banks or near another dependable water source. Gardening usually is considered women's work, though men may turn over the soil before planting, or, occasionally, work with their wives to maintain the crops. Gardeners plant both cash crops, like tobacco, and crops for household use, like vegetables and cotton. Women plant, water, weed, harvest, and process or market their garden crops. Gardens may be small "kitchen" gardens or large commercial gardens. A tobacco farmer explains that she, like other tobacco farmers in her area of central Laos, grows as many as 10,000 plants, transplanting them from the raised seed bed into rows in the garden when they are three to five inches tall (Interview #30).

> When the plants grow tall, we decide how many leaves we want each plant to have, and when they reach that size we go through and break off the top of every plant. Then it doesn't send out other new leaves; only the existing leaves grow bigger, higher quality. After breaking off the tops, the plants send up shoots. We have to remove them quickly so the leaves don't become bitter . . . then we harvest the leaves ourselves as they mature—daily, two to three leaves per plant at a time. Harvest extends over about a month. We need to water throughout, but just enough to keep the plants healthy. (Interview #30)

Usually households do not exchange garden labor as they do for paddy or swidden work, though occasionally they exchange labor in the informant's village. In a village where tobacco is the main cash crop, the informant is the owner of the tobacco garden and sells the final product, but her husband shreds the tobacco after the leaves have "aged" for a few days. She describes this as follows:

> *Informant*: After harvesting, we put tobacco leaves in a cage; we pile leaves over one another fairly tightly about three nights or four nights until they turn yellow, and we slice them.
> *Interviewer*: Who shreds or slices the leaves?
> *Informant*: Soubinh [her husband] slices.
> *Interviewer*: What if he were not home?
> *Informant*: He has to be there because this is the time we grow tobacco. Our working season. We can't go anywhere. (Interview #30)

Swidden farmers of all ethnic groups grow some onions, herbs, vegetables, and spices for home consumption. Sometimes vegetables, especially eggplant, cucumber, and long bean, are planted among the rice plants or sometimes separately. Pepper and other seedlings may be nurtured in the home garden before they are planted in the swidden.

Another gardener, this one from southern Laos, also describes garden work in her village.

> After growing rice, we have tobacco and vegetable planting on the river bank. If we are a big family, we have two or three gardens. Only a family—brothers, sisters, father working together plant a garden. Women . . . plant; heavy work like digging is for men. Each one household is doing it alone. I do mine, you do yours. In garden work, we are not in a hurry; we depend on water from the river. (Interview #12)

Animal Husbandry. Women are almost entirely responsible for raising smaller animals like chickens, ducks, pigs, and goats, though they often delegate this responsibility. Children or older people may feed the animals, cutting grass for the tethered buffalo or scattering rice husks for the freely roaming chickens, ducks, and pigs. Besides fish and frogs, chickens are the most common source of animal protein for many villagers. When relatives and friends work in labor exchange groups, a chicken from the "host" family enriches the diet of the workers and adds to the fun. When an important person visits the village, chickens are killed for his or her dinner.

One informant says that his younger siblings do the lighter work. Everyone, including the children, must tend the herd of cattle and buffalo (Interview #19). While men are more likely to plow or haul with buffalo or oxen, all family members help to care for these valuable larger animals.

Forest Foraging and Fishing. "The gathering and use of forest products [constitutes] a traditional role for women" (Fortmann and Rocheleau 1985, 254). One study in northeast Brazil found that forest product extraction is roughly equivalent to wage labor and to agriculture in its contribution to family income. In Brazil, this "subsidy from nature" is most important for poor households and for women (Hecht, Anderson, and May 1988).

Forest foraging is sometimes a principal source of subsistence for villagers as among the Mnong Gar Montagnard peoples of Vietnam's central highlands (studied by Condominas before their village was destroyed by war in 1962). Among this group, wild foods, "especially bamboo shoots, were eaten in the greatest numbers when the rice was growing but not yet harvested" (Condominas 1977, 120). Long fallow shifting rice cultivation was the main source of subsistence among this group.

Like villagers of Brazil, Vietnam, and other countries,[8] Laotians of all ethnic groups depend on forest products for subsistence and, occasionally, for income. While all villagers eat and use forest products, families growing insufficient rice regularly supplement their diets with wild foods and sometimes sell forest items. During poor crop years, most families must depend on the forest for survival.

Among the ethnic Lao, women are the main gatherers of forest food and other wild products that supplement household agricultural production, while men hunt and both men and women fish. Barber (1979) claims that fishing is a male activity, but Condominas (1970, 12) notes that "everybody fishes, all year long." Some kinds of fishing techniques are more commonly used by men, especially net casting, pumping a pond dry, and grenade fishing (also mentioned by Barber 1979, 141–43). Pumps and grenades are more available to men than to women. One informant says,

> Looking for food nearby is usually for the women, the men don't go. Women go to forest or pond and come back the same day. Oh! They go for the day for fishing in the ponds. They go to the swidden fields, or the paddy, look for frogs. The children can go along. They go for maybe two hours, like going to the market, but the forest market. (Interview #6)

Men, on the other hand, are more likely to spend overnight in the forest on a hunting, fishing, and gathering expedition (Interview #6).

Crafts. Few of the goods needed for household use can be purchased with the limited income obtained from the sale of agricultural surplus or forest products. Thus, most must be made by family members. Traditionally, women and men, young and old, contribute to household goods production. Some home-produced goods are simply used by the household, or bartered or sold in exchange for other needed items or services. But some craft processes and products have significance beyond their household uses. For example, excellent young ethnic Lao weavers in both Thailand and Laos traditionally attract desirable husbands, while outstanding older weavers are well respected. Furthermore, a distinctive woven skirt border defines a woman as ethnic Lao (Cheesman 1988). Traditionally, mothers of Lao sons determined whether and when their sons could enter the Buddhist monkhood by the timing and production of the variety of cloths necessary for their ordinations (Lefferts 1993). Craft production for marriageability, respect, cultural identity, and religious observance may be displaced by competing systems of value and competing factory-produced items as a unique culture is assimilated into larger economic and social systems (see Ehlers 1990 for a Guatemalan example and Weiner 1986 for a Papua New Guinea example).

Women in all three Laotian ethnic groups are responsible for cloth production, but a number of women make other items for sale or barter, including, for example, alcoholic beverages, snack food, floor mats, and thatch for roofing.

Ethnic Lao women are traditionally responsible for the production of family clothing from its beginning in the planting of a cotton crop through its completion in the weaving of cloth and the sewing of the final garment (see Photo 3.2). Some villages traditionally specialize in silk production. Although household men might construct a silkworm-raising shed, weave bamboo trays for raising the silkworms, or help construct a loom frame, most of the cotton and silk work is carried out by women who distribute the fruits of their labors to family members as appropriate. Cloth produced beyond family requirements is sold or bartered. Some Lao weavers obtain cotton from Khmu women in return for producing cloth for the use of Khmu households. One southern weaver reports,

> In one year we members of our household make fifty to sixty skirt lengths of material. Generally everyone [every woman] in every house does it. The house with three people do three looms; the house with four, do four! The house with two women; there are two looms, then. These are the women's responsibilities. From age ten, eleven, or twelve girls know how to do this. They watch us, and do it together. During the reactionary period [i.e., before 1975], the youngsters aged thirteen, fourteen, fifteen know how to weave and know how to knit, too. For myself, I know everything. After finishing, I sell it for money. (Interview #16)

Until recent years, mothers taught daughters designing and weaving skills when girls were still young, and adolescent girls spent long hours weaving at the loom under the house, especially during the slack agricultural season. Often young women, weaving into the evening under their houses, were

PHOTO 3.2 This woman of Luang Prabang Province can remove the seeds from one kilogram of cotton per day with her manual gin.

visited by small groups of flirtatious young men. Part of her weaving, traditionally, was for her trousseau. Also, however, she hoped to impress one of her regular visitors and his parents with her artistry and industry. If family clothing needs were met, weavers bartered their cloth for other goods or sold it for a profit.

Through the practice of textile arts, village women exert a certain amount of control over the gender definition and activities of various family members. For example, traditionally, to support the ordination of a son, a mother must weave a voluminous amount of the required material: 33 square meters of white cloth for his robe (which is then dyed saffron, often in the monastery), a colorful silk sarong and one or more shoulder cloths, a patterned head cover, pillow and mattress covers to decorate gifts accompanying her son into the temple, and a female-patterned cloth to enfold his alms bowl. Her skill and dedication in preparing the requisite donations determine the occurrence and timing of her son's ordination (Lefferts 1993). Sponsoring a son's ordination earns merit for the mother by her contribution of her son, as well as by her sponsorship of the ordination. Her son, dressed in fancy clothing as he enters the ordination and then in a monk's robe, all of fabric skillfully prepared by his mother, is, in some ways, the mother's spiritual representative (Lefferts 1993).

Blouses, shirts, and trousers from factory-made cloth replaced homemade clothing in many villages by mid-century, and by the late 1960s many women in more accessible villages were wearing skirts of cloth manufactured in Hong Kong or Japan. In more remote areas, ethnic Lao women continued to make family clothing unless they were displaced by war. Older women in one Luang Prabang village report, however, that they stopped silk-raising in the 1960s when the previous government prohibited silk-making since it was a sin to boil and kill silkworms, a necessary step in thread production (Alton 1993, A–9). By the early 1970s, Barber (1979) reports that most weavers of Phone Sung had stored their looms some years previously. However, during the same time period, women in Hat Saifong district near Vientiane produced voluminous amounts of elegant silk cloth for skirts and elaborately patterned skirt borders for sale locally and in the capital city.

In addition to textiles, Lao women traditionally ferment rice in water to make alcoholic beverages. Part-time village specialists distill the more potent spirits using a primitive still, often made of easily available materials like a barrel and a dish pan. Rice wine and spirits are commonly sold or exchanged within the village. Women, especially ethnic Lao women, make snack foods like noodles only on special occasions or as a business. Floor mats and thatch are commonly made by villagers to cover and furnish their own homes, but may, on occasion, be sold or exchanged.

Marketing. Before 1975, village entrepreneurs and market sellers of local goods were frequently ethnic Lao women. Except for trade in large livestock, markets traditionally are populated predominantly by women as both sellers and buyers. Businesspeople in towns (e.g., Indian cloth merchants, Chinese jewelers, and Vietnamese restaurant owners), both before and after 1975, are often not Laotian, however. Most villages have one or two storekeepers who frequently traveled to larger towns or to a nearby national border to purchase goods. Merchants often visit villages to purchase crops or products for sale in larger towns. Often these village traders were Lao women.

One village businesswoman started a small all-purpose retail business on the porch of her house. She sold medicines, groceries, sweets, and noodle soup. She talks about how she got started:

> I bought things in Vientiane, like candies, medicine, tobacco, aspirin, other medicines, brought them to our village and sold them. Elder sister, auntie [fictive kin terms] who didn't have enough, had no money, would come get something from me. Maybe bought something worth 8000 and would give . . . rice [in exchange]; I'd take whatever they could give. (Interview #28)

The store gradually expanded to take over most of the house. She loaned money to relatives who bought a taxi. When they left the country before 1975, they gave her the taxi. Her modest house grew into a pharmacy, a grocery, a small restaurant, and a taxi stand. Her husband drove the taxi, but she was the businesswoman.

Another informant describes how she sold her produce to traveling merchants. "No problem, as long as we have products, they come to buy them at our place. Market women come to buy them at our garden and they take them to sell in Vientiane market" (Interview #10). In Hat Saifong district where I lived in 1968, women gardeners, assisted by family members, grew a large variety of cash crops for sale in the Vientiane market. Early every morning a village truck transported village products and women vendors to Vientiane, returning after the vendors completed their sales. Both of these informants and the Hat Saifong village were located within 32 kilometers of the Vientiane market. Informants who lived in more remote areas reported less market activity.

Ethnic Lao women, then, are traditionally major participants in the household economy, contributing their farming labor to paddy rice production, and managing the swidden from planting to harvest time. A woman's garden, small animal husbandry, forest foraging, and craft products are consumed in the household. Any surplus products customarily are hers to barter or sell. Women are traditionally the marketers, so some women sell not only their own products, but others' products as well, often returning with goods to sell in their own village.

Traditional Sources of Political and Community Power

Lao society does not have rigid social classes. Traditionally, members of royal families constituted an hereditary elite, but few members of that elite lived in villages. Buddhist monks, male elders, and school teachers are accorded respect. There is little socioeconomic stratification in rural villages with little or no occupational differentiation. Existing stratification is based on wealth and occupation, and seems to vary by stages in family cycle. Household prosperity appears to be most dependent on the availability of labor to produce a surplus for sale. The time of greatest prosperity during the family cycle is when the oldest daughter marries, the younger children are productive workers, and the older parents are still healthy and working in fields. A family at this stage has maximum labor power. As children marry and move out, though, the custodial child begins the family cycle anew as parents begin to withdraw from fieldwork.

The basis of village social control is the need to maintain a good reputation. Numerous family economic and life-cycle activities can only be performed with the support and cooperation of fellow villagers. Villagers withhold this support from those who are dishonest, lazy, or uncooperative. In extreme cases, people may be accused of witchcraft and ejected from a village (see R. Ireson 1996).

Women were less directly involved than men in local and national politics and government before 1975. Beyond the village women traditionally are politically visible only in supportive roles as secretaries and banquet preparers. Some village and town women probably play indirect political roles facilitating interfamily and interfaction communication to resolve disputes or otherwise strengthen extended family ties for political ends. However, the Lao national "state" historically has not had a strong presence in most villages, so the control of women by a male-dominated central government has not dramatically affected rural women's lives until recent years. On the other hand, the tendency for more women than men to remain in their natal villages after marriage has enabled women to maintain and solidify family and (sometimes fictive) kin networks. As a result, women are often active in community and neighborhood affairs, even though their husbands are the customary household heads.

Ethnic Lao women's traditional community activities include participating in town meetings and community work projects. Ethnic Lao villages are customarily headed by a single village chief who manages village-governmental relations, organizes community projects, and mediates local disputes. He is advised by a group of middle-aged or older men. Some of these elders sit on the temple committee as well. These two organizations, the temple committee and the village elders, constitute the only local political organizations.

Occasionally a village designates a chief of the village for women who might organize women's responsibilities for a village festival or, less commonly, hold a separate meeting for women on a matter of villagewide importance.[9] Often, though, the wife of the village head organizes women's activities as necessary.

> *Interviewer:* Is the wife chief of the village? In Salakham village, there are chiefs of village for men and women separately; how about your village?
> *Informant:* There is only one place for chief of village in my village—men and women come together at the same house. (Interview #38)

Village heads in different villages call villagers to official meetings in different ways. The village crier may call out news of the meeting from a central place in the village;[10] or the village head himself may sound a gong or drum on a large wood block, or he may personally invite each family to the meeting.

Commonly, each family sends a representative to the meeting, though sometimes both husband and wife attend. One woman observes how formal male authority is reinforced by the way in which village leadership calls a meeting. She says that "in some places, they go to inform [*pao*] at your home; sometimes they walk on the street and inform 'tonight there's this or that, there will be a meeting at the temple. If dad isn't home, son should go; if son isn't home, dad should go.' I heard them say it like this" (Interview #24). Villagers most often report that meetings are for household heads, but in most villages this results in a predominantly but not exclusively male meeting. One woman from central Laos reports on the meeting to discuss the annual ceremony honoring the village spirit:

> Yes—the lord for that domain (spiritual)—would come by the village chief's place to inform of the need and procedures to be followed—the chief then would sound the drum or *ka loh* [wood block] for the villagers to gather at his place to meet and discuss the plan—they met right next door to us so I knew and heard everything. . . . Mother and other villagers came to the meeting; family heads. (Interview #17)

In the village of the previous northern woman, she recounts that:

> *Informant:* When the *chaa paao* [village crier] announces a meeting, tomorrow we will go, everyone wonders what it is, set the time aside. We help each other if someone can't go. Eat dinner and then go to the meeting at the headman's house. They ring the gong in a small village.
> *Interviewer:* Who goes to the meeting, men or women?
> *Informant:* Either men or women can go to the meeting.
> *Interviewer:* Does one person go?
> *Informant:* Yes, one person goes. (Interview #38)

The same custom is followed in southern Laos, according to this woman informant who says that "if my husband can't go, I will go" (Interview #13). Yet another informant reports that in her village only men attended village meetings.

Informant: Only men go to the meeting, then come back and let the family members know and go to help.
Interviewer: For example, if there are jobs that need women to help, don't women go to the meeting?
Informant: Usually not.
Interviewer: How do they know what to do?
Informant: Our husband comes back to let us know; if there is no work for women, men go to help. (Interview #12)

When villagers agree to carry out a project, each house sends a worker on designated days. A woman from southern Laos describes the building of a diversion dam, which also created a village fishpond:

In the village, there is a river; people build a dam. This is the head monk's idea. They use money from the temple. The money mostly came from the people. The temple keeps it. It was used for a dam. . . . It is a diversion dam. To divert the water. This dam is not for fish, but it results in water and fish at the same time. . . . It takes many months to build. Everyone comes to help one another. The majority is the adults . . . both men and women. . . . Dig . . . the big rocks, . . . haul stone, break the stone. We don't use explosives, but our own hard labor and energy. (Interview #34)

A central woman says that "Oh, our village does work, like with a school, we *vaan* [contribute exchange labor], help, call to work, the village meets, decides 'such-and-such a day we will build a school,' and have this or that person to help. The women can help too, the husbands and wives can work, the kids can help, carry wood, help" (Interview #28). Another woman from central Laos says that "the village head tells them [household representatives] that they will dig a well. All the men should go help. He announces like that and leads them to dig. And then we go to help or work. The women also help pull the mud and dirt out from the well" (Interview #11).

Some informants report community projects that were carried out mainly by men. A central woman reports that in her village "for collective home construction and building projects—men did the work. Women just helped with food; preparing meals and drinks for the workers" (Interview #33). However, one female informant reports a road-building project that was disproportionately carried out by young women:

My uncle, the village chief, also called on people for help in the project. Work was done at night under the torch light, after there had been a candlelight vigil at the temple ground on the *"van sin"* [religious day]. The road was large and wide enough for two vehicles to pass each other to and fro. Works involved digging and hauling dirt. . . . The road gave access to Nasaytong and Vientiane from our village. I helped for two weeks. . . . Those who came to help . . . they came to work for us; we had to feed them. The work was done by women—mostly young girls. . . . They came empty-handed—we had all the tools. (Interview #17)

Not everyone contributes labor to village projects. Sometimes both non-Laotian and local merchants residing in the village contribute money instead of labor. A northern informant reports that "if they [Vietnamese merchants] don't work with the others, they give something, money . . . or food . . . to help." His wife adds that "mostly the trader women contribute money" (Interview #41).

Finally, ethnic Lao women traditionally use their communication and problem-solving skills to resolve some village disputes. In one central Lao village, the new farmer's association (composed only of men) was confronted with a land dispute. After a contentious meeting that upset a number of the members,[11] the issue was evidently the subject of many private conversations for several days. At the next meeting of the association, the issue barely surfaced. It had been resolved quietly with the informal assistance of village women.

So, even though ethnic Lao women do not traditionally represent the village to government beyond the village or carry primary responsibility for organizing villagewide activities, senior household women often participated in village meetings, and both men and women of all ages contributed to most villagewide projects. Women, as well as men, mobilize village labor in a number of villages. Sometimes informal discussions between husbands and wives and, in turn, between the women of different households, help to resolve village disputes.

Education and Traditional Sources of Power

While boys traditionally learn to read and write during one or more sojourns as novices in the village Buddhist temple, girls learn how to weave, sew, and market from their mothers, aunts, and grandmothers. Both learn agricultural, hunting, and foraging skills from older same-sex relatives. While both weaving and marketing require some arithmetic, girls do not formally study math. Children of both sexes learn skills necessary for successful lives as village farmers by observing and by following the instructions of older, usually same-sex relatives and neighbors. Children's games often consist of modeling adult activity, like farming, cooking, or marketing. Adolescents, at least if supervised, can perform nearly all adult subsistence tasks.

Before 1975 in the cities and in nearby villages, boys were more often sent to school, but secular and Christian schools were open to both boys and girls. A number of these girls then became teachers. Many villages did build secular schools and were assigned government teachers before 1975. Both girls and boys then attended the village school. Usually only a few boys and virtually no girls from rural schools were able to continue their education in the district or provincial capital.

One informant remembers the establishment of a school in her village near Vientiane. "During my older sisters' and brother's days, there was no school; you could only study with the monks in the temple. After that, in 196(?), I don't remember. There was a school by the village women's organization, a teacher . . . they taught at the school. I remember from when I was about 10"[12] (Interview #28). Another informant talks about how children learn:

> The kids, as they grow up, see their father, mother work; they call them, say, "Child, come help your father." If it's a son, he helps his father; if a girl, she helps her mother. Steam rice, carry water, help her mother. The mother has to tell her the details. Do this, do that. . . . All would know what to do by age twelve to thirteen. They see their friends, everyone else does the same, they know it, and parents don't have to tell them in detail any more. (Interview #13)

Village projects often offer opportunities to learn skills, as well as to socialize and to contribute to community improvement. One temple dormitory project benefited boys, rather than girls, however.

> No work assignment was designated . . . just young people did the packing of the ground before pouring the cement slab. . . . As the evening came around they would sound the drum and the young people would get excited about going out . . . because it was an opportunity to get out to socialize . . . young people would get "energized" and motivated to do work. . . . The monks . . . had the skills to do the work and oversee . . . the operation; also the village chief/*tasseng* [sub-district chief] would go to oversee the project . . . and sometimes they did not. Sometimes they dropped in briefly . . . leaving it up to the children and young people to do the work. If it was . . . major work the monks would do it. Every morning after waking up and having breakfast, they start working. The general policy set forth by the head monk was that of using the construction as an . . . opportunity for the novices and other monks to learn skills as they are involved in the construction project. This project and program was spearheaded by the Rev. Choui. . . . Those who graduated from the program and construction project would leave with skills to make a living in carpentry, masonry, and others. (Interview #37)

Girls are sometimes involved in fund-raising activities for both schools and temples. A village resident and head teacher reports that teenage girls helped raise money for the construction of a new primary school building.

> First and foremost is money. How to raise funds for the project. . . . This is a true story, OK; that particular year the Army Corps of Engineers staff were competing for the attention of the young girls in our village so they tried to outdo each other . . . (laughter). Each and everyone of them was in on the competition for donations (laughter). Yeah! This is how it was. . . . Yeah! (Interview #24)

When it was built, nearly all school-aged children in the village attended school, with many of them completing primary school, an uncommon experience for most Lao village children at that time. Adults and teenagers, though, do not attend the school or study. Even this head teacher's wife never learned to read and write Lao. Her intelligence and motivation to learn were reflected in her skills in remembering and executing detailed *ikat* (tie-dye) weaving designs and graceful dance movements.

In short, customary education reinforces the traditional division of labor, while "formal" education is traditionally available only to boys through the temple. In the latter part of this century, though, more and more secular schools are enrolling a growing number of girls as well as boys. However, traditionally education beyond the home is not a resource available to girls or women.

Religion, Cultural Ideologies, and Traditional Sources of Power

Most Lao are Theravada Buddhists and animists. A few have converted to Christianity. Ideally every young man becomes a Buddhist monk for at least a short period. Today fewer young men are ordained. Monks officiate at religious ceremonies and festivals, as well as at household ceremonies and funerals. Spirit practitioners are usually older men, and mediums of both sexes are known. Spirit practitioners officiate at weddings, birth-related rituals, and numerous informal animist ceremonies called *baci* or *soukhuan*, which mark life events like recovery from illness, return from travel, or the completion of a new home (Ngaosyvathn 1990).

Lao believe in spirits that reside in certain locations such as streams, fields, or groves of trees. Villages are often protected by tutelary spirits, and a goddess guards the rice crop. Village spirits, the rice goddess, and some other spirits regularly received offerings in the past. Malevolent spirits sometimes possess people or cause illnesses that can be exorcised by a shaman.

As in other parts of Southeast Asia, religious teachings reinforce gender inequality. Prerevolution ethnic Lao ideologies of gender inequality are based on Buddhist teachings and practices. Monks and male village elders traditionally dominated temple committees and the ritual aspect of religion, but women are major supporters of the temple through regular contributions of food and other goods. Women plan and prepare family rituals, though most of these ceremonies are conducted by male elders. This gender-based division of labor is supported by Buddhist teachings. In Buddhism, women are viewed as more deeply attached than men to worldly objects, at least partly because of their importance as mothers. The mother-nurturer image is the dominant female image in popular Thai Buddhist texts (Keyes 1984).[13] Her nurturing in these texts is not limited to the family but extends also to sustaining Buddhist institutions by regular ritual observances and by providing sons for the monkhood. Economic activities are not positively valued in Buddhist teachings. In fact, monks are prohibited from handling money. Kirsch (1985, 304) argues that men are more attracted to religious and associated political roles because of the positive Buddhist sanction connected to those roles, while "women are 'stuck with' . . . economic specialization." Van Esterik (1982, 78) agrees, noting that "women and men alike recognize that detachment and release are Buddhist ideals. But . . . this belief does not mean that women are, in fact, inferior to men. Instead, it motivates women to support the institution where these ideals are practiced, while they go about the business of living."

The major opportunities for religious leadership and participation are customarily open only to men who became monks. In villages, women participate in and support a variety of religious activities but always act in the role of supporter or helper. A village man from southern Laos notes that women are participants at the annual ceremony for the village spirit.

> *Informant*: Yes, you have to *liang baan* [have the ceremony for the village spirit]; can't live without it.
> *Interviewer*: All women and men do this together?
> *Informant*: Yes, they all go, including children.
> *Interviewer*: The monks lead this?
> *Informant*: No, not the monks. (Interview #27)

Another informant remembers that, in her central village, the one responsible for the village spirit shrine and for officiating at the annual ceremony was a man specializing in this village service (Interview #35).

Girls and women serve the local Buddhist temple in a variety of ways. While "elders served in different organizing committee roles . . . for the temple affair, elderly women and younger ones participated in the sermon and prayers in the religious functions . . . also did various tasks such as receiving guests at the temple gate and pinning flowers on the guests' garments and collecting

donations as . . . admission fees" (Interview #17). One woman describes her
work for a village religious festival:

> *Interviewer*: What was your work for Boun Phavet; what were you expert in?
> *Informant*: Sometimes I cut and arranged flowers; sometimes I told them [other
> women and girls] to carry water, fill the jugs of the monks.
> *Informant's husband*: She was a member of the women's committee.
> *Informant*: In the old regime, we had to make papaya salad; we helped each
> other; we did that. Divided the work. . . . The elderly women are responsible
> for preparing the *phaa khuaan* [ceremonial "tree" used in animist/Brahmin
> ceremonies for good luck and prosperity]. (Interview #24)

Young women also helped to celebrate at temple festivals, often by dancing.
One informant, a member of a dance troupe, describes her activities. "When
others wanted us [the dance group], they would talk with the group head who
would talk with the parents of the young women. . . . For a . . . temple
festival, they had us go dance" (Interview #29). Such a village dance group
performs popular versions of classical court dances that require weeks or
months of regular practice. Young women not a part of such groups take part
in ordinary circle dancing (*lamvong*) at festivals to raise funds for the temple.
One temple committee recruiter describes his activities:

> There was a *phaved* festival of 1967. . . . It was me who had to go recruit the
> young women who come to dance. I had to talk with their parents . . . at their
> homes. Sat down and chatted, saying "Now, we're going to hold a festival. And
> we would like to stage a circle dance . . . to raise funds for the temple so I'm
> talking to you folks about having your daughter(s) involved to help as valuable
> resources." They never did refuse . . . they sent their children. (Interview #37)[14]

Sometimes girls or women help with temple construction projects. Informants reported that girls had helped in constructing a temple drum, a temple
building, and a well on the temple grounds. Both women and men earn religious merit through their activities in support of the temple and the *sangha*,
the Buddhist monkhood. Being a monk is the major source of merit open to
men. Although women cannot be ordained, they may sponsor an ordination
to earn merit.

Women, then, traditionally contribute to village religious activities by
participating in both animist and Buddhist ceremonies and festivals; by preparing some aspects of temple or spirit festivities such as food, water,
decorations, or ritual items; by contributing their labor or special skills (e.g.,
their strength in digging or hauling or their dancing); or by sponsoring a son
or brother for the monkhood. Unspoken in the informant reports is the traditional daily preparation of rice and other food for local monks. None of these
activities is a source of power for a woman in this life. Although a woman

may be respected for her religious activities, the subsidiary nature of the activities reflects her subordinate status in this realm. However, the merit earned through various religious activities may ensure her a better position in her next life.

Traditional Sources of Power in the Domestic Arena

Lao family organization shares many characteristics of other Southeast Asian family systems. There are no large and well-defined kin groups. Lao women, like Lao men, retain their family identity upon marriage and share any inheritance with their siblings. Descent is bilateral, with paternal and maternal kin having similar importance for the individual. Surnames, now passed from father to children, were adopted only during this century in response to French colonial law. Wives commonly take their husbands' last name, though sometimes an in-marrying husband may take his wife's last name. Several observers of Lao village life were influenced by earlier Western analysts of Thai social organization, which characterized Thai social organization as "loosely structured," but the concept explains little (Barber 1979, 77–81). It seems to refer to the flexible division of labor and the high level of individual variation accepted within Thai and Lao society. Further, it may also reflect bewilderment over the lack of strong patriarchal control over women and families common in traditional European, North American, and Japanese families (see Potter 1977, Ch. 1).

Courtship, marriage arrangements, and residence after marriage all reflect the Lao view of men as more adventurous and of women as more domestic. Young people often marry others from their own village and may marry cousins. Parents or the young people themselves may propose possible marriage partners, but parents of potential partners are usually consulted. Parental approval is necessary before traditional marriage negotiations can begin. The practice of marrying more than one wife occurred but was uncommon before 1975. Either party may initiate a divorce, though it is discouraged.

A Japanese observer characterizes associations between young ethnic Lao men and women as extremely free and open (Ayabe 1961, 16). Groups of young men visit young women in their homes, usually in the evening while the girls are spinning or weaving. Banter and indirect allusion to love or sex may be part of the conversation. Before the days of rock and roll and the guitar, a member of the group might be an accomplished player of *khene* (a bamboo mouth organ) and, ideally, the young people sang their bantering conversation. Most young men are reportedly looking for a mate who is hard-working, pleasant, and nurturing, though a beautiful girl will receive more offers than a plain girl (Barber 1979, 348–49).

Ideally, when a young woman has chosen the young man she prefers, he, through a respected go-between, proposes marriage to her parents. In Phone Sung the parents then convene a group of respected villagers to discuss his character and moral standing (Barber 1979, 341). If the young man is not well known, a member of the group talks with a friend from the young man's village. If the group determines that the young man is an acceptable mate, the group then considers his wealth, education, job, religious training, and the daughter's characteristics in determining an appropriate bride price. Parents, with the help of their respected relatives, can choose to reject a man as unsuitable for their daughter. She, then, has little recourse. She must either accept her parents' choice or disobey her parents and elope. When she becomes pregnant and lives with her chosen husband, parents often relent.

Mothers and female relatives teach girls to be skeptical of the intentions and trustworthiness of men. Even parents may find them unreliable as family laborers or supporters of their parents. Instead, young men often concentrate on traveling, having adventures, and visiting young women wherever they go. Barber (1979, 344–48) particularly seems to revel in the recounting of "love" conflicts since they reveal some of the underlying social patterns: the importance of status (*piap*) and of appearance, and confirmation of more general gender roles with men as the active adventurers and women as the reactive homebodies.

When the wife's parents have accepted the potential groom and agreed on the bride price, which usually includes gold, one or more animals, and, in recent decades, cash, astrologers are consulted and the parents choose an auspicious wedding day and time. The marriage ceremony itself occurs in the bride's family home and follows the pattern of the Brahminist/animist ceremony used for many kinds of life events (Ngaosyvathn 1990).

Newly married couples often reside with the wife's family for a few years, though patrilocal residence is not uncommon. Most couples subsequently establish an independent residence. Since the youngest daughter is usually last to marry, she and her husband often remain in the parental home, caring for her parents and eventually inheriting the house and at least some of the paddy land. These patterns are tendencies, rather than rules. Ayabe (1961) and Branfman (1978), however, find that a much higher percentage of women than men in their study villages were born in that village. Perhaps as many as 92 percent of the families in Pha Khao reside matrilocally (Ayabe 1961, 14). Among Phone Sung residents sixty or older, twenty-one are living with married daughters and only seven are living with sons (Barber 1979, 321).

The traditional Lao tendency toward matrilocal residence with the family home and much of the paddy field passing to the daughter caring for the aging parents ensures that a number of women are embedded in a kin-based network of social and economic relations and have access to or even control over important economic resources. The strength of adult women's local kin networks enables many women to demonstrate some authority in family and community even though men are the formal household heads. Women demonstrate this authority mainly by representing their household to the larger community and by controlling the labor of family members. Other domestic tasks, though, like household chores, regular and frequent births, and the care of infants and children, seem to diminish women's power and autonomy.

Even before she inherits, a married daughter resident in her parents' house compound influences the flow of information and resources between the "household head" (her father) and her in-marrying husband. However, neither husband nor wife has much economic power as young adults living in the parental compound.

Men as Formal Household Heads. In extended family households, the senior husband/father who is still physically active is considered the family head. After the older couple distributes the inheritance,[15] the husband of the daughter inheriting the family home and caring for the parents becomes the family head. In a single nuclear family household, the husband/father is considered the household head and, formally, the representative of the family to the larger community. Female-headed households are not common, but single women, either widows or divorcees with children, are recognized by the community as legitimate heads of households.

Representing the Household to the Community. As a result of customs favoring residence in the wife's village, the wife's relatives are more likely involved in household activities including agricultural labor, house construction, and the mediation of domestic arguments. Although a man is nearly always the household head, women sometimes represent the household to the community by, for example, requesting assistance for harvesting or a house-raising.

Some report the normative pattern reflecting male headship in the family:

Interviewer: Whenever you work like this, *vaan*[16] harrowing, *vaan* transplanting, *vaan* harvesting, is it the husband who calls the friends to help, or can the wife also call them? Who calls them to help?
Informant: The husband, of course.
Interviewer: You don't go call them? Do others send the husband?
Informant: Some families the wife goes. But for us, it's the husband who goes to ask friends to come help. We women fix the food.
Interviewer: According to true customs, who should go look for the friends, *vaan* them to help? Who is best to go?
Informant: It's the husband, of course. (Interview #11)

Others assert that either of the responsible adults in the household can request assistance or invite participation of other villagers. One informant says that "both of us invite them to our house ceremony. Husband and wife go to invite others and when we go to help them, both of us go" (Interview #24). Another describes this as "an adult's job; the adults, the heads of the households run the events [rice paddy labor]. She [the mother] could request agricultural labor too; most of the time it is the father. If the houses are close enough, the mother would go" (Interview #21). A third reports that a "man or woman goes to invite people to her house ceremony. The mother or the grandmother could do it. Not children" (Interview #28).

Still others declare that any family member can invite participation or request labor (including also Interviews #34 and #32). "In our house, for example, my household will do *naa vaan* [exchange rice paddy labor] tomorrow; I go up north through the village, along this row, to this house, that house. My wife goes on that row, my child on that, however it is appropriate, and tell them" (Interview #4a).

In some families or villages, though, it was more common for mainly women to invite the participation of other villagers:

> *Interviewer*: Who went to ask the villagers to help with raising the house? You did or someone else?
> *Informant*: It was my wife, my mother who went to sit and chat, yeah! . . . It was my wife—most of the time she did. It was done the day before. (Interview #37)

Two respondents' answers directly reflect the matrilocal residence pattern. In one family, "It was my parents who went around asking people, *vaan* relatives in the village, mostly my mother, asking relatives" (Interview #36). A woman informant remembers how it happened when she was young: "As we were prepared to transplant within a week's time we would begin to . . . call on our friends and relatives, that is, mother did. I was too young. . . . After mother made a complete round of calling face to face—total forty families—she would, then, tell me to prepare the food and other necessities" (Interview #17). Another female informant says that she invited other villagers to help with their house-raising, but that it would be acceptable for a man to invite villagers, "if his wife was tied up with children" (Interview #14). One man says he never invited or requested the assistance of other villagers:

> *Interviewer*: Did you go talk to the village?
> *Informant*: My wife does it. . . . I don't go (laughs); I never do.
> *Interviewer*: Who do you go ask?
> *Informant*: Go to the relatives . . . the villagers. (Interview #26)

Another informant agrees: "It is the mother to do so. The father is not supposed to be involved in this. If the mother can't go, the female neighbor can also do it for you" (Interview #18).

Depending on the village and the household, then, mainly men, mainly women, both, or occasionally even a teenage daughter or son may request or invite the help of neighbors, or, as we will see later, contribute their labor in response to such a request from another community member.

Family Disputes. One informant reports that neighbors, who are often relatives of the wife, mediate family arguments, though intractable spouses may seek redress from higher authorities: "For small things, husbands and wives, the old people from nearby houses come to consult. They say this isn't a big deal; let's just solve it without going to the *pho baan* [village head]" (Interview #13). But if the argument is more serious, the issue goes beyond the circle of neighbors and kin. "If it's more serious, it goes to the *pho baan*, who will talk to them. Says—this isn't a big matter, let's just get along, apologize to each other, OK? Then it's done with. If it's a bigger thing, or they don't want to listen to the *pho baan*, then it goes to the province, to the *chao khoueng* [province governor]" (Interview #13). A woman's interests are taken into account by this conflict resolution process.

Control over Family Labor or Resources. The pattern of formal male headship with some level of female authority is also reflected in informant descriptions of who, in the household, delegated community labor. "It had to be the family head" who decided, says one man (Interview #31). "It is the father who will tell you who is going to help," says another man (Interview #3). Two women informants have a somewhat different view of family decision making. One woman says that "the parents decide" (Interview #13), while another, whose husband was often away, says that "mostly the father doesn't designate." Instead, she discussed the request for family exchange labor with her older children, found out who was available, and sent the available child. If all the older children were busy (working in the swidden, teaching, working for hire), she went herself.

Female authority may be evident within the extended family as well. One male informant in a clearly male-dominant household reports that at one stage in the life cycle of his extended family, the oldest sister was the "principal elder" and controlled access to the extended family granary.

> Yes, our parents divided the land and gave to every one of us . . . but we were still working together as one unit. Talking about (laughter) . . . our family and relatives, we all shared the same storehouse and gave adequately to everyone, yeah! Older sister . . . my older sister, the mother of Bualiphan. Right, she was the principal elder . . . even those relatives in Vientiane came to get grain from . . . our main storehouse, yeah! . . . Generally speaking the farm produced over thousand [unit not specified] . . . that's a lot of rice. (Interview #31)

In short, traditional male household headship is commonly tempered by the wife's kinship or long friendship with other villagers and, for some women, their status as heir of the family home and property, often giving them the authority to act in the community on behalf of their households, to control some family labor or resources, or to have their interests protected in family disputes.

Household Maintenance. Women in their reproductive years are usually the principal female laborers in the family. They are almost entirely responsible for daily household and child-care tasks, in addition to frequently experiencing pregnancy and birth. These domestic tasks and physical changes fill their time and tax their energy while yielding little or no power or even autonomy. This work produces no marketable products or resources for future use except daughters who, as they mature, begin to share some of the household workload. Lao men and children depend on women for their everyday needs. Women are traditionally responsible for most of the food processing, cooking, water carrying, fuel gathering, and housework. For example, one man from central Laos says, "If we seriously think about it, there are jobs men do, there are jobs women do, too. The women are more engaged in household chores—cleaning dishes, cooking, carrying water" (Interview #18).

With high infant and child mortality, coupled with a need for family labor and no viable birth control practices, women are regularly subject to the hazards of pregnancy and childbirth. Family size was and is still large. Households average six members. In my 1969 study of seventy-two households in six ethnic Lao villages, the average number of total live births for all women over forty was 7.7 (C. Ireson 1969, 4). Of all children born alive to mothers in the seventy-two households, 17 percent died in the first year, while 39 percent had died by the time they reached eleven years of age (see Table 3.1). At the time of this survey, 12 percent of all sample females ages eighteen to forty-five were over three months pregnant and an additional 41 percent were breast-feeding their children. Being tired and ill are common for women, so common that they are often unremarked. Although the average iron intake was 5 percent above the daily standard,[17] mainly from fermented fish paste eaten by all family members in soups and sauces, Lao women need considerably more iron than men and are commonly anemic (C. Ireson 1969, 13).

Mothers are principally responsible for their children. Although fathers often play affectionately with their children, they seldom take responsibility for their care unless the mother is sick or away from home. When adults must work, mothers carry nursing infants with them and leave their other young children in the care of an older sibling. Parents prefer to leave their younger children in the care of an older daughter, but if there is no daughter in the family, the older son will be the child caretaker. Children as young as eight or nine will sometimes be responsible for younger children. Grandparents too old for fieldwork may sometimes also care for younger children.

TABLE 3.1 Percentage Child Mortality by Ages

% Died	By Age
5	1 month
17	1 year
21	2 years
27	4 years
30	6 years
39	11 years

Source: C. Ireson 1969, 4.

A female informant identifies work around the house and weaving as "women's things." She also notes that she was responsible for the care of children, including her younger brothers and sisters, her children, and those of close relatives, and her older parents. She lists some of her domestic responsibilities as "taking care of children and watching our parents because my husband has gone to be a policeman. I have younger siblings and relatives and have to watch them so they could do their homework. There are a lot of other things" (Interview #16). She implies that if her husband were home, he would help with these tasks, and, in fact, most ethnic Lao men do play with children and teach boys basic skills all men must know.

In the seventy-two households I surveyed in 1969, parents, mainly the mother, cared for the children, but the main child-care worker in one-fifth of the families was the child's older sister and in one-tenth of families it was a grandmother. When the mother has work to do, children often help or do "child's work." However, children in less than one-fourth of surveyed families carried water or cared for younger children (C. Ireson 1969, 6).

Informants in the more recent study remember a variety of childhood responsibilities. One older son, explaining how his younger brothers and sisters helped with the lighter tasks, says, "The younger ones would do lighter works such as carrying water, gathering firewood, making rice, and help cook in the family . . . or pounding rice" (Interview #19). Both boys and girls may carry water, gather firewood, and steam rice, though few adult men are regularly responsible for these domestic tasks.

By age five, girls help with household work and by age nine, boys pasture cattle or buffalo. Girls learn to carry out other daily chores for family maintenance, like cooking, carrying water, sweeping, or foraging for food on the margins of the village. A girl traditionally learns to grow cotton, spin, and weave intricate patterns from her mother by the time she is twelve, and she continues to weave during the agricultural "off" season for the rest of her life.

Play groups are most often composed of boys, although younger girls and an older girl carrying her younger sister or brother may also participate or watch. Boys are not expected to carry out family chores until they are older, though they sometimes carry water and fuel. The chores they are assigned often send them afield, rather than keep them at home where they can be closely supervised. Thus boys learn to be independent and are freer to play with their peers who are also, for example, grazing the family water buffalo on the rice stubble outside the village. Both boys and girls learn to fish with baskets and nets.

While housework, child-bearing, and child-rearing provide ethnic Lao women with little control over resources, other aspects of domestic life may do so. Some level of traditional female authority and even extra-household leadership is evident in many households and villages. Women exercising this authority are often older women in well-established households living in their natal communities. Ethnic Lao women often represent their households to the community, mobilizing village labor for agricultural work or a house-raising, for example. They may allocate family labor or control the allocation of other family resources. Finally, their interests may be protected by the community in internal family disputes.

Rural Khmu and Hmong Women and Traditional Village Life

Khmu and Hmong women are traditionally less likely than ethnic Lao women to share household power with their spouses or to engage in production or commercial activities that produce goods or profits that they control. Nonetheless, the subordination of rural Khmu and Hmong women is not complete. Some women are able to exercise control in some aspects of their lives within traditional rural society.

The Khmu[18] are the largest midland Lao group in northern Laos. Khmu legend claims Luang Prabang as a Khmu city. In annual court rituals practiced in Luang Prabang, a related midland Lao group, the Ksak, are acknowledged as the original inhabitants of the land with special powers over the spirit world. The Lao consider the Khmu their "older brothers" because of their indigenous status. The Khmu of Luang Prabang, though, consider themselves inferior to people of other groups. Khmu protagonists are often tricked and deprived of their rights in one common folktale theme (Smalley 1964, 113). With no extra-village political or military organization, and in this century with little representation in colonial or Royalist governments, Khmu have been unable to defend themselves against the better-organized and governmentally connected ethnic Lao. Some writers believe that the Khmu originally cultivated rice paddies in flat valley floors but were driven into the hills by in-migrating lowland Lao who seized the most desirable agricultural land for themselves (Taillard 1989).

Hmong are the most numerous of highland ethnic groups, and the best known to Westerners because of their role in the Second Indochina War and the subsequent resettlement of many Hmong refugees in North America and Europe. Hmong migrants to Laos during the last two centuries followed a path curving from China through the highlands of Vietnam, Laos, and western Thailand, and Hmong still inhabit some areas in these countries.

Khmu and Hmong Villages

Khmu most often live on hillsides or mountain ridges in bamboo and thatch houses raised on low wooden house posts. Villages of 15–150 families are most common, though larger villages may develop in more favorable locations (Proschan 1993, 139). Teenage boys sleep in separate men's houses, which also are used for male guests, meetings of elders, and occasionally as a workshop (LeBar 1965, 7). A fence surrounds the village, its gates decorated with crossed swords to protect against evil spirits (Lindell et al. 1982, 4). Villages are semipermanent. Khmu move when tragedy strikes: epidemic illness, fire, or many deaths in childbirth (Proschan, personal communication, 1991).

Khmu tend to have darker skin than most Lao, though many Khmu and Lao have intermarried, with the children most often raised as Lao. Khmu and people of related groups were taken as slaves by Vietnamese, Cambodian, and Thai as recently as the last century (Lebar, Hickey, and Musgrave 1964, 95). Some Khmu villagers are apathetic, showing signs of cultural disintegration in the face of political powerlessness and extreme poverty. Traditional symbols of prestige—gongs, jars, and buffalo—are gone or nearly unavailable. Khmu living in more accessible villages or with long-standing relationships with Lao communities are often acculturated to Lao life, speaking Lao and even, in some cases, adopting Buddhism (LeBar 1965; Smalley 1964).

Hmong reside on the upper slopes or tops of mountains at elevations above 900 meters. Hmong villages or individual household units within the village move when their fields are completely depleted and no additional land is available to clear and farm (see Xiong and Donnelly 1986, 212–13 for an example of such a migration). Male household heads decide when and where to move (Xiong and Donnelly 1986, 213). With productive land, though, many Hmong villages in Laos are stable, maintaining the same location for several generations (R. Ireson 1990, 21; 1991, 5–6). Settlements are traditionally small, often consisting of just a few to a few dozen households, although in recent years, war, and then the current government have promoted settlements of larger size, either for protection and delivery of relief supplies or for easier administrative control and service. High population growth and the dearth of unoccupied land have also affected migration opportunities.

Village houses are often strung along the saddle of a ridge or just below the peak of a mountain with the main access by foot or animal path. Wood and wood shingle or bamboo and thatch homes are sometimes large enough to accommodate more than one nuclear family. Many Hmong were uprooted by the Second Indochina War, and many of these chose to flee Laos in 1975. Since land scarcity was becoming acute in some areas, this mass exodus relieved land pressure on the remaining households (Cooper 1986, 29-30). High population growth since that time may soon cause land scarcity once again.

Traditional Sources of Economic Power

Khmu Village and Household Economy. Agriculture supplies the main source of Khmu sustenance, supplemented by foraging, hunting, trapping, and fishing in the forest and streams, and the raising of a few domestic animals. Several varieties of "sticky" rice are grown in hillside swidden fields. The preparation and maintenance of the swidden is similar to that described for the ethnic Lao, but Khmu seem more skilled at maintaining the fertility of their swiddens. Khmu by preference systematically rotate from one swidden to another. Under indigenous conditions, the Khmu rotational system produced an adequate livelihood without major environmental damage.

Khmu farmers cultivate nonrice crops like corn, beans, vegetables, and tubers, along with rice in upland fields. Cotton is a particularly important crop for cash and barter, though some families also grow, ferment, and sell tea leaves. Many households plant a variety of vegetables, tobacco, spices, and fruit trees in and near their village. Tobacco appears to be an important social lubricant. Conversations often begin with the offering of tobacco or fermented tea leaves, while a man who is interested in a young woman might go to "get some tobacco" on the porch outside of her room (Lindell et al. 1982, 10). Forests and streams provide an amazing variety of foods and other products to Khmu families, particularly important when crops are ravaged by disease or drought.

Traditionally, buffalo ownership is a sign of prestige. Cattle and buffalo, along with smaller animals, forage freely in the area surrounding the village, to the occasional detriment of a poorly fenced garden or field. Large animals are not used as draft animals. Instead their main use is for sacrifice, but when they are slaughtered for other reasons, owners share the meat throughout the village. Some Khmu own horses for riding or packing. Horses are more valuable than other animals and are not sacrificed or eaten. In recent decades, Khmu poverty has limited large animal ownership (Lindell et al. 1982; Smalley 1964).

Khmu Women and the Economy. Khmu women are known as horticulturalists, producing food and cash crops. Although some Khmu women may
physically keep the family savings, it is under the husband's authority. Women
traditionally trade a few surplus goods locally, though they have little
experience with the world beyond neighboring forests, fields, and villages.
Unlike ethnic Lao and Hmong women, Khmu women are not usually skilled
at crafts like weaving or stitchery.

Dependent on swidden cultivation of regularly rotated fallow fields and
regular trapping, fishing, and foraging in forests and streams, many Khmu
families have been poor though nearly self-sufficient. Both men and women
participate in the major agricultural tasks of field clearing, planting, weeding,
harvesting, and carrying the crops to the village (Proschan 1993). However,
women are more likely to regularly perform these tasks, especially planting,
weeding, and the harvesting and carrying of nonrice crops. Men are responsible
for felling trees in the potential swidden and for burning the field.

In most swidden systems, the ground is not cultivated. Instead, the man
pokes holes in the cleared ash-fertilized soil while the woman drops seeds in
the holes. After planting, women maintain the field until harvest, though
household males may occasionally help. This involves cutting weeds, and
planting and harvesting a variety of vegetables, fruits, and, perhaps, other
grains. It is not unusual to see a lone woman cutting weeds by the hour in a
swidden high on a hillside. Chansina et al. (1991) report that, among swidden
farmers in Sepone District of Savannakhet Province (mostly of midland Lao
groups), swiddens are weeded three times during the growing season. They
estimate from the reports of one village that a one hectare swidden would
require 130–180 person-days of labor simply for weeding (Chansina et al. 1991,
37). The entire household harvests upland rice, though Khmu and Hmong men
only occasionally help carry the harvested rice to the granary in the village
(raw data from R. Ireson, 1993). Swidden agriculture is not mechanized and
generally does not require draft power. Tools for both men and women are
simple: an axe, a machete, a curved knife for weeds, a basket for collecting ripe
produce, and a carrying pole for transporting harvested rice. Khmu swidden
farmers traditionally use their swidden for only one or a few years before
returning it to fallow. Tayanin and Lindell (1991) report a sustainable long
rotation of fallow fields in Tayanin's Khmu village. Although Khmu
traditionally do not plant gardens, they do raise animals. As with the ethnic
Lao, Khmu women are responsible for small animal husbandry. Chickens are
often sacrificed in rituals.

Women regularly forage for wild roots, shoots, leaves, fruits, berries, and
mushrooms. Men, on the other hand, regularly check and reset their traps and
snares in the forest (Lindell et al. 1982). Hunting is also important traditionally, though large game animals are becoming rare. Girls and women do

most of the fishing; however, a number of people may work together to capture all the fish in a section of stream bed (Tayanin and Lindell 1991).

Men make ingenious traps and skillfully weave baskets and other items of bamboo and rattan. Women often crochet net bags whenever their hands are not occupied with other tasks (Lindell et al. 1982). Blacksmithing, a male task, seems to be limited to the repair of the small inventory of agricultural tools. A Khmu woman may often trade cotton to a lowland Lao weaver in exchange for cloth. She gets one-half of her crop back in woven cloth, while the other one-half pays for the weaver's cotton-processing labor. A few acculturated Khmu women gin and weave the cotton they grow (Smalley 1964), but most purchase or barter for cloth. Some Khmu women traditionally make other products for use or for sale. Like ethnic Lao women, part-time village specialists ferment rice husks in water to make a mild alcoholic beverage and distill more potent spirits. Floor mats, thatch, baskets, and other items from natural products are commonly made by villagers to cover, furnish, and use in their own homes, but these items may, on occasion, be sold or exchanged.

On a typical morning in a Khmu household, men check their traps and give salt to their cattle while women husk and cook rice and carry water. Elderly women may feed the animals while older men may sharpen knives. After breakfast, all household laborers walk to upland fields. In the fields they may plant, weed, or harvest, or visit a nearby forest to hunt (men) or forage (women).

While there are few daily activities that cannot be done by either men or women, some tasks are commonly gendered as follows:

> Tasks associated with men are hunting and trapping, felling trees, blacksmithing, and long-distance trade that requires sleeping away from the village. Tasks associated with women are planting rice, carrying water, gathering forest plants, feeding animals, and trade with nearby villages. Both men and women perform most agricultural tasks of clearing brush, cultivating, weeding, harvesting, and carrying. (Proschan 1993, 140)

Young men are the only villagers that leave the village for long periods of time. They often travel to Thailand for wage work or may join the army. Men sometimes also work for local Hmong, Lao, or Chinese in nearby villages or towns to earn small amounts of money or food. Traditionally, according to Lindell et al. (1982), women, children, and older people hardly ever leave the village and its surrounding fields and forests. Men alone take goods to town to sell so they can purchase salt, clothing, needed tools, and household goods (Lindell et al. 1982, 14). Proschan is quoted earlier as stating that women engage in local trade. While small-scale local trade may give women control over the income (or goods) from some of their products, most major market exchanges are controlled by men, rather than women, even if women have produced the goods sold (implied by Smalley 1964, 116). Ethnic Lao observers report that Khmu women work harder and have a more difficult life than women in highland or lowland groups (Lao Women's Union officials, personal communication, 1985). Chronic food shortages are relieved by men's hunting or wages, as well as by women's forest foraging.

Hmong Village and Household Economy. Hmong villagers grow their food staple of white (nonglutinous) rice in their lower swidden fields and plant opium in higher elevation fields. Villagers grow corn as animal feed. Women are important producers of rice and nonrice swidden crops like tobacco, corn, squash, melons, tubers, vegetables, bananas (Vang and Lewis 1984, 154), and cotton, nearly all of which are used for household consumption. In the recent past, corn and other grains that thrive at higher elevations provided the staple food, though this has gradually changed in Laos and Thailand (Tapp 1989, 46–47). Women are involved in all aspects of household agricultural production and often function as laborers for their husbands or male household heads. However, production tasks are not predominantly the responsibility of women, as they tend to be among the Khmu. Women are generally not financial decision makers for family or household. The Hmong farm their swidden fields much like the Khmu with a similar division of labor, with one major exception. Hmong farmers often continue to farm the same field until the soil is too exhausted to regenerate secondary forest (Geddes 1976; Keen 1978; Lemoine 1972). In addition to food crop cultivation, Hmong women have major responsibilities for opium poppy cultivation.

Opium is an important dry-season crop, as it provides the income necessary to supplement chronically inadequate rice and corn production in many villages. Opium is an ideal cash crop for isolated farmers who must transport goods to market along mountain trails. It is compact and light; does not spoil; is not affected by heat, cold, or moisture; and yields high returns. Further, labor requirements do not conflict with labor needed for corn and rice cultivation, and because poppy does not deplete soil rapidly, a poppy swidden may be used for a number of years (Westermeyer 1982, 44). Increasing reliance on opium cultivation over the last forty to sixty years has enhanced male dominance. Women cultivate, harvest, and prepare opium for sale, though often with family help, while men control the salable product and the resulting profit (Cooper 1983).

Cooper (1983) closely links mode of production with gender inequality, suggesting that husbands and wives had a more cooperative and less unequal relationship decades ago when subsistence swidden rice production was the main economic activity. All household members contributed to rice production as they were able, and all members benefited from the full rice granary. The male monopoly over tree-cutting and therefore over the conversion of forest into cropland still gave men a productive edge over women, though, even under the swidden rice system.[19]

With the increasing importance of the large-scale cash-crop cultivation of opium, which Cooper (1983) dates from the first half of the twentieth century, men gained more control over members of their household, particularly their wives and sons. The relationship between husband and wife became more like that of master and servant (Cooper 1983, 175–76). Women carry out many of the difficult tasks of opium cultivation like clearing underbrush, carrying tools to and from the field, preparing the soil for planting, and intensive weeding, though the husband must clear larger trees from a new swidden once every five to ten years (Cooper 1983, 176). While much of the opium production work is carried out by household women, the male head decides when and whether to sell the crop or to consume it, what to buy with the proceeds, what to give to his wife or wives, whether to use part of the profits to hire wage laborers the following season, and how much to keep for his own use (Cooper 1983, 173).

Men are solely responsible for selling opium, though a woman can sell if a merchant arrives in the village when the husband is gone, but he has already instructed his wife to sell (Sirivanh Yeuthao, Project Officer, Quaker Service Laos, personal communication, 1993). He then controls the income from the opium crop. Thus, the husband appropriates the surplus value created by his wife's labor. If he decides to keep some of the profits, often converted to silver, he will bury the silver in the forest without telling anyone of its whereabouts (Sirivanh Yeuthao, personal communication, 1993). With the Hmong shift to greater dependence on opium production, the wife spends "a greater proportion of her life in productive labor than does the husband," while she is not compensated for the profits she has generated for her husband (Cooper 1983, 176).

Traditionally men hunt, though women are the main forest gatherers, often foraging every day. With increasing land pressure and dwindling forests, hunting and foraging are declining in importance. Many Hmong men successfully raise cattle and horses in the less disease-ridden higher elevations of their villages, while women raise pigs and poultry. Trade in cattle, opium, peaches, and other products that grow in the cooler highlands has probably been an integral part of the Hmong economy in Laos for decades. These goods are exchanged for rice and other needed items.

Hmong women make one elaborate set of clothing each year. Young women, particularly, take special care to produce lovely garments, since they will first wear them during the New Year's festivities in the company of many young men. Hmong clothing preparation, depending on the subgroup, requires skill in embroidery, applique, and batik-making, in addition to weaving and sewing. Traditionally, though, these items were not bartered or sold for additional income. Women specialists may also distill alcoholic spirits from corn mash for home use and local trade. Hmong men trade cattle and cash crops for rice, the preferred staple, and other needed items. While men are the main traders, some women may engage in petty trade with the consent of their husbands or fathers (see Xiong and Donnelly 1986 for an example).

Traditional Sources of Political and Community Power

Khmu Politics and Women. Everyday village social life is oriented toward the rhythm of food production, harmony with the spirits, and interaction within the household and village. The Khmu have no political organization beyond the village, though Lindell et al. (1982) note several "vague indications of an ancient unity" like the prior right to the land acknowledged in Lao state ceremonies, linguistic similarity among Khmu groups, and a division into more than ten geographically based units covering most of northern Laos, which include the Lamet, a related midland group. The authors (Lindell et al. 1982, vi, 2, 3) suggest that perhaps these units are remnants of an earlier now-forgotten administrative structure. In any case, the Khmu have clear economic links to people of other ethnic groups and were incorporated into the Lao national network of political administration during the colonial and Royalist periods. The village headman may be proposed by villagers but must be selected also by the district administration. As past slaves to the Lao and other groups, Khmu traditionally have had little political recourse when their rights were violated.

Most Khmu villages are not highly stratified by wealth. Household rituals involving the whole community and substantial bride prices tend to redistribute money and personal property. Men are clearly superior to women among the Khmu, however. Family authority lies with the husband, while the oldest male of the oldest generation of the dominant local lineage commands the respect of local villagers. Male elders witness intravillage agreements, make important village decisions, and resolve internal problems when they arise, though all adults, including women, may participate in the general discussion before the elders decide.

Hmong Politics and Women. Most Hmong prefer to live with members of their own clan, so that a respected clan elder can perform necessary clan ceremonies. Villagers cooperate on community projects and house-building, and may go together to the forest to forage or collect firewood. Other intravillage assistance seems to be based on clan or, more specifically, on extended family relationships. Poor families, devastated by serious illness or death of a laboring adult, are assisted by family and sometimes other clan members so they can become self-sufficient again. Families of opium addicts similarly receive "welfare" assistance from related families.

Class stratification in Hmong villages is shallow, partly because of customary family and clan assistance to poor or young families. Most households produce most of what they need, bartering or purchasing the remainder with income from opium or cattle sales. Only families with an opium addict are likely to remain impoverished throughout their family cycle. As among the ethnic Lao, wealthier families are those with many working members.

There is no Hmong political organization above the village level, and even the village committee or headman is an administrative creation of the Lao government, representing the village to the district and provincial government. Resolution of problems and conflicts and local decisions are made by a gathering of male lineage elders, with informal participation of others, including women (Tapp 1993), but Hmong women have no authority, says one informant. Their status is lower than that of men and they are on the periphery of decision making. Women do not drink, so when men are sitting around a table drinking and discussing important matters, women literally have no place at the table (Sirivanh Yeuthao, Project Officer, Quaker Service Laos, personal communication, 1993). Observers agree that decisions are made by the husband, though they report that wives are often actively involved in discussions preceding these decisions (Cooper 1983; Westermeyer 1982, 30). Many Hmong families fled Laos in 1975 after the Second Indochina War, though seldom was this women's decision.

Traditional Sources of Educational or Religious Power

Both Khmu and Hmong children are informally trained in adult skills by family and community members. A few children, mainly boys, attended school before 1975. Men are usually the ritual practitioners among the Khmu and Hmong. Although women may be herbalists, this specialty confers little power. In both groups, men and women seem to acknowledge male superiority.

Education, Religion, and Khmu Women. Education of Khmu children is informally carried out by adult family members, older siblings, and storytellers (Lindell et al. 1982), and children work under the supervision of their parents to learn the skills and knowledge necessary for a life of foraging, hunting, and slash-and-burn agriculture. Deep feelings of inferiority, undoubtedly related to past servitude, are inculcated from early childhood in both girls and boys (Lindell et al. 1982, viii). Traditionally, few Khmu children of either gender attended school.

Traditional Khmu religion is animist and centers on spirits of ancestors, village, house, forest, and swidden. The village ritual specialist safeguards community welfare by presiding over periodic villagewide ceremonies and sacrifices for village and area spirits, but has no independent political power (Lindell et al. 1982, 6–7). The ritual head inherits his or her office from a parent or close relative. Shamans are spirit healers and medical practitioners.

Through close contact with the spirit world and specialized knowledge of ritual, sacrifice, and botany, a shaman is able to predict the future and communicate the spirit's prescription for an illness. Khmu shamans and ritual heads are particularly well respected for their knowledge of the spirit world. Lindell et al. (1982) say that Khmu shamans are always men. However, Smalley (1964) notes that Khmu shamans may be either male or female. A Khmu woman may inherit village ritual headship from an older relative and thereby become the organizer of village rituals to ensure village well-being.

Education, Religion, and Hmong Women. Like Khmu and ethnic Lao girls, Hmong girls learned needed skills from their mothers and other female relatives. Girls were much less likely to attend school than boys, and hardly any girls were allowed to continue their schooling after completing the school available in a very few Hmong villages before 1975.

Hmong are traditionally animists. Everyday activities and illnesses are intimately linked to the spirit world, so shamans are held in high regard. Shamans treat illness by restoring the patient's soul spirits. The male household head also honors ancestral and house spirits with regular rituals. Herbal medicine is practiced by a number of skilled women (Tapp 1993). Significant numbers of Hmong have converted to Christianity. Christian conversion may have led, at least in some groups, to less obvious social subordination of women (Sirivanh Yeuthao, personal communication, 1993).

Traditional Power in the Domestic Arena

Home, Family, and Khmu Women. A sizable Khmu village contains members of several marriage alliance groups (LeBar 1965; Proschan 1993) with one or several local lineages. These groups exchange women unilaterally. That is, one group is a "wife-giving" group in relation to another group which is a "wife-taking" group (Lindell et al. 1982). Villagers' prime loyalties are focused on the head of their local lineage. As the oldest man of the oldest generation of the family, he represents his kin not only in wife exchange but in rituals of sacrifice to the ancestors (Lindell et al. 1982). Households may contain only one nuclear family or may include several generations and several nuclear families. The father wields the most authority, though some Khmu mothers may keep the family purse. Parents, mainly mothers, and other relatives including older siblings, aunts, or cousins may care for children (Proschan 1993). Unmarried teenage sons reside in a separate community house where they learn hunting, trapping, and craft skills from older men (Proschan 1993).

Descent tends to be patrilineal, but relations with kin of both mother and father are important (Proschan, personal communication, 1991). The property of a mother goes to her children. If the mother dies when the children are young and the family still resides with her parents, the children will stay with the mother's parents. If the mother dies when the children are older, the children may live with the husband's family (Smalley 1964, 116–17).

Most marriage partners are selected by the young people themselves. Polygyny is accepted but uncommon because of its cost. Festival days and parties following ritual sacrifices and feasts for ancestors are the scene of much courting, though an interested young man may visit a young woman at her home. Marriages include the giving of a substantial bride price and feature food and free-flowing alcohol. The husband normally moves into the bride's household for several years of bride service, though the young family may return to his natal household or establish their own nuclear family when the husband collects sufficient money or goods to pay the bride price in full. Newlyweds move immediately to the husband's village if he pays the full bride price at the time of marriage (Proschan 1993). Girls may marry as young as fourteen years, though their husbands tend to be older.

Women are responsible for family water, firewood, and entertainment products, like wine, tobacco, and fermented tea. Men look after the family basket, container, and tool supply and may also gather firewood. Smalley (1964, 116) notes that men are considered better cooks than women. Kinship relations, residence patterns, and the high bride price systematically disadvantage women. Lineages reckoned through the male line, formal male authority in household and community, and the tendency toward patrilocal residence, at least after the first few years of marriage, make it unlikely that a Khmu woman will reside in a community of relatives and lifelong neighbors. Unlike many ethnic Lao women, then, a Khmu woman is less able to exercise informal power either within or outside her family. The high bride price often requires a man to migrate for wage labor, to return only when he has amassed enough money to pay at least part of the bride price. Often he returns to marry a young bride. The difference in age exacerbates the tendency toward male dominance among married couples, though residence for a few years with the wife's family may mitigate this tendency initially.

Home, Family, and Hmong Women. Unlike the bilateral ethnic Lao, or the more patri-centered marriage-alliance system of the Khmu, Hmong kinship is organized around exogamous patri-clans divided into lineages (all descendants, through the male line, of an historic male ancestor), sublineages (the largest kinship unit capable of collective action), and extended families (Dunnigan 1982). Descent is patrilineal, with a wife joining her husband's clan at marriage. Children are members of the husband's clan. If the husband dies, the wife may marry one of his younger brothers.

The authority of men over women is a constant theme in Hmong social organization. This authority is reinforced by residence with the husband's family after marriage. Formally proposed and negotiated marriages between the men of the involved families are the norm, but marriage by abduction (or elopement, if the girl has accepted her suitor) is not uncommon. The abduction is usually regularized by negotiation and payment of bride price after the fact. Richer or older men may have more than one wife. Traditionally, sons continue to live with their parents after marriage. Extended family households farm the staple crop(s) together, maintaining one granary. Individual nuclear families or even individuals within the household may grow a cash crop or sell crafts or other goods, keeping the profits for their own use.

Women are responsible for nearly all housekeeping, though men sometimes cook. Women rise earlier than household men, build the fire, husk the rice for the day, fetch the water, chop the firewood, and prepare the meal. Certainly if there are guests, and sometimes even within the household, women eat only after men have eaten their fill. In the evening, the situation is the same: women do most of the chores, eat after the men, and retire early while men continue to visit around the fire (Cooper 1983, 176). Girls and women are responsible for food processing like rice husking and corn grinding. Girls and grandmothers, as well as mothers, care for small children. When household members go to the swidden field to work, children are cared for in the field house.

Although women have no authority, wives are often actively involved in discussions preceding household decisions (Cooper 1983; Sirivanh Yeuthao, personal communication, 1993; Westermeyer 1982, 30). While researchers commonly report that men decide financial and inheritance matters, women themselves may report that such decisions are joint (Quaker Service Laos file notes, 1990). Parents continue their interest in their married daughters, partly because of the advantages of cross-clan connections (Cooper 1983). In a situation of land scarcity, her parents may "sponsor" the request of the husband and their daughter to live in their village and be allocated land. However, they may lose touch with her if her husband lives far away or decides to migrate.

The substantial bride price necessary for a Hmong marriage reinforces male dominance but also provides some protection against maltreatment of the wife. If, for example, the wife runs away and initiates a divorce (a rare situation), the case proceeds to a formal clan "hearing," and if the presiding headman or elder finds the husband guilty of a major offense (e.g., beating with insufficient cause), the divorce is granted and the husband forfeits the bride price (Cooper 1983, 181–82; Thao 1986). Wives unable to obtain redress for suffering at the hands of their husbands may commit suicide, an indication of their limited power and options.

Life Cycle Variations in Women's Power

Ethnic Lao Women

There are perhaps four periods in her life when an ethnic Lao female has some social power or autonomy: as a breast-fed baby, as an attractive young woman, as the "matron" of an established family, and as an old woman. Babies of both sexes are indulged, while attractive young women receive the attention of many young men and are also able to begin their own independent business enterprises. Married women with young children must work hard to produce enough for their young family. A woman with a nursing baby is either constrained to stay home with the baby or to take the baby with her as she works. As a result, most younger mothers stay close to home.

As the matron of an established family, though, she keeps the family purse and makes major family financial decisions jointly with her husband. She is assisted in her work by her children as she grows, gathers, or weaves items for family use or for sale. Older children can care for younger children while she travels to a market town to sell her produce. She controls the distribution of her production and the money or goods that she obtains from their sale or barter.

An old woman is respected by her children and grandchildren and may become an even more regular supporter of the temple. Maintained by an adult child, she is free of all onerous economic duties and from many of the social rules requiring modesty of younger women. In fact, she and her women friends are free to be impolite, assertive, and even lewd!

Khmu and Hmong Women

An unmarried Hmong girl between the ages of twelve and fifteen years has more control over her life than at any time before and after adolescence. During this period she is free to accept or reject the advances of a variety of suitors, married or unmarried. This short period between puberty and marriage may be the happiest time in a Hmong female's life. An older woman may attain some level of autonomy also if she can produce opium on her own swidden and if she has a resident daughter-in-law to cook for her. Normally, though, even an older woman will not have the resources to purchase or clear an opium swidden herself. A son, however, might buy or clear one for her (Cooper 1983, 184–85). Unfortunately, little information is available on changes in Khmu women's lives and power throughout the life cycle.

Events through the socialist period and current economic liberalization have not changed these cycles of female power and autonomy, but have affected the economic and ideological basis for women's power and have altered women's opportunities and arenas for the exercise of this power.

Summary of Women's Traditional Sources of Power

Ethnic Lao women have benefited from some of the same organizational patterns and cultural ideas supporting relatively high female status in other parts of Southeast Asia. The family was and is bilateral, with a tendency toward matrilocality. State control, especially in rural areas, has been weak, sporadic, or nonexistent. Ethnic Lao women have been economically and commercially active. Gender complementarity rather than opposition is valued. As in other Buddhist areas of Southeast Asia, Buddhist ideology relegates women to a lower spiritual status than men, while legitimating women's economic activities. In short, rural Lao women traditionally have access to resources through their economic activities and consequent involvement in household decision making. Besides working in the fields, foraging in the forest, and raising small animals, many also have other skills like making cloth from either cotton or silk. Women customarily control the income from several of these activities, though most of their products are usually directly consumed by their families. The importance of women in the kinship system reinforces women's authority in the household and, informally, in the village community. Although men are formal heads of households, temples, and villages, some level of female authority and even extra-household leadership is evident in some households and villages. Women exercising this authority are often those living in their natal communities, older women in established and prosperous families, and women carrying the practical day-to-day responsibility for their family because of husband absence or incapacity. Women were traditionally limited or diminished by their lack of access to the monkhood, political decision making, and education.

Khmu women traditionally share only a few of the organizational patterns and cultural ideas supporting relatively high status in other parts of Southeast Asia. Certain bilateral elements in Khmu kinship organization enable some Khmu women to continue residing with their kin group after marriage, giving them allies and a work support group, though authority is vested in the male household head. While Khmu women do trade a few surplus goods locally, their traditional economic activity does not seem to extend very far into the commercial arena. Khmu women are mainly horticulturalists and producers of much of the household food and cash crops. Khmu women do decide what cash crops to grow in their swiddens, and they may occasionally sell the crops themselves. Weak state control, combined with a lack of Khmu political organization, has historically left villagers at the mercy of better-organized Lao in-migrants who may have uprooted entire Khmu villages, taking the most fertile agricultural lands, an historical development that disadvantages all Khmu. Unlike ethnic Lao and Hmong women, Khmu women are not usually skilled at crafts like weaving or stitchery. Men are usually the shamans and ritual practitioners. Khmu women, as well as many Khmu men, are limited by their lack of education and experience beyond village life. Extreme poverty in some Khmu villages ensures that all efforts are focused on obtaining enough to eat rather than on improving the household economy or the quality of village life.

TABLE 3.2   Traditional Arenas of Power and Autonomy for Women
             by Ethnic Group

Ethnic Group	Economic	Political	Cultural/ Religious	Education	Domestic
Lao	Yes	Some: Informal and indirect	Some	No	Yes
Khmu	A little	A little	No	No	A little
Hmong	No	No	No	No	A little

   Hmong women do not share any of the organizational patterns and cultural ideas supporting relatively high female status in other parts of Southeast Asia. Instead, patriarchal patterns and ideas more common in China than in Southeast Asia seem to have greater influence. While state control has historically been weak in Laos, Hmong are recent immigrants from an area with an historically strong and, indeed, dominant state. Hmong clan authority may also act, in lieu of state control, to circumscribe women's power traditionally. Women seem to be "other" rather than complementary to men. Hmong society is organized into exogamous patrilineal clans. Descent is patrilineal, and marriage nearly always patrilocal. As a result, married women may lose regular contact with their parental household and become dependent on their husband's family. Hmong women are involved in all aspects of household agricultural production but rarely have control over the commodities they produce. Few Hmong women customarily engage in commerce, keep the family purse, or are key household decision makers. Before 1975, few Hmong were literate in Lao, the language of government and commerce; some men, but few women, spoke and understood spoken Lao. Most Hmong are animists though some are Christians. As among the Khmu, men are the shamans and ritual practitioners. In short, women's status is low and may have declined with increased dependence on opium as a cash crop, since men control women's labor to produce this crop, which is then completely controlled by the male "owner." Women's traditional power seems limited to sexual autonomy in early adolescence, but with the possibility of some control over her personal economic production as an older woman. (See Tables 3.2 and 3.3 for tabular summaries.)

Tradition and the War Years

Between 1945 and 1975, war sporadically disrupted traditional village life for many. Men were drafted and women alone carried out as many subsistence and community tasks as they could, sometimes while enduring bombing and propaganda from one or both sides. To escape bombing, sometimes entire villages moved into caves or into the forest. One northern ethnic Lao woman, for example, raised eight children with the help of her mother. She was aided in rice paddy cultivation by traditional labor exchanges with other families in her village (Interview #5). Trained women loyal to the Pathet Lao found that their skills were used without prejudice during the war as they variously established a nursing school, directed a hospital department, and taught in school (see Chapter 8 for details).

An ethnic Lao soldier describes how his family survived while he was away:

After I got married I left my wife and took command of the Forest Tiger soldiers. But my wife built a house and had paddy and swidden fields to raise food. If you have a buffalo and paddy fields to farm, you can eat. And we [wife and children!] sold small items at our house. I bought good land, then bought buffalo, oxen, oxcart, a bicycle, and cart—bought by myself. But I didn't use them, my siblings used them because I was away. I farmed rice there only from 1967 to 1969 . . . but if I had free time I would check on my family. Her siblings looked after her. Sometimes I had time to come out of the camp to plow the paddy or swidden fields; sometimes I could work a full day, other times only a little. But there was no problem or lack. (Interview #6)

It would be interesting to compare this report with his wife's evaluation of her situation during his absence!

Other women found it difficult to survive in an all-female household during wartime like the ethnic Lao family described earlier that depended on the male labor of the son. This family was unable to continue paddy farming when the son was drafted. He returned after only two years, but during that time his family lost or soldmost family possessions. Family members contributed their labor to a relative's rice crop and received some rice in return, but it was insufficient for their needs. Some other families in the village, otherwise not directly affected by fighting, were similarly affected. Traditional labor exchange networks were insufficient to meet the heavy demands for male labor in that village (Kiang McIntosh, personal communication, 1993).

Somkhouane, married to a soldier working in military intelligence, said that before she became an entrepreneur, "there was nothing. At the end of the month I got his money [salary], took that money and used it to buy things like candies, medicine, tobacco, aspirin, other medicines in Vientiane, and brought them to our village to sell at the house. After that I had enough to

TABLE 3.3 Traditional Sources of Women's Economic Power

Sources	Ethnic Lao
Participation in economic activities; types of activities	Very active: agriculture, animals, foraging, textiles, trade
Cultural meanings attributed to economic participation (ideology)	Females seen as economically responsible. Buddhism views women as more tied to material world.
Economic resources: control over land, labor, water, or other productive resources; control over her own products; distribution of surplus	Inherits land and goods. Controls own labor except for rice production. Sells own surplus production (except rice) and controls own earnings. Keeps family purse; makes decisions jointly.

eat" (Interview #28). May Xiong describes how she lived alone in the Hmong military town of Long Cheng while her soldier-husband was at the front, maintaining herself and her husband (during his occasional visits) by using his salary as capital for petty trading, much like Somkhouane. This was an unusual occupation for a Hmong woman. May never returned to rural life (Xiong and Donnelly 1986).

Life changed with the 1975 revolution, even rural life. The most striking change, beginning in 1973, was an end to fighting and bombing. Many internal refugees and demobilized soldiers returned to their war-destroyed homes and fields to begin rebuilding, while some urban residents and strong Royalists left the country entirely or were sent to "reeducation" (prison) camps. During the immediate post-liberation period, many entrepreneurs like Somkhouane and May Xiong left Laos. Somkhouane left during the late 1970s when restrictions against private enterprise were strictly enforced, but others quietly stashed their capital until they felt more confident that the new government would not penalize them.[20]

With peace, socialist ideologies about gender, government policies imping-ing on women's lives and roles, and the Lao Women's Union have changed the environment in which rural women live and work. As villagers reestab-lished themselves after the war and as elements of the socialist reorganization reached into the countryside, women's labor and cooperation were expected.

Khmu	Hmong
Very active: agriculture, animals, foraging, minor trade	Active: agriculture, smaller animals, foraging, textiles
Women valued as hard workers.	Females seen as lacking cultural authority. Importance is as laborers and reproducers of the lineage.
Inheritance insignificant. Does not control land. Labor devoted to subsistence. Little control over products, surplus. May keep family purse but financial authority vested in husband.	Possibility to own field to produce cash crop as an individual, but son or other relative must clear and give it to woman. May voice own views. All authority vested in husband.

In Chapter 4, I profile particular women and describe several post-1975 villages of each ethnic group in order to highlight cultural and individual sources of power and subordination in women's lives and work. I then describe how socialism and, later, economic liberalization have affected women's activities in Luang Prabang villages.

Notes

1. The information used in this chapter to describe traditional pre-1975 life is generally drawn from pre-1975 pre–socialist sources and is reported in the "ethnographic present" when appropriate. Quotations, however, retain the verb tenses used by the interviewees themselves. Even today, women still carry out a number of traditional activities and retain or lack control over some resources and goods as they did traditionally before 1975.

2. 2.4 acres = 1 hectare

3. With a life expectancy of about fifty years, adults who support the household and are pillars of the community are those whose oldest children are productive laborers and who are themselves physically strong and vigorous. "Middle age," then, usually includes adults between the ages of thirty and forty-five to fifty years.

4. The study from which much of the information in this section is drawn, "Patterns of Cooperation in Rural Laos" (C. Ireson, R. Ireson, Keopraseuth, C. Meksavanh, T. Meksavanh, and Vansi, 1988), was carried out with funding from the Social Science Research Council under the Indochina Studies Program. It is more fully described in the preface. Quotations cited by interview number refer to this study.

5. At that time, young men who were the only household male were supposed to be exempt from the draft.

6. Buffalo and cattle are turned out to range freely during the agricultural "off" season.

7. The mat or mats described by this informant form a threshing floor approximately 20′ × 50–60′.

8. See Belsky and Siebert (1983) for Filipino examples and Liemar and Price (1987) for Thai examples.

9. This statement was made by a woman from northern Laos (Interview #38).

10. In Houa Phan Province, some villages have tall platforms, like bamboo lifeguard towers, for the town crier.

11. A number of ethnic Lao customs function to avert or avoid face-to-face conflict, confrontation, or expression of anger.

12. From the informant's reported age, we can infer that her school was built in the very early 1960s.

13. Thai and Lao Buddhism are very similar.

14. The custom is for one man to pay for an entire round of dance. He is called up to receive a set of flower garlands, which he distributes to his friends who then invite the other girls sitting in the dance area.

15. This usually happens some time after the older couple withdraws from heavy agricultural labor.

16. *Vaan* refers to the process of requesting exchange labor.

17. The daily standard of the U.S. Food and Nutrition Board in 1969 was 10 mg/day.

18. Also spelled Kmhmu (Proschan 1993) and Kammu (by the Swedish Kammu Studies Group of Tayanin and Lindell (1991) and their colleagues). For rich ethnographic description of life in one Khmu village, see Tayanin 1994.

19. During fieldwork, Cooper observed that women could steadily chop heavy undergrowth with their machetes and chop firewood with an ax. But he had no success when he tried to persuade Hmong women to attempt tree-felling (Cooper 1983, 177–78). See Friedl (1975) for a more detailed discussion on the implications of the male monopoly on land clearing.

20. For a discussion of the economic problems facing the Lao government with the collapse of the war economy, see Evans 1990 and 1991.

4

Women of Luang Prabang

When their reproductive and household tasks are reduced, women are able to increase their economic production and, according to my theoretical framework, if cultural, political, and economic factors allow, to increase the economic resources under their control. Furthermore, macro-level political and economic changes can have a positive effect on women's economic activities, control over factors of production, and control over marketable surplus production. This chapter illustrates these relationships in one province, Luang Prabang, demonstrating specifically (1) that changes in domestic work were related to increased production and (2) that political and economic changes through the socialist and liberalization periods had a positive impact on women's economic power under some circumstances. Continuing economic changes may, however, undermine rural women's economic power in the future. Women from the three focal ethnic groups, conditioned by the different kinship, religious, and cultural patterns described in Chapters 2 and 3, responded differently to changes in domestic labor and to political and economic changes. I draw most information in this chapter from data gathered between 1986 and 1990 in fourteen villages participating in a women-focused development project aimed at improving rural conditions by alleviating women's drudgery while supporting and supplementing women's productive capabilities.[1] I augment this information with data from two other studies of rural Luang Prabang villages (Håkangård 1990; Luang Prabang Rural Micro-Projects 1990, 1991—hereafter LP Micro-Projects).

I begin by describing Luang Prabang Province and profiling villages and individual women of each ethnic group. I then depict aspects of village development, focusing on changes in women's domestic workload, women's production, and women's ability to control surplus production and other economic resources. I conclude by demonstrating the effect of changes in domestic workload, economic production, and economic policies on rural women's power and by analyzing the different effects on women of the three different ethnic groups.

Luang Prabang Province

Luang Prabang, the focal point for my examples of women's power, auton-omy, and subordination, is a northern province covered by mountain ranges: "The mountains are rough and sharp-crested with steep . . . slopes and narrow V-shaped valleys. Although the mountains are not particularly high, not exceeding 2,300 meters, they form a massive . . . block of tangled and forested highlands" (LP Micro-Projects 1990, 3). The Mekong River and several of its tributaries—the Ou, Khan, and Seuang Rivers—flow through the province, providing major transportation routes. The climate, as in all of Laos, is affected by the monsoon and is tropical or subtropical with three seasons—a rainy season and a dry season with two parts: cold/dry and hot/dry. The most com-mon forests in the province are tropical moist deciduous forests. These are closed, high forests with canopy trees of many types including some semi-evergreens, with teak and other commercially valuable trees at lower eleva-tions. The understory is usually comprised of bamboo and other evergreen shrubs. Logging, land clearing, or fire may lead to the invasion of bamboos and tough grasses. Dry dipterocarp forests are also common. These are more open forests resembling savannah woodlands. Pine forests are also found at higher elevations (LP Micro-Projects 1990, 9–11). Commercial logging and shifting cultivation under conditions of increasing population density have led to the loss of much of the primary forest in the province, and only 7 percent of the land is covered by such forests today (LP Micro-Projects 1991, 13). A limited road network, including a few paved roads, links some areas of the province, while many villages are accessible only by trail or river. Some roads and trails are passable only in the dry season in November or December until late May or June (see Map 4.1). Luang Prabang is home to people of several major ethnic groupings including the three considered in this study: ethnic Lao including Laotian Tai (30 percent), Phu Thai (4 percent), and Lue (4 percent); Khmu (47 percent); and Hmong (13 percent) (UNICEF 1992, 12).

The provincial capital of Luang Prabang is the former Royal capital and boasts several thousand inhabitants, but it has few industries except tourism, government service, and cottage industry production. The main manufactured products include rice noodles, pottery, textiles, and boats (LP Micro-Projects 1990, 43). Food and imported goods are plentiful in the markets. Outside Luang Prabang city, most families are subsistence farmers who produce most of what they need to survive. For occasional cash needs, a family may sell an animal, forest products, agricultural produce, or home-manufactured goods.

Rice production dominates agriculture, and farmers use two main systems: paddy farming and shifting or swidden cultivation. Because there is little flat or nearly flat land in the province, potential paddy land is scarce. The farming systems of villages studied in 1990 are reasonably representative of the prevalence of each type of system. In five study villages in 1990, 17 percent of

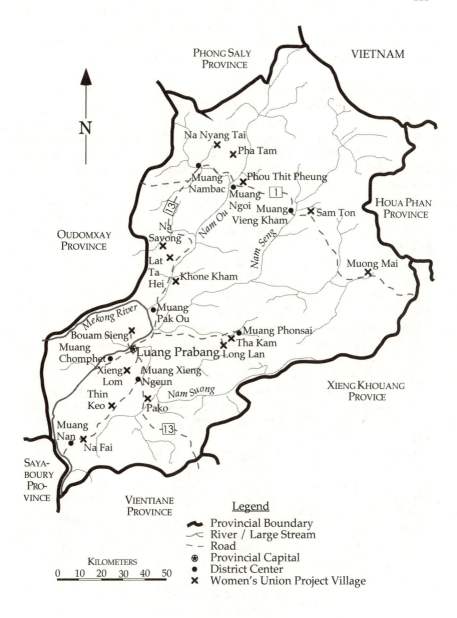

MAP 4.1 Women's Union Project Villages, Luang Prabang Province
Source: Quaker Service Laos in C. Ireson 1990, Appendix A.

the informants reported that their household depended only on paddy farming, while more than one-half (52 percent) reported using both agricultural systems, and the remaining one-third (31 percent) reported depending only on swidden cultivation (C. Ireson 1990). Even the families of civil servants and disabled veterans who receive a salary and/or rice ration depend on their own production for a major part of their livelihood.

Provincial government authorities, which include both provincial administrators and Party leaders, are responsible for specific development priorities in the province, following the general policy directives of the central government. National and provincial resources are meager, though a number of international development agencies are active in the province. Government offices are understaffed with few technically trained people. Few staff have extension or adult education experience or training. These governmental limitations are evident in the lack of services or infrastructure available to villagers even in accessible and "progressive" villages.

Primary schools of at least one or two grades exist in most villages, but the buildings are often temporary with ill-attending, poorly paid teachers. Most district centers house a middle school. The only high school is in Luang Prabang city. The educational system disproportionately educates ethnic Lao boys. According to data gathered from study villages, more men than women are literate, and a higher proportion of ethnic Lao are literate than adults of other ethnic groups.

Provincial health and medical capacity are even more limited than educational capacity. The province has thirty-two doctors, including seven who teach at a training school (LP Micro-Projects 1990). Staff are hampered by old and broken equipment, lack of medicines, and inadequate education. The provincial hospital has little outreach capability. A few district hospitals are functional. A very few villages have health clinic buildings, but they are rarely staffed or supplied. Common health problems reported by village committees in the study villages are malaria, diarrhea, dysentery, polio, and tuberculosis. Fevers, parasites, and respiratory diseases are too common to be mentioned. Measles epidemics periodically infect village children. Infant mortality is high, estimated at 140 per 1,000 births (LP Micro-Projects 1990, 47). In the previous year, one study of a village with sixty-six households revealed that five mothers died in childbirth.

Impact of Socialism and Economic Liberalization on Luang Prabang Women

Socialism

Lao socialist ideology, as we have seen, encourages women to "build socialism" (i.e., to participate in activities for community betterment, to increase production of needed goods, to continue maintaining their families, and to support the new state). Prevailing ideologies about gender, government policies impinging on women's lives and roles, and the Lao Women's Union have changed the environment in which women live and work, although socialist liberation and more recent economic liberalization have not yet dramatically transformed rural lifestyles.

Some changes have occurred, however. When some villages collectivized their paddy rice production and established cooperative stores, family, village, and regional economies were modified, though many village cooperatives dissolved with the introduction of liberalized economic policies in the late 1980s. The economy is still only partly monetized, with most households maintaining subsistence-oriented production practices. The traditional division of labor by sex and age remains mostly intact. A few women are directly involved in Party politics and government administration, even at the local level, though women are more visible in support roles. Monks are, in principle, state officials. Although the power and vitality of the Sangha, the organization of the monkhood, has been coopted by the state, spiritual and ritual functions of the local temple persist in Buddhist (mainly ethnic Lao) villages, and traditional Buddhist ideas and practices continue to reinforce gender stratification. Traditional ideas about gender found in each ethnic group are challenged by socialist ideology. The intensive post-liberation adult literacy campaign greatly improved the literacy of urban and rural adults, and girls and boys attend government schools that exist in many rural areas today for the first time. Family life has changed little since the revolution. These changes, coupled with a number of new policies—a Laotian version of socialist ideology and the maturing of the Lao Women's Union—have affected women's activities and access to resources. This combination of changes has thereby altered the power, autonomy, and subordination of rural Lao, Khmu, and Hmong women.

Liberalization

The effects of subsequent economic liberalization of the 1980s are much more visible in cities and towns, but changes have also reached the countryside. As I mention in Chapter 2, the policies associated with the New Economic Mechanism (NEM) overhauled the structure of incentives so that market mechanisms and the private sector were more prominent in order to encourage private and foreign investments and to further economic growth. As a result of the NEM, agriculturalists were permitted to market their crops through private as well as state channels, cooperatives were de-emphasized with land assigned to households, and cash payment of taxes was required of all (see Chapter 2 for further discussion of NEM). The implementation of NEM policies occurred as communism in eastern Europe and the Soviet Union was collapsing. Aid programs to Laos from these countries collapsed along with communism in those countries. As a result, the Lao government welcomed increased aid from capitalist countries, non-governmental organizations, and United Nations agencies.

These national policy changes resulted in several important transformations for rural Luang Prabang farmers, including the establishment of private crop marketing companies, increased marketing and access to markets, increased rural production for cash, and the inauguration of rural development projects funded by foreign donors.

With changes in economic policies, three crop marketing companies were established in Luang Prabang in 1989. Agents for the companies distribute seed and purchase the crops produced. The companies reach farmers near Luang Prabang city and in accessible villages in other parts of the province. Some of the crops purchased are sold locally or within Laos, while other crops are sold to Thai merchants. Some sesame, for example, is used locally for producing confections, while most is sold to Thailand for producing oil (LP Micro-Projects 1990). The crops purchased by the companies—sesame, peanut and other legumes—are mainly grown by women farmers.

With economic liberalization, marketing is once again an acceptable activity. Ethnic Lao women were forced to curtail their commercial activities after the socialist revolution. Their skills were rarely used in the failed state-store network, nor by local, male-dominated buying and selling cooperatives. Now, however, some ethnic Lao women tend village stores, sell their own and other village products in the nearest market, and sell their products to traveling petty traders. Some Lao women are seeking markets for their own production beyond the local area, in either national or international markets. Khmu women are less likely than Lao women to be commercially active, while few Hmong women appear to be involved in marketing in the province.

Women in all groups appear to be increasing their production in response to increased market opportunities. Their understanding of the market for their goods, though, is rudimentary. One staff member of a foreign aid project purchased a lovely fabric at an ethnic Lao Lue village, paying above the market rate for the piece. In short order, women of that village produced dozens of identical pieces and proudly confronted the next project visitor with stacks of fabric for purchase (Douang Deuane Bounyavong, personal communication, 1992). Women of this village, assisted by project staff, are now seeking a broader market for village fabrics.

In the early 1990s a number of foreign assistance agencies were funding development projects in the province, many more than operated in the province in the mid-1980s. These projects affect villages by targeting some village members for project inclusion, by hiring villagers to build or maintain project facilities, or by working with the village committee to plan and support developmental changes for the village. Project personnel may provide a limited market for items produced by villagers (vegetables, textiles) and support small hotel, restaurant, and house construction businesses in the provincial capital. Women may benefit from these projects if their village is targeted and if their products are purchased by project personnel, but until recently most projects have ignored women as project beneficiaries. One project, for example, trained several hundred village men in fruit tree production (women in all ethnic groups are more likely to be responsible for horticulture), while hiring local village women as agricultural laborers at the fruit experiment station since men would not work for the food that was offered in lieu of wages (Sisouvanh 1992). Two ongoing projects and one planned project, though, have specifically targeted women. Data from these projects form the bulk of the statistical information presented in this chapter.

Activities of Rural Women

Women studied in 1986 and/or 1990 include those from three ethnic groups (Lao, Khmu, and Hmong) in a variety of village settings ranging from accessible well-established paddy farming villages in wide valleys to remote newly established upland farming villages on mountain slopes. The study focuses on women in their productive years (i.e., women from about ages sixteen through fifty). The educational level of the study group ranges from a few who are relatively well educated (some secondary school) to those who have not attended school or adult literacy classes and who cannot speak, read, or write Lao, the national language. Study villages are located in six of the ten districts of the province. The rural women were studied as part of the preparation for and evaluation of an ongoing development project sponsored by the Luang Prabang Women's Union and supported by the American Friends Service Committee.[2]

The population in study villages is young, with one-half of the population below sixteen years old, according to data gathered from informant interviews in five study villages. The birth and infant mortality rates are high, with older women (n = 10) in study villages reporting an average of nine births each, with six to seven surviving children. Almost one-third of the reported child deaths occur to newborns, with more than one-half of the deaths occurring within the first year of life. An additional one-fourth of the reported child deaths occur before age five. Despite the high number of infant deaths, the population growth rate is estimated to be a whopping 3.2 percent per year (LP Micro-Projects 1990, 20) for a doubling time of twenty-two years! Birth control methods and programs were unavailable before 1994, though women seem to want families of just four children. The average household size is 6.5 people in study villages[3] and most often consists of a nuclear family, though surviving grandparents and other relations may also share the household with a nuclear family. Female-headed households are not common, nor are those with no adult women.

Subsistence resources vary greatly between villages and within villages. Only one-third (32 percent) of the informants reported that their household had sufficient rice for family needs every year in the last five years, while over one-third (39 percent) reported shortages in at least three of the last five years. The average period of rice shortage varied from one to six months, with a mean of three months per year. Besides rice, nearly every village informant (91 percent) ate vegetables the day before they were interviewed, but fewer than one-half ate either fruit (47 percent) or meat/fish (38 percent).

Economic well-being seems to vary by accessibility to good agricultural land and the availability of family labor to work it. Accessibility to fertile land varies markedly by ethnic group, with ethnic Lao groups generally having access to better land. Other sources of family livelihood besides crop production for consumption and sale include animal raising, forest products gathering, hunting, and craft sales or barter. The varied housing in rural Luang Prabang reflects variations in economic status. Some households in the old paddy-rice-growing ethnic Lao village of Na Fai live in spacious two-story houses of sawn wood with tile roofs, while most households in the relatively newly established Khmu village of Sam Ton live in small pole and bamboo houses with thatched roofs on low stilts. Even Na Fai has some housing like that in Sam Ton, though it usually houses new in-migrants.

Inheritance of fertile paddy land, most common among the ethnic Lao, provides the basis for social class distinctions. Sufficient labor and access to other factors of production (e.g., water, animal or mechanical power), however, are still necessary to convert paddy ownership into economic well-being. In groups or villages that rely mainly on upland rice production where hillside land is plentiful (a common situation in many villages until just a few decades ago), household and collective labor was the most important determinant of economic sufficiency. So children of a poor family may see their socioeconomic level increase markedly as they enter adolescence and add to household labor resources. Socioeconomic differences, then, are most obvious in ethnic Lao villages relying mainly on paddy production. Because upland rice fields produce less rice than paddies, villages with little access to paddies (commonly the midland and upland groups) are generally poorer than villages based on paddy agriculture. Socioeconomic differences, then, sometimes reflect ethnic differences. Inheritance differences by ethnic group provide some economic resources for ethnic Lao women, though not generally for women of the other groups. In all groups, though, women's labor is of vital importance to household survival and economic well-being.

Women in all villages are responsible for rice hulling, water carrying (see Photo 4.1), cooking, child care, gardening, highland field weeding, forest foraging, and small animal raising, though their older children or husbands may assist them. They share other subsistence tasks with the other adults in their families. Many ethnic Lao women are skilled cotton processors and

PHOTO 4.1 This Hmong woman near Phou Thit Pheung is hauling water in bamboo tubes. She suffers, as many upland women do, from goiter.

weavers, while other women have various other craft skills (e.g., jute bag making, embroidery).

Rural Women and Their Villages

Three women from different villages and ethnic groups illuminate somewhat different cultural and individual sources of power and subordination in women's lives and work. All three women are working members of fundamentally subsistence-oriented households that draw on various aspects of their natural environments to sustain themselves and their families. All engage in some aspects of agriculture, animal husbandry, forest foraging, fishing, and hunting. In addition, most are skilled in making items needed in their everyday lives. All are able to produce or gather products for sale when necessary. All are integrated into the larger governmental structure of the Lao People's Democratic Republic and all have some access to limited markets outside their village. Khmu, Lao, and Hmong cultures and social structures differ, however, so the division of labor varies somewhat, as does the meaning assigned to particular tasks and to femaleness itself.

Ethnic Lao Village Life

Na Fai. Na Fai is a larger, long-established paddy farming village that even in 1986 was nearly wealthy enough to support some specialists, mainly weavers and seamstresses. Located on a road between the provincial capitals of Luang Prabang and Sayaboury in southwest Luang Prabang Province, Na Fai lies in a valley 2 kilometers from the district center. Many village houses are large, supported high above the ground on tall posts, and permanently constructed from sawn lumber with tile or tin roofing. The village school offers five years of education. Many children attend school for the full five years, and a number, including more girls than boys, continue their education at the middle school in the district center. Many women, as well as men, are literate in Lao. In 1986, the village installed a drinking water system that delivers water to several spigots throughout the village. Women have long grown cotton and woven cloth for nearby villages and for export to Thailand.

Na Nyang Tai. Na Nyang Tai was destroyed during the war, but it now appears prosperous by Luang Prabang village standards. Many rebuilt homes are sturdily constructed of sawn wood with lofty tile roofs and decorated gables. The paddy farming Lao Lue ancestors of Na Nyang Tai residents have lived in the same northwest Luang Prabang Province site for hundreds of years. A wide stream runs by the village, which is surrounded by a large area of rice paddies. The women produce dyed cloth for work clothes and patterned fabric for curtains, tablecloths, and decorative blankets. They also make mattresses from kapok covered with sturdy, decorated, hand-woven cloth. In 1988 the district established a ten-day rotating market in the area, providing an outlet for village products. Despite the prosperous appearance, villagers marketed few goods in 1988, did not have a rice surplus, and all but two women were illiterate.

Aspects of Ethnic Lao Women's Lives. Na Fai is unusually wealthy for a rural Lao village in Luang Prabang. Its favorable location in a fertile valley on a main trade route to Thailand accounts for some of its wealth. Nonetheless, the skills and activities of Na Fai women are similar to those of other rural ethnic Lao in the province. Women of Sieng Lom, for example, another ethnic Lao village located near a river and on a bad road 13 kilometers from Luang Prabang city, can weave too, but for income they grow tobacco and garlic, rather than cotton. The rich silt deposited every rainy season on their riverbank gardens enables them to grow a variety of annual plants and vegetables. Lue women in Na Nyang Tai also grow crops for sale.

Two villages of ethnic Lao Lue demonstrate the textile production skills of ethnic Lao women. The women in Na Nyang Tai make mattresses and comforters filled with kapok, and weave plain and patterned cloth. They use or sell the cloth, mattresses, and comforters they make, although local marketing possibilities in their area are limited. Women in the Lue village of Khone Kham, located on the Ou River, are known for their production of indigo-dyed cotton "homespun" cloth for use in making sturdy work clothes. They grow both the cotton and the plants that produce the indigo dye. Many of the older women have permanently stained blue hands from handling the newly dyed cloth. They sell and barter this product to nearby villagers. One Khone Kham woman reported that she trades cloth for the care of her two cattle by a ridge-dwelling Hmong family. Interestingly, few women in either of these villages are literate. Nearly all Lao weavers and seamstresses also farm and forage for household subsistence and income.

Boun Soum, Seamstress of Na Fai. Boun Soum, her husband, and their six sons live with Boun Soum's mother in a sturdy, two-story, sawn wood house. All of her babies survived, though her youngest, a one-year old, is too thin, so she will nurse him for longer than the sixteen months she nursed her other children. The family has fertile paddy land and enough labor to eat well. Yesterday the family ate three meals including pork for breakfast, vegetable soup for lunch, and bird for dinner, plus rice at every meal. Boun Soum attended school through the fifth grade, quitting when her father died and her labor was needed by the household. Her three younger siblings, though, did not stop and were able to continue their studies after receiving scholarships to study abroad. Her elder brother has married and received a cash inheritance already, but her mother has not yet given out the remainder of the estate.

Since Boun Soum is living in her mother's home and caring for the sometimes asthmatic older woman, custom dictates that she receive the house and at least some of the family paddy land. Each elder person determines his or her own pattern of bequests, though, so Boun Soum does not assume that she will automatically inherit the house and paddy land.

Boun Soum studied sewing for three months in the district center 2 kilometers away and now owns a sewing machine. She much prefers sewing, housework, and child care to field work, though sometimes she must do agricultural work. Yesterday she steamed rice, prepared all the meals, fed the chickens and ducks, and sewed for a neighbor in exchange for field labor. Her mother watched the preschool children, and both women did housework. The first floor of her home is for sewing, visiting, and selling cloth, clothing, and corn. Since the village has both a rice mill and a water system, little of her time and energy is used for rice milling or water carrying. Her husband is responsible for nearly all the agricultural labor, including rice cultivation in both paddy and upland fields and growing a few garden crops. Occasionally he fishes and gathers bamboo shoots from the forest. Sometimes he sews his own clothes, or helps with housework or with collecting firewood. Boun Soum herself keeps the family purse and is responsible for financial decisions. Boun Soum would like to sew full-time for pay, perhaps teaching others to sew as well (see Photo 4.2). Her expertise is recognized by other village women who selected her as vice-president of the village women's union.[4]

Khmu Village Life

Thin Keo. Khmu war refugees established Thin Keo village in the mid-1970s at the end of the second Indochina war. The village is located on an unpaved all-weather road 7 kilometers from the district center of Sieng Ngeun and about 30 kilometers from Luang Prabang city on the road to Na Fai. In 1986, villagers were still underfed, unhealthy, virtually uneducated, and poor. The women worked long hours, often continuing to work immediately before and after giving birth, but were timid toward outsiders and seemingly unassertive in village decision making. They grew three cash crops (sesame, peanuts, and cotton), but rice was usually insufficient for their needs. They had a small area of irrigated paddy field for double cropping, but most crops including rice were produced in upland fields worked mainly by the women. The only two services or items of infrastructure available to Thin Keo residents in 1986 were the road and a government-provided teacher. However, residents were responsible for building the school and paying the teacher. The school was a temporary building with a dirt floor, woven bamboo walls, and a thatched roof, and the teacher was rarely paid.

PHOTO 4.2 Boun Soum much prefers sewing to agricultural labor.

Other Khmu Villages. The impoverished condition of Thin Keo villagers is shared by other Khmu villages in the province. A survey of seven villages in a small area indicated that four of the five Khmu villages were poorer, both in grains and in cash income, than the one Lao village, and that the same four villages were also poorer than the one Hmong village, as indicated by average household expenditures (LP Micro-Projects 1991, Figures 4 and 5). Similarly, a 1990 study of eight Luang Prabang villages indicated that Khmu households were less likely to be self-sufficient in rice than were Hmong or Lao house-holds (Håkangård 1990, 18).

Disease is rampant in Sam Ton, a Khmu village in northern Luang Prabang. The village suffered drought and lost most of its crops in 1987. Deaths exceeded births in 1990 with dysentery killing the most people. Malaria and polio are also endemic, while tuberculosis and malnutrition are common. Opium use and marital infidelity often cause family disputes. Sam Ton is located high on a scenic ridge, but the available agricultural land is steep and not very fertile, and the village spring dries up every year for two months requiring all-day trips to the valley floor, 900 meters below, for water. Villagers live in constant and well-founded fear of not having enough food to eat.

Two grades of primary school are located in a temporary building much like that of Thin Keo, and a number of women reportedly can read and write "some" Lao. Because they are desperate to change their situation, twenty women are currently studying to become literate so they will be included in the women's union project. Most Khmu are animists, practice spirit worship, and rely on shamans for help with illness, spirit possession, and other common problems. The village head in Sam Ton has identified these customs as regressive. Thus, since the selection of the village as a "development village," he has outlawed these traditional practices. Villagers reported that at first they were afraid, but nothing bad happened, so now they have also begun to plan ahead and to wash their clothes and kitchen utensils more frequently.

Government officials and other researchers note that Khmu skills in agriculture, production planning, commerce, and finances are limited. An incident in Sam Ton demonstrates this lack of basic technical skill and also illustrates villagers' lack of experience with the world beyond their village. The government and foreign donors gave the village women's union a rice mill, mosquito nets, and cement and reinforcing steel to build a school. The village committee, including several men and the president of the women's union, were responsible for using these items. Villagers paid transportation expenses for these items, correctly installed the rice mill, and immediately began sleeping under the mosquito nets. But, since they did not know how to design a school or lay cement, and since the district carpenter was chronically unavailable, they hired roving Vietnamese laborers to build the school by the deadline imposed by district officials. Villagers paid the Vietnamese in full for the work when they began working and, in addition, agreed to feed them every working day. The work took much longer than anticipated, though it was properly done. Ultimately, the villagers ran out of rice and the district again stepped in and fired the Vietnamese crew. So, after paying huge sums, in village terms, for the transportation of construction materials and building costs, the villagers were left with no more money or resources to convert to money, a marked rice shortage, and an unfinished school. This incident illustrates lack of knowledge of basic design and cement work, naivete in dealing with non-Khmu (Vietnamese laborers, district officials), and women's circumscribed participation in dealing with outside inputs for "their" project.

Aspects of Khmu Women's Lives. Women still do much of the agricultural work and all household work, while men fish, hunt, and clear the swidden field once a year. Some evenings or early mornings husbands may care for children so wives can fetch water, hull rice, or gather firewood and forest foods. This division of labor by gender has been little affected by government proclamations of equality, socialist reorganization, or recent economic liberalization. It is not uncommon for a Khmu woman to give birth a dozen times and lose one-half of her children at birth or from disease (LP Micro-Projects 1990, 21–22). Women's survival past age fifty was dramatically lower than that of men in three out of five Khmu villages surveyed in 1991. Researchers attribute this to hard labor and many births (LP Micro-Projects 1991, 19, 21, 22).

In addition, rural Luang Prabang Khmu produce few marketable products, though they may sell products like bamboo shoots or tree resin gathered from the forest. They seldom have rice or other crops to sell and often produce an inadequate supply for their own use. Most Khmu still live in isolated settlements and are viewed as backward and stupid by many members of lowland and highland ethnic groups. The resulting discrimination perpetuates these dismal conditions. Better connection of Luang Prabang to Thai markets resulting from economic liberalization may generate more male labor migration (common before 1975) or induce more women, like Phing of Thin Keo, to grow cash crops.

Phing, Farmer of Thin Keo. Phing, at thirty-two, has already given birth to seven children, although only four are still living. Her oldest child is nine and the youngest is five months old. Her household has eight people, including her husband, his mother, his younger sister, Phing, and her children. She weans her babies when they are eighteen months old, or when she is six months pregnant, whichever comes first. They have plenty of paddy land and two buffalo (unusual for the people in her village), so they have enough food to eat. Phing studied reading and writing during the intensive literacy campaign carried out by the new government shortly after the revolution in 1975 and says she can read and write "a little." She would like to have only four children, two girls and two boys, but knows no way of controlling her fertility. Phing cares for pigs, chickens, and ducks in the yard near their house, carries water, husks rice, and sweeps the house and yard. Her mother-in-law cares for all the children but the baby, and often cooks.

Phing is an excellent horticulturalist, but with a nursing baby and a husband who is often busy with the business of the village cooperative, she has little time to devote to the production of sesame and cotton for sale. They grow rice, corn, sesame, cotton, vegetables, cassava, and fruit trees in the family's highland field. They can work their highland field for five years before the soil is exhausted; they then must clear a new area. The day before being interviewed, Phing was feverish so she did not go to the highland field. But usually she carries the baby and her lunch on the ninety-minute walk to the fields, where regular weeding is needed during the growing season. The family exchanges labor with other households for land clearing, and her husband builds the fence and burns the cleared area. Phing herself is responsible for maintaining the crops during the growing season. Occasionally, her husband comes to the highland field to help. On those days he spends part of the time hunting wild boar and other forest animals, and carries firewood back to their village. Like the other Khmu women in the village, Phing does not weave but grows cotton to exchange for finished cloth. To improve her life she would like easier and faster ways to carry water, pound rice, and obtain firewood. She also wants to plant more cash crops, especially cotton and sesame. She can successfully grow these crops now but is interested in advice on how to increase yields. Her family's survival depends largely on her efforts. This year, revenue from her cash crops will enable the family to roof their new house.[5]

Highland Hmong Village Life: Phou Thit Pheung

This Hmong village is perched high on a mountain, very near the top. The village is named after the mountain: the village of the mountain of the "pheung" spirit. Spirit involvement is also evident in everyday life as shamans minister to the sick and those in difficulty. Although it is an established village of forty-five years, it is not rich. Few villagers are literate in Lao and health problems abound. The houses are nearly all temporary structures of bamboo and thatch, but the village is self-sufficient in rice production and sold rice in both 1989 and 1990. Other products sold include sesame, soybean, cucumber, coffee, and animals (pigs and cattle). While a number of Hmong villagers in Luang Prabang and other provinces continue to grow and sell opium as their major cash crop, Phou Thit Pheung villagers say they do not. Ten village women are studying Lao and have the authority to meet with government officials, though this is a new phenomenon.

In 1985. while I was traveling on other business with a carload of male provincial and district officials, our car stopped at Phou Thit Pheung. It was the middle of the day so the curious group that gathered around us was made up of children and women. The women stood some distance away from us while a local official from our group spoke briefly to the children and shy women. A child was dispatched to find a person who could speak with us. While the two groups remained standing at some distance from one another,

I asked why we were waiting. The women were too shy to talk, my companions said, and they probably didn't speak much Lao anyway.

Four years later Phou Thit Pheung was included in the Luang Prabang Women's Project. When I next visited the village in 1990, several women came running up to my pickup truck almost before it had come to a stop. The president of the women's union eagerly helped me from the truck, enthusiastically telling me about pots and pans, mosquito nets, and evening study sessions, and introducing me and my fellow travelers to some of the other women and men who gathered to greet us. Speaking in fluent Lao the entire time, this lively woman then escorted me to her home where she showed me the fruit tree seedlings she had recently planted. She gave me a tour of her house and garden, and we discussed the virtues of a raised cooking stove rather than an open hearth for cooking. She introduced me to her shaman husband after he finished the healing ritual he was conducting for their sick son, and we then returned to the larger group to conduct "official" project business. During the remainder of the day, I discovered that the village women's union president was not the only Phou Thit Pheung woman who spoke and understood Lao.

Women's Changing Resources: Development Project Villages

The lives of the women and the villages described in the previous section have changed since 1986, sometimes dramatically. All the villages studied were subsequently included in a women-oriented rural development project. While involved in this rural development project, residents in project villages were also subjected to nonproject sources of change as the local and regional economies transformed in response to new national economic policies. In Luang Prabang between 1986 and 1990, these changes involved the establishment of crop purchasing companies and increased marketing activity.

Some project inputs disrupted village life and disturbed the existing distribution of power within the village, with a range of effects. The varying village responses to these inputs to the village women's union and the varying benefits that villages reaped from the project reveal much about women's power and subordination in each participating village. Some villages were unable to use inputs well, at least within the 3-year project period, while other villages made good use of the inputs, realigning village dynamics in the process.

The Luang Prabang Women's Project entitled "Improving Labor Productivity of Luang Prabang Women"[6] aimed to improve the lives of women and their families by relieving some of the women's everyday labor burden so that women would be able to engage in more productive or more remunerative work in cottage industry, handicrafts, agriculture, or other activities. It focused on approximately 1,100–1,200 women in fourteen villages in eight of the ten

TABLE 4.1 Luang Prabang Women's Project Villages

Village	Year[a]	Ethnicity	HH[b]
Thin Keo[c]	1: 1986	Khmu	50
Khone Kham[c]	1: 1986	Lao (Lue)	51
Na Fai[c]	1: 1986	Lao	133
Sieng Lom	1: 1986	Lao	105
Na Nyang Tai[c]	2: 1988	Lao (Lue)	165
Na Savang	2: 1988	Khmu	44
Sam Ton[c]	2: 1988	Khmu	55
Tha Kam	2: 1988	Khmu	44
Bouam Sieng	3: 1989	Khmu	61
Long Lan	3: 1989	Hmong	70
Muong Mai	3: 1989	Khmu	112
Pha Tam	3: 1989	Hmong	26
Phou Thit Pheung[c]	3: 1989	Hmong	37
Pako	3: 1990	Hmong	28

[a]Began during which project year; date of baseline survey.
[b]Number of households at time of baseline survey.
[c]Villages included in the evaluation study; see Map 4.1 for village locations.

districts of Luang Prabang Province, providing assistance to the village women's union in each village. Project assistance was targeted to the specific labor-saving needs and productive capabilities of the women of each village, so project activities varied somewhat by village. The planned project period was three years for each village, with four or five villages beginning the project in each of three consecutive years, for a total project period of five years. Data were gathered and the project was formulated in 1986, though project implementation did not begin until 1988. Additional data were gathered in 1990 half-way through the project period in order to evaluate the accomplishments and problems of the project.[7] (See Table 4.1 for a list of project villages and Map 4.1 for village locations.)

Village women's unions first received project inputs designed to ease women's nonproductive but very necessary domestic work. While this varied by village, depending on what the women of each village identified as their most burdensome tasks, unions most commonly received rice mills and gravity-flow drinking-water systems. Blankets, mosquito nets, and kitchen utensils went to the poorest villages as well. A few villages requested imported materials for constructing child-care centers. One village, Na Fai, received a cotton gin. Only after these labor-saving inputs were installed or in use were more production-oriented inputs added, including, depending on expressed village interest, animal husbandry, training in fruit production and aspects of textile production, and production-related tools and supplies (hand tools, pushcarts, vegetable seeds). Other inputs to improve the quality of village life, such as materials for and training in the manufacture of water seal toilets, imported materials for school construction, and adult literacy materials, were also included when requested by the village women's union.

Project Results

Several important things changed, especially in the more successful project villages. Changes occurred in women's balance of reproductive to productive work, in the types of productive activities women pursued, and in the resources controlled by or available to women.

Reproductive Work: Women's Household Work. Women in all the project villages that were evaluated (except Khone Kham) experienced a decrease in their labor burden of two to five woman-hours per day in each household by use of rice mills, water systems, and the cotton gin. Village women and women's unions interviewed during 1986 almost unanimously included rice hulling and water carrying in their listing of hardest and most time-consuming tasks. At that time many reported that someone (nearly always a woman) in the household spent, on the average, two hours a day hulling sufficient rice for the daily meals. In reports of hour-by-hour activity, many women reported hulling rice for two hours very early in the morning. Water carrying, often shared with children, usually occurred more than once a day, occupying from less than one hour to several hours depending on the season and the proximity of the water supply.

Even years later village women, village men, and even province officials reported that a woman's life, indeed life generally in project villages, is now comfortable and convenient. "We don't pound rice and we don't carry water far," many say when asked about project benefits. Women in most project villages now report that they no longer get up very early, yet they leave the village earlier to go to their fields and gardens. Women in villages that grow cotton and make cloth still find this work difficult, though it has been substantially alleviated by the ginning machine operated by the women's union in Na Fai. Na Fai weavers report that the best ginner among them can hand-gin one kilogram of cotton per day. Now Na Fai cotton producers machine gin 18–22 kilograms of cotton per hour.

In short, project labor-saving equipment installed in project villages has saved at least two woman-hours of labor per household per day. The operation and maintenance of rice mills and water systems are handled by just a few people, some of whom are paid for their work.

Changes in Production. Women in most project villages increased their production for sale, especially their production of nonrice food crops, cotton, and pigs. Although quantities of agricultural products were not systematically measured in either time period, it appears that agricultural production has increased in all first-year and second-year project villages visited during the evaluation period. Most of the same items were produced in both time periods, but most were produced only in small amounts for family use during the initial period. By 1990, some families were producing goods for sale. Sesame and cotton are the most common cash crops in both periods. Table 4.2 shows the increase in types of cash crops grown from the baseline to the evaluation periods. In every village but Sam Ton the change is marked.

Agricultural products for sale are included in Table 4.2 if more than one individual, the village committee, or the village women's union reported village production of the product for sale during the baseline period and in 1990. Cotton production in Na Fai has increased noticeably with project provision of a ginning machine and the involvement of the United Nations Development Programme-supported Textile Center, another project of the Lao Women's Union, in providing long staple cotton seeds and purchasing the ginned cotton. Short staple cotton is still grown for village use, but long staple cotton has become an important market crop. The sales of indigo-dyed cloth in Khone Kham, Lao skirt lengths in Na Fai, and decorative weaving in Na Nyang Tai continue but have not obviously increased.

The production of pigs has also increased remarkably from the baseline period to 1990 in two villages where the village women's union report the use of rice bran from the rice mill for pig raising. In Sam Ton the number of pigs has increased 2.5 times, from 87 to 220 pigs in two years, while in Na Nyang Tai the pig population increased thirteenfold from 1988 to 1990 (see Table 4.3).

Nonrice crops, pigs, and cotton are mainly produced by women. All first- and second-year project villages visited during the evaluation showed an increase in the production of at least one of these types of commodities.

Increased Availability of Economic Resources. Clearly, project activities in all but the one unsuccessful village of Khone Kham added to the resource base of the women, either individually or collectively through the women's union. For example, Na Fai women collectively used rice mill proceeds to repair the

TABLE 4.2 Crops Cultivated for Sale During Baseline and Evaluation Periods

Village	Ethnicity	No. of Crops Baseline	No. of Crops Eval.	Sesame	Cotton	Peanut	Tobacco	Banana	Soybean	Coconut	Other
Na Fai	Lao	2	5	x	x	x	x	x	x	x	
Na Nyang Tai	Lao	1	7	x	x		x	x		x	Garlic Onion Mango
Khone Kham	Lao	1	5	x	x	x			x		Sugar Cane
Thin Keo	Khmu	3	5	x	x	x					Corn Redbean Roots
Sam Ton	Khmu	2	1	x	x						
Phou Thit Pheung	Hmong	1	4	x					x		Cucumber Coffee

TABLE 4.3   Change in Village Animal Population Between Baseline and
Evaluation Studies

Village	% Change in Large Animals (Buffalo, Cattle)	% Change in Small Animals (Pigs, Goats)
All five villages[a]	+ 18	+ 11
Four villages (excluding Khone Kham)	+ 41	+ 47
Na Fai (Lao)	+ 257	No measurable change[b]
Na Nyang Tai (Lao)	- 17	+ 1200
Thin Keo (Khmu)	No change	- 46
Sam Ton (Khmu)	- 5	- 167

[a]Only one data point for Phou Thit Pheung.   [b]Data incomplete.

access road into their village, and Thin Keo women used rice mill proceeds to pay for the transport of project goods and to buy hardware for the kindergarten. Individually, Na Fai women have profited from the cotton gin and from rice bran as pig food, while other villages (Na Nyang Tai, Sam Ton) also have used rice bran to increase pig production.

Some village women reported small increases in their own and household income and resources, but this was observable only in an increase in large animals in Na Fai, and in the new construction of houses in most project villages. (See Table 4.3 for changes in large animals.) Increases in income and resources are sure to benefit women and their children only if women participate in family decision making about the use of these increased resources. This is most likely to happen in ethnic Lao households where women are often the producers and marketers of products and where women usually keep the family purse. This is less likely to occur in Khmu and Hmong households. One Khmu woman from Sam Ton, for example, mentioned that she produces goods and her husband markets them. In 1986 the Khmu women of Thin Keo were less likely than the ethnic Lao women of Na Fai, Sieng Lom, and Khone Kham to keep the family purse and to acknowledge a share in household decision making about sales and purchases.

Increased economic resources in project villages do not therefore necessarily lead to increased individual economic power for women. Collectively, though, village women have augmented their control over economic resources. In a number of villages this collective change in women's control has led to increased respect for women and for the village women's union, though not without some initial problems in project implementation. Noticeable improvements in village quality of life due to project activities (especially clean drinking water, water seal toilets, school construction) have also enhanced respect for the women's union in a number of villages. Measurable gains in some villages included lower childhood mortality, improved health, and increased school attendance in all villages but Khone Kham. In villages receiving mosquito nets or water systems, villagers perceive that the incidence of malaria or gastrointestinal diseases has declined, though other health problems remain. Villagers also report fewer arguments among household members about who will make yet another trip to the nearby stream or who will get up early to pound rice.

Local and National Economic Changes

About the time rice mills and water systems were becoming operational in project villages, the effects of Lao government economic policy changes began to reach the countryside with the establishment of private agricultural marketing companies, approval of private entrepreneurship, and access to internal and Thai markets. Time freed by project labor-saving interventions appears to have been channeled into increased production of goods for sale, which resulted in reported increases in income and village quality of life. Na Nyang Tai women, for example, reported clear links between these project inputs and production. They reported that the time and energy they were saving were being used to study, to weave more, and to grow more products for sale. Local and national economic changes stimulated the development of markets for women's increased production, markets that did not exist even a few years previously.

Project Implementation and Women's Power

These beneficial results occurred only after villagers adjusted to changes in social relations necessitated by successful project implementation. Not all villages adjusted successfully. (Khone Kham, for example, did not.) The different ways in which villages handled the operation and maintenance of project rice mills and water systems illustrate marked differences in village social relations. Rice mills and water systems were introduced to project villages by a training course to villagers selected by the women's unions and village governing committees of the first villages to participate in the project (henceforth called Year One villages). The trainees, including both women and men, then returned to the village to carry out their responsibilities. For the water system, additional help from district or province technicians in design and construction was obtained.

In many cases, mere training and technical help were insufficient. Women's union ownership of the facilities was not clear, and, in all Year One villages, at some point either women abdicated control over at least one of their facilities (the rice mill or the water system) or village men usurped control. This required provincial women's union intervention, sometimes with the additional assistance of provincial and/or district officials. Union and government officials re-explained project objectives, persuaded village committee men to relinquish control, and encouraged the village women's union to take charge again. In subsequent project years, both men and women in new villages were more thoroughly aware of village women's union ownership of and responsibility for these facilities before entering the project. The differences between the way three ethnic Lao villages handled the project rice mill and between two of these villages' management of the water system illustrate the variation in various village responses to changing social relations.

Rice Mills. In Na Nyang Tai (Lao), a Year Two village, the rice mill is competently operated and maintained by the women's union and is well used by villagers. While we were there, the responsible woman started the motor to demonstrate its operation to us, and almost immediately several people appeared with baskets of rice to mill. Initially there was some disagreement about payment for milling and the use of the bran, but these problems have since been satisfactorily resolved.

The introduction of the rice mill to Na Fai (Lao) also caused problems. A family operated an older, less efficient rice mill in the village at the time the women's union rice mill was installed. The new mill was cheaper and milled the rice better, so most people began to use it. The mill-owning family wanted to run the new mill on contract to the women's union, though they were not allowed to do so. About the same time, the new mill broke after it was secretly filled with kapok. Village women's union representatives claimed it was sabotaged by the competing family. This dispute was resolved only with the intercession of the Luang Prabang Women's Union project coordinator and the district chief. The old mill was retired, and the new mill continued running under women's union auspices. The village dissension caused by this disagreement is fortunately no longer apparent. Pig raising, common during the baseline survey, continues to flourish with the rice bran from the new mill. Rice milling was provided to a road-building crew encamped nearby in exchange for repairing the road into the village. Women's union members are now operating both the rice mill and the cotton gin, but some villagers still doubt their competence in doing so.

Although Na Fai was a Year One village, village men did not attempt a rice mill takeover. Instead, the women surrendered control over the project-provided cotton gin. Women from the beginning were hesitant to take responsibility for the ginning machine and apparently did not maintain it properly. A few months after the village installed it, the women abdicated control, turning its operation, maintenance, and profits over to the male leaders of the village and cooperative. The village women's union was otherwise not very active the first two years of the project. The village committee, not the women's union, received all aid goods and reported to the Luang Prabang Women's Union, saying that because the women's educational level was very low, the men had to take charge. But, in fact, Na Fai women are well educated by Luang Prabang village standards.

Ownership, maintenance, and operation of the rice mill has been a continual problem in Khone Kham. The rice mill belonged to the old cooperative, defunct since the mid-1980s, so ownership of the current rice mill is evidently in doubt. The two young people who were trained, under project auspices, to operate and maintain the rice mill were not supervised by the women's union. Money "earned" by the mill after several months was duly recorded by the two operators but was nowhere to be found, according to the village head. He therefore unilaterally decided to turn the rice mill over to the family of the head elder. The new rice-mill operators must pay a small sum to the women's union every year for the use of the mill. Not all villagers agreed with this, but at the time of the evaluation visit no one had yet been willing to ask for a village meeting to discuss the issue. Currently, only the richer families can afford the cost of milling, and since rice is in short supply, few households have enough rice to mill. In addition, the milling plates now evidently need repair or replacement, so rice is milled incompletely.

There appear to be at least two causes of the problems in Khone Kham. First, villagers have learned from previous aid how to "accept assistance" from outside sources. But these inputs were not made in a way that promoted village decision making and self-sufficiency. Instead villagers came to expect governmental help in maintaining and repairing governmentally provided inputs. Second, village leadership and organization do not promote mutual respect, intravillage cooperation, or village improvement. Teachers do not stay long at the village, and a village daughter, trained as a medic, stopped practicing in the village because the village did not pay her.

Water Systems. The Na Nyang Tai (Lao) women's union oversees the water system, calling on men of the village committee when repairs are needed. The committee and the union have plans to install a reservoir at the head of a portion of the system to ensure more regular water flow. Mothers have trained their children to use the public faucets properly, so most are in good condition. In Thin Keo, a Khmu village, neither women's union nor village committee seems to tend the water system. Undisciplined children have broken most of the faucets, but the piping system is still functional so water continues to be delivered to the village.

Control Over Project Resources. As in Khone Kham, an "elite" group of related families in Thin Keo appropriated project resources. This occurred only after the income- and resource-creating aspects of the project became evident to families containing the village head, the women's union head, and the only well-educated villager, a man. At one point the village committee took over the rice mill. Later the educated man and the village head ordered the killing of an animal bank buffalo, without seeking permission of the women's union, in order to celebrate the departure of a student teacher. When the project coordinator learned about the buffalo, she was very angry. She went to the village and asked them to buy another buffalo to replace the one they had killed, threatening to withdraw the project if they did not. So the two "elite" men assessed the other villagers for the cost. During this process, the women's union head favored her family, rather than protecting the interests of the village women's union, so she lost respect of some of the women. These control attempts divided the women and undermined the women's union head.

Several of these problems seem related to issues of village stratification and to shared understandings in the village of appropriate female and male behavior. Higher status villagers attempt, usually successfully, to extend their influence from other village arenas (village or lineage leadership, entrepreneurship, or relative wealth) to controlling the new resources introduced into the village by the Women's Project. Higher status villagers are invariably male. Further, in none of the three ethnic groups are the following project-related behaviors viewed as appropriate for women: the operation and maintenance of engines or mechanical systems, direct communication with outside government officials, and acceptance of goods for the use of village development. Other activities required by project participation were acceptable only for some, mainly ethnic Lao participants, including record-keeping and travel to the provincial capital. The project, then, required modifications in women's roles and gave women direct control over new resources. Furthermore, if village women's union leaders were not from "leading" village families, the village status hierarchy might also be challenged and altered by project activities and resources. Successful project villages were those that responded to project activities and inputs by transforming some aspects of gender and status relations in the village.

Obviously, project implementation has been most successful in well-organized villages and where the village governing committee helps and supports the village women's union in carrying out project activities. However, it is not always easy to know in advance whether such project-supportive village dynamics will occur. Some villages that had inactive or nonexistent women's unions in 1986 and in which women's education and status were clearly inferior to those of men were still able to develop successfully as project villages. In several villages, as in Na Nyang Tai for example, respect for women and for women's union activities has increased, according to reports of either the village committee or the women's union committee itself. Women in these villages can now deal directly with government officials, control important village resources, and mobilize village labor in service of these village resources. This project-related economic and political power may be gradually affecting other areas of village life as gender roles and the village status hierarchy shift. More students are studying in project villages, but more than one-half of the new students are still boys in some villages. The percentage of girls continuing their education beyond the village, however, has risen in three villages. Women are now involved in literacy classes in two villages, though women's literacy level continues to be much below that of men in all villages except Na Fai. A women's union representative is included in the village committee in three of the six villages evaluated, including the most successful (Na Nyang Tai) and least successful (Khone Kham) of the six villages.

In sum, when women's household tasks are streamlined, women are able to increase their economic production. Further, the macro-level changes resulting from the expansion of the Lao Women's Union and the Luang Prabang Women's Union into rural development, as well as the liberalization of national economic policy enabled many women to increase their income or household resources because there was a local vehicle for women's development (particularly the alleviation of domestic tasks) and a market for women's increased production. In addition, in some villages these changes and the additional resources provided to women collectively by the project are altering gender roles and improving women's positions within the village.

Ethnic Differences in Women's Responses

Observations

Women of all ethnic groups can benefit from women-oriented rural development projects and economic changes, but they begin from different points, with different sets of resources and skills, and differences in decision-making authority and village-level political power.

Lao women in project villages generally have access to better agricultural land, have less onerous work demands, have skills that can be used to produce products for sale, have experience with marketing and speak the local language of commerce (Lao), and are more likely to be literate.[8] In addition, Lao villages are more likely to have access to transportation, schools, rice mills, or other services and facilities. Lao villages have a political advantage over villages of other groups since the state is predominantly administered by Lao men or minority men who have assimilated to lowland society norms. This advantage may be declining in northern provinces where, increasingly, minority men are attaining top posts. However, it still appears that ethnic Lao are disproportionately selected for "development" while ethnic minorities are slated for resettlement[9] to areas where they can be more closely controlled.

Hmong villagers, in particular, are sometimes suspected as possible supporters of anti-government guerrilla activity (C. Ireson and R. Ireson 1991).

Khmu villagers suffer from stereotyping as "backward," an image reinforced by their lack of skills generalizable beyond their daily subsistence activities and their usually limited experience beyond their village. Khmu village social organization appears less supportive of political solidarity and mutual defense, and has historically made the Khmu vulnerable to land grabs by better organized and politically connected Lao villagers. Their limited access to good agricultural land thus may be partly a result of political factors, rather than preference for upland agriculture.

Hmong villagers commonly grow opium and raise cattle. These two products ensure a regular annual income and provide a buffer against misfortune like the drought and epidemic described in Sam Ton. Nonetheless, Hmong villagers, like the Khmu, are usually not literate in Lao, are usually less healthy and well nourished than the ethnic Lao, and rarely send their children to school. Similarly, Hmong and Khmu women are less likely than Lao women to make financial or agricultural decisions within the household and, the Phou Thit Pheung women's union notwithstanding, are less likely to have the authority to deal directly with government officials or to engage in commercial activities.

In Thin Keo and Sam Ton, Khmu villages with more than the usual range of problems in project implementation, some problems were related to women's and men's low levels of education, skills, and experience in dealing with the world beyond the village. These villagers have left cement in the open where it hardened, or incorrectly mixed it, and have had more difficulty establishing working relationships with ethnic Lao officials from the women's union and with other officials. These and other Khmu and Hmong villages have in some cases been handicapped by the physical isolation of their villages and by women's inability to speak and write Lao. However, exceptionally motivated villagers, both female and male, competent village leadership supportive of women's union activities, and additional project inputs, training, and advising enable even very poor ethnic minority villages to develop.

In general, Lao women in project villages are not obsessed with problems of food security and health, and have some of the skills and authority necessary to take immediate advantage of the opportunities offered by a rural development project and other changes associated with economic liberalization. Khmu and Hmong women, on the other hand, are more affected by health and nutrition problems and most Khmu women are preoccupied with immediate survival needs. Khmu women have few skills to take advantage of opportunities resulting from economic liberalization, while Hmong women have little authority to do so. Both suffer from lack of language, literacy, and experience outside their own cultural and ecological niche. Thus, it seems necessary to preface village economic development projects with literacy training and basic household supplies (mosquito nets, blankets, pots) in the poorest villages. Food security, though an immediate and pressing worry in most Khmu villages, is also a concern in Lao and Hmong villages. Expanded economic opportunities will not be viewed positively by women from any group if they threaten subsistence activities and crops.

Sources of Ethnic Lao Women's Advantages

Information from two other recent studies of Luang Prabang villages supports the foregoing observations. Also, data from the Luang Prabang Women's Project baseline survey when disaggregated by ethnic group provides further confirming evidence.

The purpose of both of the other two studies was to assist in the design and implementation of two separate development projects[10] and both included villagers from the same three ethnic groups. One study was carried out by the Lao government with support of the Commission of the European Communities. This study included seven villages in an area 15 kilometers southwest of Luang Prabang city, which were selected for participation in a variety of rural micro-projects (LP Micro-Projects 1990, 1991). The other was undertaken by the Swedish International Development Authority in conjunction with their upland agriculture project in the province and contains information from nine villages in two southern districts of the province —Luang Prabang and Muang Nan (see Map 4.1) (Håkangård 1990). As with the data from the Luang Prabang Women's Project, the villages were not chosen to be representative of all Luang Prabang villages of that ethnic group. Furthermore, the data were gathered during relatively short field visits of one or two days per village and data quality depends on the goodwill and good memory of individual villagers and, for some items, on the good record-keeping of the village administrative committee. However, villagers chosen for "development" are often pleased to be consulted and seem to produce accurate information, with the possible exception of Hmong when questioned about opium or household finances. When two of these three studies (LP Micro-Projects 1991; Håkangård 1990; C. Ireson 1990) report the same type of information for each village, information from the studies is combined in one table; otherwise, related information is presented separately. Altogether these three studies provide similar data for six ethnic Lao villages, ten Khmu villages, one mixed Khmu/Lao village, and four Hmong villages in Luang Prabang Province.

Resources. Lao villagers do seem to have access to more resources than either Hmong or Khmu villagers. They have more paddy land, have greater access to commercial agriculture markets, are more likely to be self-sufficient in rice

TABLE 4.4   Estimated Average Amount of Paddy Land per Household
            by Ethnic Group

Ethnicity	No. Villages	No. HH	Average Hectare Paddy per H H
Lao	5½	538	0.47
Khmu	10½	420	0.23
Hmong	5	197	0.06

Sources: C. Ireson 1990, Appendix D (using all 14 project villages). LP Micro-Projects 1991, 10.

(found in one study only), and have lower rates of child mortality and malnutrition. Two studies, however, show that Hmong households are more likely to be self-sufficient in rice and are richest in both small and large animals. Khmu fare best on only one measure in one study—the percentage of school-age children attending school. The details follow.

According to combined findings of two studies, Lao households, on the average, have twice as much paddy land as Khmu households, while few Hmong households have paddy (see Table 4.4). Håkangård indicates that, while few Lao cultivate only paddy rice, Lao households are much more likelyto cultivate both upland and paddy rice (see Table 4.5).[11] No Hmong households in the two villages she studied cultivate paddy rice, while only about one-fourth of Khmu households cultivate paddy rice in addition to upland rice.

Since 1989 new cash crops have been introduced by three commercial agricultural companies. Villages contacted by these companies are near Luang Prabang town or on a road (LP Micro-Projects 1990, 27). Lao villages tend to be more accessible than villages of the other two groups, with Hmong commonly least accessible, often living on mountain ridges requiring several hours of walking along a track.

Households in the one Lao village studied by Micro-Projects staff produce enough rice to meet nearly three-fourths of their yearly need, while Khmu households meet only one-half of their need and households in the one Hmong village studied meet only 35 percent of their yearly rice need (see Table 4.6). Hmong households in the other two studies fared much better, with 81 percent of them being self-sufficient in rice, while 68 percent of Lao and only 19 percent of Khmu villages were self-sufficient (see Table 4.7). Khmu villages are particularly disadvantaged in this important measure of food

TABLE 4.5 Percentage of Households by Ethnic Group Cultivating Two Types of Rice Lands

	% HH Cultivating				
Ethnicity	Paddy Only	Paddy & Upland	Upland Only	No. HH	No. Villages
Lao	4	44	52	27	2
Khmu	0	26	74	25	3
Hmong	0	0	100	16	2

Source: Håkangård 1990, 7.

TABLE 4.6 Rice Production per Person by Ethnic Group

Ethnicity	Production/Person in kg	Est. Yearly Need Met (%)[a]	No. Villages
Lao	106	73	1
Khmu	72.8	50	3
Hmong	51	35	1

[a]Authors estimate 140–150 kg/person/year required rice consumption.
Source: LP Micro-Projects 1991, Figure 4.

security since they have fewer animals to sell than do the Hmong and do not cultivate a lucrative crop like opium.

Hmong households are richer than households of both other ethnic groups in their possession of large animals (buffalo and cattle) and pigs. The differences are particularly notable in the average number of pigs raised by a Hmong household (2.7 animals) in comparison with pigs raised by Khmu or Lao households (1.6 and 1.2 animals, respectively; see Table 4.8).

Given the relatively small sample of each study, the low number of infant and child deaths, and the short period (one or two years) for which these data are available, calculations of infant and child mortality are likely to be unreliable. However, these calculations give us some measure of the relative levels of mortality. Table 4.9 includes birth and infant mortality information

TABLE 4.7 Rice Sufficiency for Annual Household Need by Ethnic Group

Ethnicity	HH Suffi- cient (%)	HH Insuffi- cient (%)	Est. Avg. Shortage	No. HH	No. Villages
Lao	68	32	2.9 mo.	310	5
Khmu	19	81	3.9 mo.	144	5
Hmong	81	19	3.0 mo.	52	3

Sources: C. Ireson 1990, Appendix D.   Håkangård 1990, 15.

TABLE 4.8 Animal Husbandry by Ethnic Group and Household

Ethnicty	Buffalo	Cattle	Pigs	Av. No. Anmls./HH Buf./Cattle	Pigs	No. HH	No. Vllgs.
Lao	519	73	484	1.5	1.2	397	5
Khmu	263	63	487	1.0	1.6	314	8
Hmong	22	139	247	1.7	2.7	93	3

Sources: C. Ireson 1991, Appendix D (baseline year data used).   LP Micro-Projects 1991, 15.   Håkangård 1990, 17.

from both the baseline study year and 1990. This indicates that rates are high for all groups, but lowest for Lao and highest for Khmu. The incredibly high Khmu infant mortality rate for the baseline years was partly due to a measles epidemic in Thin Keo and a dysentery epidemic in Sam Ton. Håkangård asked her informants how many of their children had died but did not determine the age at death. Nonetheless, her findings are similar, showing that, while the number of child deaths was high for all groups, it was highest for the Hmong and lowest for the Lao (see Table 4.10).

Nutritionists from the Micro-Projects staff examined the majority of children in its seven project villages, finding that Hmong children were most likely to suffer from malnutrition and show the most severe symptoms, while Lao children were least likely to be malnourished and were unlikely to be severely malnourished (see Table 4.11).

Village records from Micro-Projects villages indicate that, among children

TABLE 4.9 Estimated Infant Mortality Rate by Ethnic Group[a]

Ethni-city		Total Population	Births	Deaths <1 Yr.	Est. IMR	2 Yr. Avg. Est. IMR
Lao	Baseline	1573	46	7	152/1000	123/1000
	1990	1804	64	6	94/1000	
Khmu	Baseline	602	24	16	660/1000	427/1000
	1990	716	36	7	194/1000	
Hmong	Baseline	279	12	2	167/1000	139/1000
	1990	286	9	1	111/1000	

[a]Based on data from two years, the baseline survey year and 1990.
Source: C. Ireson 1990, Appendix D.
LP Micro-Projects (1991, 6) reports an IMR of 140/1000 for Luang Prabang Province, and estimates a combined IMR of 123/1000 for the 86 Lao, 168 Khmu, and 36 Hmong households in the project area, based on 10 months of data.

TABLE 4.10 Child Mortality by Ethnic Group

Ethnicity	Total Births (No.)	Children Died[a] (No.)	% Died	Interviewees (No.)
Lao	98	28	29	18
Khmu	128	42	33	22
Hmong	54	25	46	16

[a]No information on age at death.
Source: Håkangård 1990, 22.

ages six to fifteen, most Lao and nearly all Khmu children were registered as attending school (see Table 4.12). All Hmong boys but only one-half of Hmong girls were registered.

In short, Lao villagers have more material and health resources available to them than do either Khmu or Hmong villagers. Whether women can use resources to take advantage of emerging opportunities depends partly on their skills and their authority to do so.

TABLE 4.11 Percent of (Malnourished) Children Aged 0–14 by Ethnic Group

| | Level of Malnutrition | | Total Mal- | |
Ethnicity	Severe (%)	Semi (%)	nourished (%)	No. Surveyed
Lao	1	27	28	91
Khmu	8	31	39	307
Hmong	14	36	51	95˙

Source: LP Micro-Projects 1991, 17–23.

TABLE 4.12 School Attendance of Children Aged 6–15 by Ethnic Group

Ethnicity	Percent Boys	Percent Girls	Overall	Villages (No.)
Lao	95	84	91	1
Khmu	97	87	92	5
Hmong	100	52	82	1

Source: LP Micro-Projects 1991, A1–A7.

Skills. Lao women also seem to have more skills that enable them to take advantage of the opportunities offered by economic liberalization. A greater proportion of Lao women are literate and the ratio of female-to-male literacy is higher among Lao than among other groups. Lao women are more likely to have marketing experience and the language of commerce is their native tongue. Many Lao women are skilled weavers, as well as being farmers like women in the other groups.

Lao women are almost twice as likely to be literate as Khmu women, while very few Hmong women are literate (see Table 4.13). The ratio of literate women to literate men is also higher (at 51, 100) among the Lao, though the Khmu ratio is almost as high (47, 100). Very few Hmong women are literate compared to Hmong men (16, 100) (Håkangård 1990, 7; LP Micro-Projects 1991, A1–7).

Lao women are primarily responsible for marketing, whereas Lao husbands rarely engage in marketing (Håkangård 1990, 21). Khmu women and men are

TABLE 4.13 Literacy of Adults Aged 16+ by Ethnic Group

Ethnicity	Male (%)	Female (%)[a]
Lao	87	45
Khmu	51	24
Hmong	25	4

[a]Female data include women interviewed by Håkangård: 18 Lao, 22 Khmu, and 16 Hmong. Male data drawn solely from LP Micro-Projects data.
Sources: Håkangård 1990, 7; LP Micro-Projects 1991, A1–7.

both responsible for marketing according to Håkangård's informants, though anecdotal evidence from Sam Ton indicates that a woman may produce crops for sale and her husband may market them (C. Ireson 1990, 45). Hmong men are primarily responsible for marketing, though a wife may help (Håkangård 1990, 21). Some Hmong women, though, get to market as seldom as once a year (LP Micro-Projects 1990, 23). Lao women are additionally advantaged by their ability to communicate easily in the market language: Lao.

Many Lao women are competent weavers and, in Luang Prabang, Lao Lue women are particularly well known for their textiles. Khone Kham is best known for its production of indigo blue homespun fabric, which women barter for other needed goods. Na Nyang Tai women, as described earlier, make a number of different kinds of fabric products. Although in these six Lao villages women produce only cotton fabric, Lao women in other Luang Prabang villages also produce silk textiles. Among the four Hmong villages studied, there is no indication that Hmong women produce textiles for sale, though Hmong women elsewhere are noted for their batik, applique, and cross-stitch work. Khmu women do not weave or do other textile work, though they sometimes crochet jute handbags.

Autonomy/Authority. Lao women are somewhat more likely than Khmu or Hmong women to have the autonomy or authority to take advantage of economic opportunities. Lao women are also much more likely to have financial authority and decision making capacity in the household than are Khmu or Hmong women. Lao women, because of their marketing experience, are more likely to have experience dealing in "public" beyond their village, though in none of the groups do women customarily have political authority.

The average age at marriage of women informants interviewed by Håkangård was about the same for Lao and Hmong women (17.2 and 17.3,

TABLE 4.14 Average Age at Marriage by Ethnic Group

Ethnicity	Avg. Age (yrs.)	n
Lao	17.2	18
Khmu	15.7	22
Hmong	17.3	16

Source: Håkangård 1990, 7.

respectively), while Khmu women reported marrying at younger ages (15.7) (see Table 4.14).

After marriage Lao girls commonly stay in their natal home for at least a few years. Most commonly, a daughter, often the youngest one, and her in-marrying husband remain with her parents, eventually inheriting the house and much of the paddy land. A Hmong girl, on the other hand, moves to her husband's household at marriage and comes under the sway of her mother-in-law or another older woman of the extended family household. With an older marriage age and matrilocal residence, Lao women are less likely to fall under the domination of the husband or the husband's family. Unless the new husband is working off the bride price for his wife by laboring for her parents, a new Khmu wife also moves to her husband's household.

Lao women are much more likely to report that they alone or they in conjunction with their husbands are the decision makers in their households, while Khmu men are the main decision makers, though they sometimes consult their wives. Hmong men, either the husband or a senior man of the husband's clan, are the main decision makers, though Hmong women may have a limited sphere of decision-making authority (Håkangård 1990, 19). Traditionally Lao women have more experience beyond their village than do other women because of their marketing activities, but in no group are women traditionally active in village politics. With socialist reorganization of traditional village governance or with participation in a development project involving women, however, some village committees added a women's union representative. For example, in the six Luang Prabang Women's Project villages for which I have information, three villages, one from each ethnic group, added women's union representatives (see Table 4.15).

From the information available on the three major ethnic groups in Luang Prabang Province, it appears that ethnic Lao villages have more resources than Khmu or Hmong villages; that Lao women may have more autonomy and authority than Khmu or Hmong women, which may enable them to utilize

TABLE 4.15 Women Members of Village Committees

Village	Yes[a]	No	Dates
Na Fai (Lao)	X		1987–89
Na Nyang Tai (Lao)		X	
Khone Kham (Lao)		X	
Thin Keo (Khmu)		X	
Sam Ton (Khmu)	X		1987–90
Phou Thit Pheung (Hmong)	X		1988–90

[a]These women were also representatives of the Village Women's Union.

these resources; and that Lao women have more economically relevant skills than Khmu or Hmong women. It is not surprising, then, that women in ethnic Lao villages are more quickly and more effectively able to make use of development resources provided by the Luang Prabang Women's Project. Rural Lao women, then, are better positioned than Khmu and Hmong women to take advantage of the opportunities offered by rural development and economic change in Luang Prabang Province. However, there is great variation between villages of the same ethnic group and between women within the same village, so that some Khmu and some Hmong women are also benefiting from development and change. On balance, though, without special efforts to address these ethnic differences in resources, autonomy/authority, and skills, development and economic change may widen the existing social and economic gaps between ethnic groups.

Conclusion

The detailed examination in this chapter of one women-oriented rural development project supports two major theoretical tenets: (1) women's everyday reproductive activities affect women's economic production and power and (2) macro-level political and economic structures and policies affect women's economic power and everyday lives. Analysis of ethnic differences evident in the project villages, as well as in villages surveyed for two other projects, further suggests that ethnic Lao village women are better positioned to benefit from rural development and economic change. This positive outcome for mainly ethnic Lao women may sharpen existing socioeconomic differences between groups. However, some Khmu women may also be able to reduce their reproductive workload, and some Hmong women may be able to transcend patriarchal control so that women of these two groups may also take advantage of opportunities offered by economic liberalization. Chapter 5 broadens this model to other parts of the country, focusing on each specific type of women's economic production in an attempt to understand production dynamics, the relationship of each type of production to women's economic power, and the effects of women's domestic power and workload on each type of production.

Notes

1. Henceforth called "Luang Prabang Women's Project." The project was implemented by the Luang Prabang Women's Union with liaison to the national women's union; technically and administratively supported by the American Friends Service Committee (AFSC) with funding from Bread for the World (Germany) and International Women's Development Agency (Australia).

2. Donors for the LPWU–AFSC project include Bread for the World (Germany) and International Women's Development Agency (Australia). Sources of information for this and immediately following sections are derived from three sources besides my own LPWU–AFSC project-related research: two reports from the Rural Micro-Projects Programme in Luang Prabang Province sponsored by the Lao People's Democratic Republic and funded by the Commission of the European Communities (LP Micro-Projects 1990, 1991), and a research study associated with a shifting cultivation project in Luang Prabang Province sponsored by the Department of Forestry of the Ministry of Agriculture and Forestry and funded by the Swedish International Development Authority (Håkangård 1990).

3. However, the overall figure for Luang Prabang Province is somewhat smaller at 6.2 (LP Micro-Projects 1990, 20).

4. This information describes Boun Soum's life in 1986. I describe her response to economic liberalization later in the chapter.

5. This description is based on a 1986 interview. During a casual conversation with Phing in 1990, I learned that her husband works with her more frequently, her oldest children are now workers, she is growing more crops, and she and her husband have expanded their home.

6. Data and other information included in this section have been drawn from the project evaluation report (C. Ireson 1990).

7. I carried out both the initial study in 1986 and the evaluation study in 1990 and worked with women's union officials to formulate the project in 1986. Baseline data on project villages added in years 2 and 3 were gathered by staff of the American Friends Service Committee with the provincial women's union.

8. "Literacy" refers to literacy in the Lao language, since neither Khmu nor Hmong are written.

9. Ethnic minorities are resettled from previous Lao paddy area occupied during the war to scrub land, or from upland areas to "potential paddy land" (i.e., relatively flat scrub land). See C. Ireson and R. Ireson (1991) for examples.

10. With the exception of census data, most rural data are gathered primarily for the purposes of development project planning and evaluation.

11. Since her study was for a shifting cultivation project, it is highly likely that only villages with significant upland agriculture would have been selected.

5

Women's Changing Agricultural Activities

Women traditionally work in several important sectors of the village economy including agricultural production, forest gathering, craft production, and marketing. In the last two decades rural women's traditional economic activities and bases of power have been affected by changes in policy and economy, first with socialist reorganization, and then with economic liberalization. Similarly, women's balance between productive activities and reproductive activities may have shifted in response to these changes in policy and economy. My general questions, then, for each potential arena of female economic power are the following:

► Have rural women maintained power or autonomy in this traditional economic arena during socialist reorganization and economic liberalization?

► Has this arena expanded with changed social, political, and economic policies, practices, and structures? Or has this arena contracted as changed opportunities and policies enabled other groups to encroach on this traditional aspect of rural women's power and autonomy?

► Has rural women's domestic and reproductive work impeded women's production in this economic arena more or less during the socialist and liberalization periods than before?

► Have women from different ethnic groups responded differently to changes in policy and economy?

Agricultural production is essential for survival and sometimes provides cash income. Women are involved in all modes of agricultural production, though the activities of women and men are sometimes complementary and sometimes similar. The major types of agricultural production are paddy rice farming, upland or swidden farming, gardening, and animal husbandry.

Paddy Rice Farming

Traditionally in Laos, few Khmu or Hmong farmed paddies while ethnic Lao women farmed paddy rice with their husbands and families. Customarily, men prepared the seed bed, constructed paddy bunds, plowed, and harrowed, while the senior working man organized household labor throughout the cultivation season. Women traditionally uprooted and transplanted seedlings, often with the help of family men. Fields were rarely weeded, though this was a female task. All family members harvested, threshed, and carried rice to the granary. Traditionally, men sold surplus rice, if there was any, while the senior household woman usually distributed rice from the family granary to members of the extended family. In some areas women sometimes plowed, harrowed, or carried out other male tasks, if there was a shortage of male labor. With peace and agricultural cooperativization, the traditional gendered division of labor was modified by the introduction of various levels of cooperative or collective work and ownership.

Activity Under Socialist Reorganization

Women members of paddy cultivating households, mainly in ethnic Lao groups and culturally related groups (like the Black or White Thai), were necessarily involved in government-mandated agricultural cooperativization beginning in "newly liberated zones" in 1978 and before that in the "old liberated zones" (areas controlled by the Pathet Lao) (Stuart-Fox 1980). While the mechanization provided by the government to some cooperatives benefited mainly men, since it replaced male labor, women received work points in their own name. Their work in uprooting and carrying seedlings, transplanting, harvesting, and threshing (see Photo 5.1) earned points and ultimately rice for their families. Women's paddy farming labor, traditionally organized by the male household head who also controlled any rice surplus, was often hidden or seen as "unpaid family labor." Cooperatives, though directed by a few village men, made women's work more visible by paying for it in work points. A healthy woman with paddy land who did not live in a household with a laboring age man was sometimes able to feed her family with her cooperative labor. Without a cooperative and without male labor, she normally would be unable to perform all the tasks necessary to grow sufficient paddy rice for her family.

In a "model" cooperative (Don Dou) all paddy rice tasks were carried out collectively with members receiving payment in rice at harvest based on their accumulated work points, and rent of buffalo and land (Evans 1990, Chs. 5 and 7). Work points were theoretically based on eight hours of normal work by

PHOTO 5.1 Threshing the rice of her cooperative earns work points for this farmer.

an average worker "with a correct attitude to labor," but one of the cooperatives studied by Evans changed the work-point system every season in response to member discontent with it (Evans 1990, 156–58).

Workers earned work points for all tasks in collective paddy farming, but not all village cooperatives awarded equal work points to women and men for their respective contributions. Furthermore, cooperative administration withdrew the labor of some men from both paddy and upland field. One cooperative manager in Savannakhet Province reported that "lighter" tasks (transplanting of rice seedlings, often carried out by women) earn fewer points per day than "heavier" tasks (plowing and harrowing, nearly always done by men). The awarding of work points was even more blatantly discriminatory in Pong Van cooperative in Luang Prabang Province, at least in 1985 and 1986 when the village was surveyed by the Ministry of Agriculture. In Pong Van cooperative women were awarded 120 points per day for transplanting while men received 200 points for the same amount and the same kind of work. "When asked to explain this discrepancy the men laughed, and simply said men have to have more. The wife of the cooperative leader agreed with this" (Maroczy 1986, 26). The cooperative head in Thin Keo, mainly a swidden farmer himself, spent much of his time "administering": hosting visitors, attending meetings in the district center, or purchasing agricultural inputs in the provincial capital. His wife was left to produce the family food supply nearly by herself though his work points for administration did result in some rice in return. Despite some discrimination in the awarding of work points and the hardship of some women who subsidized male cooperative administrators, a woman's paddy rice work was remunerated for the first time under this system and she received a share of the harvest in her own name.

Communist officials also mobilized large groups of workers during the agricultural off-season for various construction projects including small dams and irrigation systems serving paddy rice growers. For example, villagers in one Houa Phan village wanted to replace their weir (small diversion dam) with a more permanent structure since the weir was occasionally swept away after heavy rains. This weir was one of several traditional stick-and bamboo weirs farmers had constructed across a small mountain river to divert water into their terraced rice paddies. With government design support and supervision, and with imported materials provided by an international agency, teams of village men and a few women worked steadily for several months to build a concrete diversion dam. Construction of a larger irrigation dam in northern Vientiane Province was able to command the labor of workers from several villages. Older school children in district or provincial schools were sometimes released from school to help with cooperative transplanting or harvesting.

In the hopes of producing a rice surplus for export earnings, government plans promoted the cooperative cultivation of a dry season rice crop in irrigated areas. Private land was used by the cooperative to do this, though owners were compensated by earning work points. Incentives for growing a second crop must have been inadequate, though, since much irrigated paddy land near Vientiane was unused during most dry seasons. However, a Khmu farmer in Luang Prabang Province used his small area of irrigated paddy as his own dry season experiment station, growing garlic, watermelon, and other vegetables. He discovered that garlic yielded well. While watermelon plants bloomed profusely, no melons developed! Interestingly, he, not his two wives who were responsible for swidden production, managed the paddy-grown dry season vegetable crops.

Ultimately most cooperatives proved to be no more productive than household farming, and part of the production was used for wages and social welfare purposes and therefore unavailable to households. Agricultural cooperatives did not introduce any innovations in production beyond the use of tractors for land preparation and mechanical threshers in some lucky areas. Otherwise, cooperative members continued to cultivate their rice using traditional cultivation methods and varieties, so yields per hectare did not increase with cooperativization. In fact, peasant resistance to the cooperative drive led to a decline in agricultural production (Stuart-Fox 1980, 1986a).

Activity Under Economic Liberalization

With the development of the New Economic Mechanism (NEM) and the subsequent dismantling of agricultural cooperatives, paddy farming labor and management reverted to traditional forms. Male household heads again organized family labor to produce paddy rice on family-owned land using family buffalo for draft power. Some of the still-functional cooperative tractors or threshers were available for hire in a few areas, replacing both men's and women's family labor for some tasks. In more prosperous areas near Thailand, wealthier men have purchased hand tractors to aid them in plowing and harrowing.

With strong government pressure for paddy cultivation by all groups, more Khmu and Hmong villages are beginning to dig and plant paddy fields. In Khmu or Hmong households with access to paddy, the division of labor for paddy farming is similar to that found among the ethnic Lao, though reportedly only Khmu men in paddy farming Bo Keo villages fence the seed bed or paddy, while only women weed the growing rice (R. Ireson, personal communication, 1993).

The "feminization of agriculture" is not a result solely of economic liberalization. It was already noticeable in villages closer to Vientiane by 1982

TABLE 5.1 Distribution of the Labor Force in Hat Say Fong District, Vientiane
Province[a]

	Estimated Proportion in Percentages		
Sector	Female	Male	Total
Agriculture	69.5	55.6	62.2
Manufacturing	4.7	0.8	2.6
Trade	15.7	2.6	8.8
Transport, storage, communication	5.1	14.3	10.0
Professional, technical, civil service	4.2	23.6	14.5
Other services	----	1.1	0.5

[a]Mukherjee and Jose (1982, 17) transliterate the district name as "Hat Xay Fong,"
while Evans' transliteration is "Hatsayfong" (1990). Categories with fewer than 1.0%
of workers are omitted from this table.
Source: Mukherjee and Jose 1982, 17.

(see Table 5.1).[1] In 1982 in Hat Saifong district, men were more likely than
women to work in transport and communication, or at professional or civil
service jobs in town. As the construction of major rural roads brings roadside
villages "closer" to urban centers, as has happened more recently, it is not
surprising to see some of these same changes occurring in more distant rural
areas as well.

Impact on Women's Work and Power

Women of all ethnic groups traditionally do not exercise authority over
paddy farming activities and decisions, nor control many paddy farming
resources. Their role is that of unpaid family labor, though they may take
responsibility for mobilizing neighbors to exchange labor for a task that
urgently needs to be done. As keeper of the family purse, however, an ethnic
Lao woman will be consulted about the purchase of agricultural equipment
and supplies. Family self-sufficiency in rice, the Laotian equivalent of
household food security, is in women's best interests. In rice-deficient
households, a woman's earnings from other sources must be used initially to
feed her family before she can allocate any remainder to the support of her
own projects or to other household uses. Family rice sufficiency, then, enables
women to more fully control the products and income of their other
economic ventures.

Families cultivating paddy rice are more likely to be self-sufficient in rice than are families that depend partly or completely on rice cultivated in upland fields. In Bo Keo Province, the farming systems most likely to produce rice sufficiency are subsistence and market-oriented paddy farming systems, while those relying on subsistence swidden farming or a mixture of swidden and paddy are less likely to be self-sufficient in rice (IFAD 1993, 8–12). Paddy farmers store their rice surplus in anticipation of bad years or convert it to savings in the form of cattle or silver. The cattle or silver can be sold to purchase rice during a bad cropping year. Market-oriented paddy farmers can also convert their cash crop profits into rice if they lose part of their rice crop (IFAD 1993, 24, 36). Swidden farmers, on the other hand, often depend on wild tubers, plants, and animals to supplement a meager rice supply, though they may also sell their own labor, livestock, or opium (in some cases) to purchase rice (IFAD 1993, 17, 31). Families with little savings, no cash crops, and no job must depend on forest products, particularly tubers, during years of rice shortage. These households therefore rely heavily on women's foraging to survive. Other food security strategies may involve both women's and men's activities to fulfill the annual household rice requirement.

This model is also generally applicable to the six Luang Prabang villages studied, though the correspondence between paddy land per capita and level of village rice self-sufficiency is not exact. In villages such as Na Nyang Tai and Na Fai, that depend mainly on paddy land for rice production, 86 percent and 67 percent, respectively, of households had enough rice for the entire year in 1990. On the other hand, in the one village that was totally dependent on upland cultivation for its rice production, only 16 percent of households could meet their annual rice requirement. Only one village with just 0.40 hectare of paddy field and many upland fields does not fit this pattern. In the Hmong village of Phu Thit Pheung, 86 percent of households produced enough rice for the entire year (C. Ireson 1990, Tables D–1 and D–3A). Since ethnic Lao women are more likely than women of other ethnic groups to depend entirely on paddy production, they are more likely to live in rice-sufficient households and to engage in other production activities that they themselves control.

The establishment of agricultural cooperatives changed the forms of both labor control and remuneration. No longer did the male household head organize family labor and control surplus rice production. Instead, labor was organized by the cooperative committee, workers were remunerated on the basis of earned work points, and the cooperative committee controlled the allocation of production. A woman's paddy rice work was remunerated for the first time under this system and she received, in her own name, a share of the harvest. Agricultural cooperatives were encouraged to organize child-care centers so that women could more easily work in the fields. Both the payment of work points to women and the establishment of day-care centers made women's paddy and child-care work more visible to and perhaps even more valued by both men and women.

Cooperatives, however, did not work very well. In fact, few villages had actual cooperatives; most were paper fictions that actually relied on cooperative work groups organized along traditional lines. Even the actual cooperatives were not more efficient production units than traditional units since few had access to chemical fertilizers and mechanization provided by the government. While some cooperatives produced surpluses, these were expended on equipment and social benefits. For example, Don Dou cooperative near Vientiane purchased a threshing machine, two sprayers, a tractor, a disc plow, and several other pieces of equipment with cooperative funds, while making small contributions for marriages, funerals, and support for children and the elderly. The cooperative intended to give allowances also for member maternity leave, training, self-defense (military) leave, and sickness, but never did so (Evans 1990, 102–3). The cooperative at Khone Kham in Luang Prabang Province collectively paid child-care workers who took care of young children while mothers engaged in cooperative work. Often, however, cooperative production was insufficient for the needs of the community. Furthermore, women were rarely included in the cooperative committee and did not operate tractors or threshers, so neither women's decision-making power nor skill levels were improved by this system. Finally, the dry season crops grown by some cooperatives interfered with women's other dry season activities like weaving or gardening.

Economic liberalization brought a return of the traditional paddy rice production system, but with the possibility of markets for surplus production and availability (for those with money or credit) of agricultural machinery, fertilizer, and other "modern" inputs. Woman's paddy labor once again was unremunerated and child care again became her responsibility, but if her household had sufficient land, traction, and labor, rice self-sufficiency was again likely.

Upland Rice Farming

Traditionally, women and men share swidden preparation. Together male and female workers from a household clear, burn, fence, and plant the fields. Ethnic Lao women or men may burn the cleared field, though only Hmong and Khmu men do so. In most swidden systems, the ground is not cultivated. Instead, the man pokes holes in the cleared ash-fertilized soil while the woman drops seeds in the holes. After planting, women maintain the field until harvest, though household males may occasionally help. This involves cutting weeds, and planting and harvesting a variety of vegetables, fruits, and, perhaps, other grains. Weeding must be done three times and may completely occupy household women in all ethnic groups throughout the growing season (see Photo 5.2)(LP Micro-Projects 1993). The entire household harvests upland rice, though Khmu and Hmong men only occasionally help carry the harvested rice to the granary in the village. Swidden agriculture is not mechanized and

PHOTO 5.2 Women swidden farmers constantly cut and pull weeds during the growing season.

generally does not require draft power. Ethnic Lao women traditionally market surplus crops from their swiddens, though Khmu and Hmong men traditionally sell their wives' crops.

Activity Under Socialist Reorganization

Swidden farming as a way of life requires extensive land areas with low population density. Fields farmed two to three years in succession must be allowed to remain fallow for years in order to regenerate trees and bushes that protect and restore the soil and suppress weeds, and then be burned to fertilize a new cycle of crops. Cooper (1986) suggests that Hmong in Laos were experiencing "resource scarcity" in the early 1970s because of high population pressure in upland areas. This pressure was relieved by massive Hmong out-migration to Thailand with the 1975 establishment of the new government in Vientiane. However, rural population growth continues among all ethnic groups and is estimated to be as high as 3.3 percent per year in some areas (Plant 1991, 54). In twenty years, even in areas currently not experiencing land pressure, existing swiddens now in ten- to twenty-year rotations will not be sufficient for the needs of a swidden farming population, which will have doubled in size. In some provinces, fallow cycles are already so short that soils are degrading and yields are declining. This suggests that in some areas swidden farming using traditional systems is no longer sustainable. For example, in 1979 farmers in one district in Bolikhamsay Province reported field rotations allowing twenty years of fallow for the recovery of swidden fertility (Samuelsson and Thongphachanh 1979). In 1989 farmers in a neighboring district reported fallow cycles of only three to five years (C. Ireson 1989b).

Upland rice cultivation was not as likely to be collectivized as paddy cultivation in the years immediately after 1975, though in some areas upland fields were collectively cleared, weeded, or harvested. In Thin Keo, for example, the twenty families who farmed the small area of paddy created an agricultural cooperative (most of these families also cultivated upland fields), but the twenty-seven households who farmed only upland fields did not join the cooperative. However, these upland cultivators did mobilize neighbors to help clear and weed their upland fields. Traditional labor exchange networks or more recently developed cooperative labor organizations facilitated the sharing of heavy or labor-intensive tasks like field clearing, weeding or harvesting. Upland farming villages in "old" communist areas like Houa Phan were more likely to have agricultural cooperatives than such villages elsewhere.

The Fourth Party Congress in 1986 approved the eventual cessation of swidden cultivation. Shortly thereafter, the national government prohibited the clearing of old-growth trees with strong sanctions, in some provinces, for clearing such a forest area to plant upland rice and other crops. Initially the prohibition extended to the clearing of primary forest for swidden. Eventually, however, the policy will cover all forms of shifting cultivation (Ministry of Agriculture and Forestry 1989, 1990; Vongkhamchanh and van der Heide 1989).

This policy directly threatened the rice self-sufficiency of many swidden households and the swidden products controlled by swidden-farming women, especially in combination with the rapidly increasing population pressure already discussed. When household rice sufficiency is threatened, the efforts of all family members must focus on subsistence and survival, rather than on successful commercial production, or even the production of a surplus for sale. Resources formerly available to men and women through sale or barter of household production must be channeled into rice purchases. Little discretionary income is available to either. As we shall see, many rural women still bear major responsibility for cultivating and harvesting upland field crops. These crops were and are a major source of resources for the women who also control the marketing or barter of any surplus from these fields. In order to maintain control over agricultural surplus and comply with the prohibition against swidden agriculture, women would have to locate potential paddy land, move their families, and contribute long months of labor to the construction of new paddies and a new village before they could attend to their own commercial production of crops, animals, or other products and once again control their own production. In other words, they would have to make a lengthy and difficult transition to a new livelihood and way of life.

Government documents and policy statements discussing the "no swidden" policy often blame minority peoples, including Khmu and Hmong, for damage to environment and timber caused by swidden agriculture. Government policy, as elaborated in the official Tropical Forest Action Plan and related documents, include "resettling" all swidden cultivators by the year 2000, either by physically moving them to a lowland area or by converting them from subsistence cultivators to commercial farmers of cash crops and livestock. Minority villages were especially likely to experience resettlement pressure during this period (C. Ireson and R. Ireson 1991, 929–36).[2] The national government announced the "no swidden" policy in the mid-1980s, but its implementation has occurred almost entirely during the economic liberalization period.

Activity Under Economic Liberalization

Economic liberalization brought a variety of hopes and problems to swidden farmers. Limited markets became available to many swidden-farming villagers, though inexperienced villagers often did not understand them. The most immediately accessible markets were those provided by agricultural purchasing companies. In Luang Prabang Province three agricultural companies with direct links to the Thai market were established after 1988. The companies introduced (or reintroduced) several cash crops including peanuts, sesame, soybean, red bean, and castor bean. The companies offered seed on credit and guaranteed purchase of the crop, a guarantee that they sometimes did not honor. Nonetheless, farmers responded enthusiastically to companies' overtures.

One observer noticed a decrease in rice cultivation in the area around Luang Prabang city with the advent of these companies and was concerned with a possible rice deficit (LP Micro-Projects 1990, 27). However, one Khmu farmer I spoke with in both 1986 and 1990 (Phing of Chapter 4) had roofed her house in 1985 with profits from the sale of sesame even though her family was short on rice that year. By 1990 she was able to grow and market more cash crops, while her household produced enough rice for the entire year. Her profits and rice sufficiency were reflected in a sawn wood house and satisfaction with her better life (C. Ireson 1990). With the collapse of cooperatives, village men who spent much of their time with cooperative business have once again returned to their fields. Phing's swidden crops had subsidized her husband's cooperative activities though she did benefit from sales of her sesame and peanuts. By 1990 Phing's husband and their older children worked with her in their swidden, while they all cultivated a small paddy field.

Some aid programs focused on upland agriculture in attempts to develop permanent cultivation systems appropriate for Lao hillsides and mountain ridges. The attempts have not yet borne fruit but may lead to some improvements soon. Training and demonstration projects in alley cropping, integrated farming systems, and fruit tree or other "perma-culture" production all offer hope for the eventual implementation of stable hillside cultivation systems. Some of these projects excluded women, usually to the detriment of project success, while others included women and enjoyed some village success. Rice-based integrated farming systems, introduced to villagers through some aid projects, enabled villages to integrate their farming systems so that residues from one agricultural activity could benefit another. For example, if pigs are housed on a platform over a fishpond surrounded by gardens, pig manure feeds fish, while the pond provides water and nutrients for nearby vegetable gardens. Since all of these activities (pig-raising, fishing, vegetable gardening) are carried out by women in all groups, women are often more interested than men in production systems like these (Somphone 1991).

The "no swidden" policy was reinforced during this period. Improved economic and political connections to capitalist or Western countries made the forest more valuable, in the eyes of government officials, for commercial logging and for preservation than for local livelihoods. Logging companies from Thailand, Japan, Taiwan, and other countries were granted concessions before 1993 to log forests in a number of Lao provinces. International environmental organizations sought to influence Lao government policy in favor of preserving wild areas, and the World Conservation Union (IUCN) continues to work with the national government to inventory these areas and prepare for the development of national parks (Salter, Phanthavong, and Venevongphet 1991). As a result of national policy and international pressures then, upland farm fields were limited to brush lands and fallow swiddens.

Swidden Farming Women

Thirty-five-year old Noi is an ethnic Lao swidden farmer and the single head of her Sieng Lom household in Luang Prabang Province. She has borne seven children; five are still living, though her husband took the two older boys with him when he deserted her the previous year. Her two daughters, sixteen and eleven years old, are old enough to work, but she must depend on her relatives to care for her three-year-old son while she struggles to produce food and clothing for her family. The day before being interviewed, Noi rose early to husk rice with a foot-powered treadle pounder and to carry water from the river. She steamed the morning rice, which the family ate with red pepper sauce. Leaving her son with her brother's family, Noi and her daughters walked to their upland rice fields where they grow rice, corn, cassava, tobacco, and a few vegetables. Her daughters weeded all day while Noi harvested some corn and gathered bamboo shoots and forest leaves. These she carried kilometers to sell in the provincial capital market, trudging home in the late afternoon with her earnings of 85 cents.

Noi's greatest difficulty is that she is responsible for all the work that is necessary to keep her family alive, including the heavy work that is usually done by a man, like repairing the house, clearing the highland field, and chopping trees for firewood. She is lucky, she says, to be strong and healthy. If she could choose, she would have ten children to help her with the work. Like most of the other families in her village, Noi grows tobacco to sell. She must plant and weed the tobacco plants. She then harvests tobacco leaves several times a week from January to May. During this period she will often rise at one or two in the morning to shred the tobacco leaves on a primitive wooden frame, using a small machete that must be honed every few minutes. She can only do this for about two hours because the fumes make her tired and sick. By then it's time to begin her usual daily routine. She recently earned over six dollars from the sale of cured tobacco. She is convinced that cooperative agricultural labor is the answer to her difficulties. Noi's story illustrates several important aspects of swidden farming: swidden farmers often rely also on forest foods, swidden farming requires the work of both men and women, and effective cooperatives did indeed enable female-headed households to survive economically.

The swidden-farming Khmu of Thin Keo benefited from economic liberalization. Although the socialist period did motivate them to organize cooperatively, few benefits were visible. The development of crop marketing companies and the reappearance of traveling merchants, along with inclusion in a development project that provided labor saving devices, enabled women to make some definite improvements in their lives. By 1990, the area of rice paddy had grown, the number of crops and amount of cash cropping had increased, and some families were able to sell rice as well as cash crops.

Soua, a twenty-six-year-old Hmong woman of Phou Thit Pheung, did not work in the family upland rice field the day before she was interviewed. Instead, she stayed home to care for her two sick children. Usually, however, she is the main field worker, since her husband is the village health worker. Soua even cuts and burns the upland field with only occasional help from her husband (Quaker Service Laos file notes 1990). A few months before this interview, Soua's village had decided to participate in the Luang Prabang Women's Development Project, but Soua and other villagers have not yet experienced improvements in their lives, either from socialism or economic liberalization.

Impact on Women's Work and Power

Socialist reorganization potentially benefited only swidden-farming women in villages with effective agricultural cooperatives that included upland as well as paddy farmers. The loss of family labor to "administration," attenuation of rural market networks, and the resettlement of upland farming villages had negative effects on women. Some women had less help farming, were less able to sell their produce, or had to establish new houses, fields, and trading networks in an unfamiliar area. These problems affected some women of all ethnic groups. Hmong and Khmu women, less likely to market their own produce, were perhaps less affected by lack of markets but were more likely to be resettled than ethnic Lao women. Government controls on swidden farmers appear to be politically motivated, that is, to assert more effective political control over the farmers and to safeguard resources that could be used by the state (C. Ireson and R. Ireson 1991).

Population pressure and the "no swidden" policy threaten the long-term viability of upland farming as the major source of household food. Ethnic Lao and some Khmu women sell some of their upland field crops while household well-being among the Hmong is often determined by the size of its opium crop, also grown in swiddens. With dwindling soil fertility and a shortened fallow period, households, represented mainly by women among the Lao and the Khmu, must grow more plants and contend with more persistent weeds in order to maintain their output. Ultimately overused swidden fields may be completely depleted. Clearly threats to the viability of upland field cultivation affect women of all ethnic groups, either by threatening their subsistence base or their income. Even prosperous upland farmers like some opium-growing or cattle-raising Hmong families may be negatively affected by population pressure and the "no swidden" policy.

With economic liberalization, women with control over their crops (ethnic Lao and some Khmu women) can market them once again, and cooperative administrators can return to their fields. Some rural women benefit from projects assisted by international organizations, often administered by the provincial women's union.

Gardens, Cash Crops, and Animals

The Lao word *suan*, usually translated as "garden," refers to vegetable and fruit gardens and orchards situated on flat land near year-round sources of water and cultivated mainly during the dry season. Hillside fields where farmers grow nonirrigated cash crops like coffee, pineapple, fruits, cotton, peanuts, and opium poppies are referred to by the same term used for upland rice fields (*hai*). In fact, some of these cash crops may be interplanted with rice or planted in a rice field after the first crop of rice is harvested. Except for herbs and fruit trees planted near the houses of some Khmu and Hmong families, cultivating gardens (*suan*) is limited to the ethnic Lao. Hmong cultivate poppies in separate hillside fields (*hai*) above 900 meters, while members of all three groups may plant cotton, peanuts, and other crops in separate upland fields (*hai*) or in the same field as their rice (also *hai*).

Women are almost entirely responsible for gardens in all three ethnic groups and have major and sometimes sole responsibility for the cultivation of most upland nonrice field crops except, perhaps, for opium poppies. As rivers retreat at the beginning of the dry season exposing banks covered with fertile silt, ethnic Lao women plant dry season vegetable gardens, occasionally with the help of their husbands who may turn over the soil or assist in planting. Some women horticulturalists have sizable fruit orchards or extensive vegetable or tobacco gardens. Traditionally, gardening tasks are carried out by individual ethnic Lao households, though some gardeners may depend on their women relatives or friends to help with the heaviest or most boring gardening tasks. Even vegetable production for the largest and most lucrative market in the capital city is carried out by households and sold by members of the gardening family or by private merchants. Some garden or cash crops like tobacco and opium require processing before sale, tasks primarily carried out by women. Some crops are the major source of household income, like tobacco in Sieng Lom (see Chapter 4) and opium for a number of Hmong households. Vegetables may be planted in upland fields among the rice plants or in separate fields (see Photo 5.3). While the Khmu and Hmong women are much less likely than the Lao to plant dry season gardens, they often cultivate nonrice crops, including opium, in upland fields during the dry season.

Pigs, goats, ducks, and chickens are women's responsibility among all ethnic groups, and some women also care for large animals. Women may delegate these responsibilities, though, so one often sees children or older people feeding or penning the animals. Hmong men often raise cattle for market.

Activity Under Socialist Reorganization

Gardening activities were not collectivized with socialist reorganization, but the slaughter of animals was regulated during the early years. Some villagers

PHOTO 5.3 This Na Fai woman carries a pepper seedling to plant in her upland field.

continued to grow gardens for their own use, but as government policy was implemented to suppress rural market networks and to discourage private entrepreneurship, market women stopped traveling and villagers were sometimes reluctant to sell their goods in market towns. Some riverbank gardeners near Vientiane neglected their usually profitable gardens for several years, though Sieng Lom women near Luang Prabang city continued to produce tobacco for sale in the provincial capital. Women's union members in the lowland Luang Prabang village of Khone Kham collectively planted and cared for a 2-hectare[3] plot of cotton plants during this period. Even in 1990 after economic liberalization, Na Nyang Tai women's union members chose to collectively plant an orchard of nearly 200 fruit trees near their village in Luang Prabang Province, rather than distribute the trees to individual households. Both women's unions planned to use profits for women's union activities, not for individual profit.

In the years immediately after 1975, the sale and slaughter of large and, sometimes, small animals were regulated. State livestock farms were established, but village animals were not raised collectively. Although animals were generally sold only sporadically, these regulations made it more difficult to convert household resources into cash during a medical emergency, for example, to pay for travel and hospitalization expenses. The ban on trade first with Thailand and then with China, stifled international market connections for selling large animals.

Activity Under Economic Liberalization

Government policies to encourage agricultural production for sale have been part of the drive to develop an integrated market economy under the New Economic Mechanism[4]. Although production policies are in place, they have not yet been matched by the development of adequate support services for farmers. These policies have expedited the establishment of private and state-private enterprises that have provided seeds and sometimes other inputs and then often purchased the resulting crop. Even the not-completely-reliable market provided by these enterprises has stimulated cash crop production. Neither women nor men in some groups, however, were well equipped to judge market demand or to bargain advantageously with the purchasers. Although the companies introduced new or formerly grown cash crops, they did not provide education about higher-yielding agricultural techniques or marketing. Provincial or district agricultural extension services have been nearly nonexistent until very recently. However, women are included in agricultural training and other services only in villages that participated in women's union-sponsored projects. These recent economic policies, however, may expand women's resource base by increasing their agricultural income.

Small animals ceased to be regulated well before 1988 while more market activity in rural areas facilitated the sale of these animals. As borders reopened, Lao, Khmu, and Hmong farmers were able once again to sell buffalo and cattle legally to Thai and Chinese traders. Internationally funded development agencies supported an increasing number of government development projects in the hinterland. Some of these projects targeted animal husbandry and animal health. Successful projects often facilitated increased production of animals for sale.

With limited opening of the Thai–Lao border trade in 1988 and the import and sale in Vientiane of Thai vegetables, riverbank gardens flourished again. Each succeeding year before the river receded, families attempted to reinforce their claim by camping on riverbanks or flooded field houses above the submerged garden area they sought to claim. Local markets for vegetables also revived as market women again made their rounds, and more local ethnic Lao and even some Khmu women sold their produce in district, provincial, and rotating local markets, or to agricultural purchasing companies linked with markets beyond Laos.

Women Cultivators and Animal Raisers

In Na Fai, sales of ginned cotton and other garden, fruit, and upland crops greatly increased between 1986 and 1990 (see Chapter 4). Cotton was grown for sale to the national women's union textile project in Vientiane. After training and the provision of seedlings, one trainee planted an orchard of sixty trees. The increased wealth of the village was reflected in the more than threefold increase over a four-year period in the number of buffalo owned and in the proliferation of village stores. Women's increased crop production expanded household and village wealth, though improved hillside cultivation practices may be necessary to sustain this growth in production. Na Fai women seized new marketing opportunities, perhaps partly because their subsistence needs for food and shelter were secure.

Choum, an ethnic Lao village on the banks of a major tributary of the Mekong River in a fertile agricultural district of Vientiane Province, is well endowed with resources (see Map 5.1). It is connected to Vientiane markets by both the river and a network of all-weather roads. Paddy fields are well established, water is plentiful, and the soil is rich. Schooling through middle school is readily available to all villagers, with a complete five-grade primary school in the village itself. The most difficult labor for both women and men (rice milling, plowing) is done by machine. The food supply in Choum is assured. Village women are skilled horticulturalists. During the socialist period they grew several crops, including rice, corn, and tobacco, for sale to state enterprises and the state-store network. With a more open market in 1988, they began trucking fruits and vegetables for sale in Vientiane, while

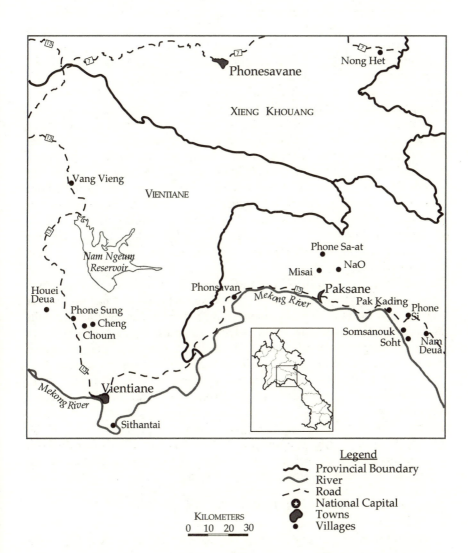

Map 5.1 Locations of Villages and Towns Mentioned in Text; Bolikhamsay,
Vientiane, and Xieng Khouang Provinces
Source: Republique Democratique Populaire Lao. 1986. 1:500,000 Map Series.
Vientiane: State Geographic Service.

continuing to sell on contract to state enterprises. Well connected to market networks before 1975, these women have a sophisticated understanding not only of their crops, but of the economic and political conditions affecting crop marketing. Few rural Laotian women have this level of experience and skill or access to such rich agricultural, economic, and social resources. Interestingly, these prosperous and skilled women have chosen to produce and sell agricultural crops rather than small animals, textiles, or products of other cottage industries (UNDP 1988, Annex III).

Lao Boua, a fifty-year-old Hmong woman of Phou Thit Pheung in Luang Prabang Province, reports that husband and wife both work in upland fields all day. The day before she was interviewed, she weeded the indigo plant garden. The leaves of the indigo plant are used for dyeing cloth. Lao Boua's husband worked part of the day with her and the other part in the upland rice field. Other family members also worked in the rice field. Lao Boua said that she also hauled water, pounded rice, fed the animals, steamed the rice, cleaned the house, and ate before she walked to the indigo field. She also collected firewood and harvested corn before returning home in the evening. She had no leisure time.

Sam Ton, a Khmu village in Luang Prabang Province (see Chapter 4), was plagued by drought and serious disease in the late 1980s and had little water for two months during a year. Despite these hardships, and their lack of skills and experience beyond the village, villagers installed a project-provided rice mill, and village women are now raising many more pigs than before. Animal and sesame sales are the only source of income for village households that rarely produce enough rice to meet their food needs.

Ethnic Lao village women in another project village dramatically increased their production of pigs. This village is self-sufficient in rice and for two years has been able to sell its goods in a local rotating market. This second village, Na Nyang Tai, is very different from Sam Ton, yet the women in both villages markedly increased their pig production after the installation of rice mills, which supplied rice bran for animal feed.

Impact on Women's Work and Power

Among ethnic Lao women, garden produce, as well as nonrice crops from upland fields, are usually grown and sold by women. Women often determine how to use the resulting income. Some ethnic Lao women neglected garden cash crop production during the socialist period, since marketing was either difficult or politically incorrect, thereby foregoing one income source under their control. With the reestablishment of regular market networks, this income source is once again available to lowland women.

Khmu villagers are often less acquainted with money and market relations than are Hmong and Lao villagers. Dependent on swidden cultivation and forest animals and plants, many Khmu families have been poor though nearly self-sufficient. Increasing land pressure and increased government administrative efforts oblige more Khmu villagers to interact with outsiders. Some Khmu women, like Phing of Thin Keo (see Chapter 4), have discovered agricultural marketing companies and are able to increase their incomes by doing more of what they already do well: grow crops. In 1990, Khmu women in Thin Keo sold peanuts, sesame, red beans, cotton, corn, and tubers. Communist commitment to minority villages, coupled with increased crop marketing opportunities, has improved women's situation in Thin Keo. According to a Khmu doctor and development worker, some Khmu women are beginning to sell some of their own products themselves (Soumountha Yuthitham, personal communication, 1993).

Hmong women labor in the opium fields of their households or their husbands', carrying out much of the work in cultivating opium poppies. Women also are important producers of rice and nonrice swidden crops, nearly all of which are used for household consumption. Men, on the other hand, are solely responsible for selling opium, and control the income from the opium crop. Thus, the husband appropriates the surplus value created by his wife's labor. Hmong women horticulturalists may be knowledgeable and skilled, but they are unable to control the products of their own labors.

The sale of chickens, ducks, and eggs is not a major source of income for most women. Poultry are free-ranging and often die or are killed accidently. Pigs, on the other hand, are often raised for market and are sometimes penned. Pig-raising women of all three ethnic groups who were unable to sell hogs freely during the socialist period once again are able to include animal-raising among their income-producing activities. It seems likely that the poorest women in Sam Ton are not able to afford the price of a piglet, so they may not be benefiting from the newly available source of pig feed.

Agricultural Training and Mechanization

Women learn their farming skills from their mothers and other female relatives. Before 1975 when there were agricultural extension services in some Royalist areas, women were taught only sewing, decorating, and cooking. Until very recently there was no agricultural training in village schools, no government extension service to teach alternative farming methods, and no agricultural credit available except through local high-interest moneylenders. Even now agricultural education and services depend heavily on the existence of women's union or provincial government projects supported by international agencies.

For example, joint provincial government–international non-governmental organization (NGO) projects in Sayaboury and Bolikhamsay Province villages train farmers to raise fish in their rice paddies. Fish eat weeds and potential pests while fertilizing the rice as it grows, thereby increasing rice yields (Sonephet of SCFA 1994). Another NGO with projects in Savannakhet Province trains villagers in integrated farming systems (Phimmachanh of CIDSE 1994). Joint Lao Women's Union–UNICEF project field workers have also trained some villagers in "rice-based integrated farming systems," of which paddy-raised fish is one part. Other components include animal-raising over a pond that is used to raise fish and to water a surrounding garden and orchard area. Even fences are part of these integrated systems. Small nitrogen-fixing trees fence the area while fertilizing the soil and providing branches for firewood. By-products from one agricultural operation are used to benefit another aspect of the system (Sombath Somphone and Ng Shui Meng, personal communications, 1988–93). Some NGO workers and their government counterparts regularly share information and have jointly carried out at least one community forestry data-collection project (Charles Pahlman, personal communication, 1993).

A number of joint government–NGO-sponsored village projects assist farmers to establish "rice banks." Grassroots development workers report that many swidden villages in their project areas produce enough rice for only half of the year. The NGO provides the initial rice, which is then loaned to needy village farmers. This type of agricultural "credit" enables swidden farmers to feed their families throughout the year and devote time and energy to the construction of paddy fields without falling deeply into the debt of local moneylenders. Government-CIDSE projects require paddy field construction as a condition of the rice loan in order to increase family self-sufficiency in rice in project areas. Farmers repay both principal and interest at the time of rice harvest. After several years the village is able to repay the initial investment of NGO rice, which can then be used to establish a rice bank in another village. Government-NGO projects often use the "bank" concept to provide agricultural "credit in kind" for a variety of village needs: cattle, buffalo, pigs, medicines (Phimmachanh 1994; Sonephet 1994).

Women are important actors in all of these projects. The district and local women's union enables women's participation at all stages: project design, implementation, and evaluation. Each village defines its own major problems and identifies its own best solutions, requesting appropriate inputs from its government and NGO sponsors. Each village then carries out the project it has designed, with assistance from a team of district workers and technicians including, in the Savannakhet case for example, district women's union, agriculture, health and education workers (Phimmachanh 1994; Sonephet 1994).

Successful villagers sometimes host "study tours" for villagers just beginning their own development process or participate as teachers in training seminars. For example, the province and national Lao Women's Union sponsored a five-day seminar on village and district development showcasing the successful Oudomxay Women's Development Project. The seminar was attended by eighty participants including lecturers from the Rice-Based Integrated Farming

Systems Project and officials and women farmers from several other provinces. Successful Oudomxay women farmers presented their projects to the seminar and convincingly expressed their opinions about development in this large group. Successful projects incorporating women farmers at every stage raise women's visibility as workers and increase women's ability to act in the "public" arena beyond their own village (Quaker Service Laos 1992).

As in other parts of the world, some agricultural tasks are being mechanized. Some cooperatives or individuals in areas near provincial capitals either own or have access to rice threshers and tractors. So far it seems that only paddy rice farming is receiving mechanized inputs. Men contribute most substantially to this type of farming. Men control and arrange tractor use, and drive the tractors or guide the hand tractors. Tractors, which can be used for plowing and harrowing, replace the manual labor only of men. Both men and women thresh rice, though, so female hand labor is somewhat relieved by the use of a rice thresher. All or nearly all of the labor replaced by machines is family labor, rather than the labor of landless workers dependent on this income source. The agricultural input that would most benefit swidden-cultivating women of all ethnic groups is a weeder. The productivity of swidden cultivators is limited not only by decreasing fallow cycles, but also by the availability of weeding labor. Weeds not removed or at least cut in the swidden choke out young food and income crops.

The socialist government offered tractors and threshers to some agricultural cooperatives, though resources did not stretch far enough to include all cooperatives. Machine use was controlled by the village cooperative committee, nearly always exclusively male, and the operators were always men. Tractors relieved paddy farming men of long hours of plowing and harrowing, but did nothing to relieve the rice cultivation labor of swidden farmers and women paddy farmers who continued to tediously uproot and transplant rice seedlings by hand. These Soviet-made tractors were very large for most rice paddies and sometimes not well adapted for paddy work, getting mired in deeper paddy mud and running over hand-dug paddy bunds[5]. So this particular form of mechanization was a mixed blessing, even for men.

Some foreign assistance projects have focused on infrastructure development. During the socialist period, the former Soviet Union and east European countries assisted in constructing roads and bridges. Route 9 east from Savannakhet to the Lao–Vietnam border was rebuilt with the assistance of these fraternal socialist countries. This road enabled Laos to ship and receive goods through the Vietnamese port of Danang. More recently capitalist and Western donors have contributed to further road construction, making more rural villages accessible to the trade and markets that grew as a result of NEM-related policies.[6] The reconstruction of Route 13 east and south from Vientiane through Paksane to the northern border of Khammouane Province was one such project. Supported by Swedish aid funds and advisors and implemented by the Lao Ministry of Construction, Transport, Post,

Communications and Aviation, its immediate impacts on agriculture, and especially its differential impacts on ethnic Lao women and men in roadside villages, are instructive.

Access to markets via the road stimulated more production of crops, animals, cottage industries, and collection of forest products along the reconstructed road. Successful production and sale enabled households to mechanize their production process. Small Japanese-made tractors and hand tractors, small diversion dams or pumps for irrigation, rice threshers, and rice mills rapidly became common in villages that had previously grown and processed their staple crop entirely with human and animal power (Trankell 1993; Håkangård 1992). This exacerbated the existing discrepancy between women's and men's agricultural workload. Like the less dependable Soviet-made tractors available to selected cooperatives during the previous decade, machines lightened paddy farming men's hardest work (plowing, harrowing, water control, threshing) while leaving nearly untouched the agricultural work of women. These men were then free to work elsewhere or to invest their profits outside the agricultural sector, most commonly in transportation (Trankell 1993, 82–83). Since women commonly share threshing work and are nearly always responsible for whatever threshing remains several weeks after harvest, rice threshers did work to women's benefit. A woman's most tedious and time-consuming agricultural tasks of transplanting seedlings, weeding swidden and garden, and transporting tools and produce between village and field were not mechanized, though she might occasionally be able to persuade a man to use his hand tractor to pull a cart of her seedlings, tools, or produce. However, rice mills replaced women's labor exclusively, since men do not husk rice in any ethnic group. Interestingly, with these dramatic shifts toward agricultural mechanization, a number of men abandoned farm work entirely to become tractor or truck drivers, while several women operated rice mills, thus increasing their income and status (Håkangård 1992, 27). Grant Evans (1990, 154–55) rightly describes this skewed mechanization process as the "feminization of agriculture."

Poor households, however, could not generate the capital to purchase or use the services of these new devices, so neither poor women nor poor men benefited from the mechanization of others' agricultural tasks. Other data indicate that an increasing percentage of households in roadside villages have either more than 4 hectares of paddy land or less than half an hectare. That is, the poor are now poorer in land, while the rich are richer (Trankell 1993, 85–88). Since few of the men and women who no longer farm have sold their land, it appears that these "specialists" are hiring poorer villagers to carry out their manual agricultural tasks or sharecropping their land with land-poor villagers. This actually increases the workload of poor women who must devote part of their labor to agricultural wage work or must grow rice for the landowner as well as for their own households. Although economic stratification increased in these roadside villages, not all village women are oppressed by these developments. Some women are able to respond to nonagricultural opportunities offered by markets now available beyond the immediate vicinity (see section on marketing, Chapter 6).

Unlike projects aiming specifically to benefit rural villagers, like the NGO projects described earlier, "national" projects aimed at increasing macroeconomic capability may ignore village needs and may disenfranchise, disadvantage, or otherwise handicap some villagers who are unable to access the "improvement." The Route 13 project did not take into account village needs for safe and all-weather transportation routes to schools and fields, or access roads to the new road. Truck traffic is alarmingly fast, often traveling at high speed through villages or careening dangerously near farmers returning from their fields or students returning from school. Furthermore, nearby villages without access roads receive little benefit from the reconstructed road. Not only rural women but also rural men sometimes receive little benefit from projects designed for foreign, commercial, urban, or "national" interests.

With economic liberalization and the concomitant increase in infrastructure development and village-based development projects, the production of cash crops and small animals for local, urban, and export markets is now an additional source of income for some women. Women may further benefit from these new opportunities if they are included in training, extension, credit, technology, or other services that are being created to promote increased agricultural production.

Agricultural Activities and Other Work

A woman participating in both paddy and swidden rice production will be occupied, with only a few short breaks, from March through December, with clearing, burning, and planting swidden; planting nonrice crops in the swidden; transplanting paddy rice; weeding the swidden continuously throughout the growing season; harvesting nonrice swidden crops, including cash crops, as they ripen; harvesting and threshing swidden rice; and harvesting and threshing paddy rice. Fortunately most heavy and time-consuming paddy rice work occurs at different times than most heavy and time-consuming highland field work, though weeds may grow rank in the swidden while women transplant paddy seedlings. Women forage and fish most intensively during the rainy season when the forest grows most profusely and when fish are abundant even in rice paddies, though these activities go on throughout the year. Many women, especially ethnic Lao women, grow garden crops during the dry season, from December through May, though many tend small kitchen gardens and orchards throughout the year. Hmong women and men plant poppies before the last rains of the rainy season. Women are the main poppy field weeders throughout the growing season from late October through December or January, and men and women collect opium sap together from January through March (Westermeyer 1982, 39–41). Women of all three ethnic groups raise chickens, ducks, and pigs throughout the year, though care is minimal. Cotton, often grown in upland fields, is harvested before the swidden rice crop and processed into cloth or clothing by ethnic Lao women during the "off" season of January and February. Hmong women must fit their cotton-processing work around the opium harvest and Hmong New Year, since the only "leisure" months in the Hmong agricultural calendar, as reported in Nong Het district of Xieng Khouang, are April and August (R. Ireson 1990, 41–42). Women regularly involved in commercial activities, mostly ethnic Lao women, cannot also sustain a full calendar of agricultural and craft activities. Instead, they may buy and market the produce of others in the village, or may provide incidental items for village sale needed by every household, hiring or exchanging labor with others to carry out their field work tasks.

A woman's household responsibilities limit the amount of time and energy she can devote to direct production, and the age of her children determines whether she must care for them continuously or whether they will contribute to her productive activities. A woman who is the only female worker in her family must spend two to five hours per day hauling water and husking rice. Other maintenance activities like gathering and hauling firewood, washing clothes and dishes, and cooking also take time and energy. None of these responsibilities are seasonal or contribute directly to production. Since all of these activities are essential for household functioning, women's productive activities must be coordinated with these basic household tasks.

Paddy rice-growing women farmers take their children with them to the paddy field where they play, work, or look after the baby in the field house or under a tree near the field. They leave for their fieldwork only after hauling water, husking and soaking rice, and cooking morning and noontime rice, and must return home to again haul water and cook. Men experience no similar constraints on their fieldwork. Fortunately, well-established villages are usually located near village paddy fields.

Swidden fields, however, are often much farther from the village. During the agricultural season in an upland village, one often sees entire families leaving the village to walk for one or two hours to their swiddens. The mother carries her baby in a sling while older children and perhaps the father lead younger children. Family members carry their lunch and tools in baskets or bags. By the time they leave, the mother has probably already been working for several hours. On the return trip just before dark, the scene is repeated, though the parents (mainly women, among the Hmong) carry firewood and food harvested in the swidden or gathered in the nearby forest. In the swidden, women and older children weed, though they may also gather shoots, leaves, or mushrooms from the neighboring forest. Men and perhaps older boys may hunt forest animals while the others weed. All rest in the crude field house during the heat of the day. If the husband has other work in the village or nearby town, the woman and children will still go to the field, since weeds require constant attention.

Gardeners and animal raisers often involve other household members in their activities. A gardener will often harvest a crop and carry it back to the village for processing under her house. Other family members may tie green onions into bunches for sale, for example, while she or other family members may dry, shred, and package tobacco for sale. Children or "retired" household members may cut or prepare animal food, though animal husbandry takes little of women's time. Free-ranging animals must be released in the morning, fed, and penned in the evening.

Conclusions: Women in Agriculture

In summary, then, Laotian women did not maintain traditional levels of economic power and autonomy in agriculture throughout the periods of socialist reorganization and economic liberalization. Changing policies, structures, and practices during these two periods changed women's economic activities and control over resources. These changes also affected the balance between women's reproductive/domestic and agricultural work throughout these periods. Paddy farming women were most affected by the socialist drive to create agricultural cooperatives. In cooperatives women received work points in their own name and may have benefited from a child-care center. Their labor was no longer controlled by the male household head but by an all-male cooperative committee. Although paddy farming women's work became more visible, household food security was not improved by cooperative production and the demands of the cooperative sometimes interfered with women's other productive activities. Swidden farmers were less likely to be cooperativized, but more likely to be resettled, often for political reasons. Increasing population pressure on upland field use, coupled with a government "no swidden" policy, threatened the viability of subsistence based on swidden farming. Since women are more likely to control the sale of nonrice swidden produce (except for opium), women's economic resources were and are even more threatened by these changes than those of men. Many gardeners ceased growing vegetables and fruits, and stopped raising pigs when private marketing was controlled, thus losing income from these sources during the socialist period. Neither women nor men benefited from agricultural extension or training during this period. Although some cooperatives were mechanized, men's paddy labor was more likely to be replaced by tractors, plows, and threshers that were provided.

With economic liberalization, women paddy farmers again became "family laborers." However, increased markets for surpluses and the availability of "modern" agricultural inputs increased the chances of attaining household rice sufficiency. This, in turn, enabled women to use their income or resources from their other production activities for their own projects, rather than for the purchase of rice. With this change women swidden farmers, gardeners, and pig farmers again had markets for their produce, so many resumed these economic activities. Road construction facilitated women's access to urban and district markets.

Women's domestic labor has continued to affect their productive labor. Child-care centers organized during the socialist period and rice mills and piped drinking water systems, more common after economic liberalization, have freed women from some of their domestic chores. During the latter period, some of women's "free" time was devoted to additional production for sale.

Finally, women from the three ethnic groups have apparently been differently affected by changes since 1975. Since ethnic Lao women are more likely than women of other ethnic groups to depend entirely on paddy production, they are more likely to live in rice-sufficient households and to engage in other production activities that they themselves control. Furthermore, ethnic Lao women were more likely to participate in agricultural cooperatives during the socialist period and were more likely to engage in marketing or other commercial ventures when controls on private enterprise were lifted. In contrast, Khmu and Hmong women were more likely to experience resettlement and were less likely to control the products of their own labor in both periods.

Notes

1. Evans (1990) noticed the same pattern in the cooperatives he studied in the same district.

2. Resettlement to potential paddy land or cash cropping and animal-raising were the only options offered by the fledgling government. No permanent hillside agricultural systems have yet been identified for Lao conditions, and no research on such systems was undertaken during the socialist period. The "no swidden" policy did not recognize differences between the Khmu system of rotation through a series of fallow swiddens and the more migratory and destructive Hmong system of continuous cultivation until complete depletion (rotational vs. "pioneering" swidden systems, respectively; Lovelace 1991, 5-6). Furthermore, policy statements did not acknowledge the sometimes destructive swidden practices of lowland Lao farmers. In addition, cash cropping options were not supported by transportation or dependable markets.

3. One hectare equals 2.4 acres.

4. See Chapter 2 for an explanation of the New Economic Mechanism.

5. A paddy bund is the low earth wall around the paddy that contains standing water.

6. These policies are related to the New Economic Mechanism.

6

Forest Gathering, Crafts, and Marketing

Forest Gathering

Forest gathering[1] is an integral part of the weekly and often daily routine of rural ethnic Lao, Khmu, and Hmong women, depending on the season.[2] While all villagers depend on gathering to some extent, families without rice supplement their diets with forest tubers and other forest products and sometimes sell forest items. During poor crop years, most families must depend on the forest for subsistence. Adult women, sometimes accompanied by other family members or neighbors, are the main forest gatherers for the household. In fact, many women consider forest gathering one of their main jobs. Swidden farmers are most dependent on forest products; their subsistence is less assured, and the forest borders immediately on their swidden fields.

Khmu swidden cultivation practices incorporate forest processes into their agricultural cycle. Tree stumps and fallow bush species are left in the otherwise cleared swidden for rapid fallow regrowth and restoration of soil fertility (IUCN 1988, 10). In Hmong and Lao swidden systems, however, all fallow tree species are cleared with no cover crops or soil-restoring trees planted to ensure rapid regeneration (IUCN 1988, 9, 10).

Easy access to productive gathering forests and plentiful stream fisheries depends on the existence of these natural resources, however. Land-short farmers engaging in shifting cultivation, especially the more destructive practices of the ethnic Lao and the Hmong, have led to steady deforestation in some areas of Laos (IUCN 1988). Today and at several times in the recent past, logging booms have also denuded large expanses of more accessible forests in Laos. For example, before 1975, especially during the brief peaceful coalition period between 1973 and 1975 when Lao borders were not closed to capitalists but bombing had ceased, Thai and other logging companies harvested many accessible stands of tropical hardwoods, usually bribing the local military commander and district officials for the privilege. For example, much of the lowland forest around Pak Kading in Bolikhamsay Province was logged at this time. This undoubtedly affected the household economies of villagers whose livelihoods and perhaps even their residences had already been drastically affected by years of war, fighting and bombing, although this is not documented. Profits usually did not accrue to villagers, but to foreign logging companies and to men who, when the government changed, most likely fled the country with their families.

However, a few Phon Sung villagers cashed in on the rush for timber that characterized the final war years during the 1970s. Two villagers purchased trucks so they could cut timber growing on village land and haul it to a nearby sawmill. Sawmill agents approached village officials with a proposal to buy a stand of timber on village land. Villagers felt they had no choice but to accept the proposal, since agents made it clear that they had already purchased the approval of the local military and district government. Barber points out how this unrepeatable activity integrated Phon Sung into a wider economic network while consolidating the economic advantage of some village households (1979, 145–47).

Activity Under Socialist Reorganization

Patterns of deforestation from both swidden cultivation and commercial logging have been affected by government policy and economic changes. But the changing political and economic environments of socialism and then of economic liberalization have not reduced the need for the forest as a source of subsistence foods, materials, and products for sale. During the socialist period, most household members probably foraged to meet their own survival needs, especially during difficult years of drought, flood, and agricultural collectivization and when marketing was severely repressed. With the lessening of market restrictions and better agricultural years, some foragers were able to sell their products. The "no-swidden" policy, first articulated in the mid-1980s, forbids the felling of old forest for agricultural purposes and proposes to settle or resettle migrating swidden cultivators who rotate crops through upland swiddens (see Chapter 5).

Although all land belongs to the state, villages informally hold forest land in their area as village commons. For example, in Bo Keo and Luang Prabang Provinces, each upland and paddy farming village controls and protects a defined land area surrounding the village, often with official district approval or initiative (see Alton 1993 for an example). Upland villages claim an area of swidden land, fallows, and forest as theirs. All household swidden fields are developed in this area. Similarly, village tree felling, bamboo cutting, and firewood gathering occurs in this area, while foraging and hunting activities may range farther afield. Paddy farming households own the right to use their paddy land, but paddy farming villages also claim an "economic resource zone" encompassing nearby forest and brush lands. Some districts have formalized the boundaries of these village commons, and the boundaries are acknowledged by all villages in the area (C. Ireson 1990, village committee interviews; IFAD 1993, 45–46; IUCN 1988, 16). Land conflicts often occur with new migrants or nonresident entrepreneurs who do not recognize these customary land rights.

Incursions of foreign logging companies have disturbed forests in the past, but foreign encroachment was circumscribed temporally by the wars and physically by the inadequate network of roads. Capitalist loggers were not allowed to continue logging after 1975, though Vietnamese logging continued in some areas. Logging after 1975, both legal and illegal, was hindered by the logging capacity of Lao enterprises, and few forests were cut.

During the latter part of the socialist period, three state logging enterprises operated in Bolikhamsay Province of central Laos. These enterprises harvested and processed timber. Before 1989 they also exported some of their logs. The enterprises replanted very little of the logged area, though two had nurseries and made some efforts to enlist local villagers' labor to plant seedlings. Profits from the companies returned to the coffers of the "owners": the Ministry of Agriculture and Forestry, the provincial government, and the army. Two of the three received technical and capital assistance from the Swedish government. Nearly all enterprise foresters and other technical employees were men. A few wives and daughters of enterprise employees also worked for the enterprises, though not in the forest or in decision-making roles (C. Ireson 1989b).

Activity Under Economic Liberalization

Government policy and practice are in conflict with rural livelihood systems. Many rural Lao of all ethnic groups depend heavily for their subsistence on land-extensive swidden cultivation and forest gathering and hunting. In a situation of high population growth, government policy initiated during the socialist period limited swidden cultivation, required district approval for any village logging, and did not effectively safeguard village forest use rights, though new policies may do so. The ban on agricultural clearing of forest with large trees, though, may have enabled village foragers to maintain access to nearby productive gathering forests, at least until the forest was logged commercially. Sale of timber and processed wood is usually one of the major sources of foreign exchange for Laos. Legal logging has been carried out by a number of governmental units since decentralization of budgetary and administrative control beginning in 1986. Provinces, ministries, and the armed forces have all controlled logging activities in their jurisdictions, with little oversight by a central government and no effective regulation of forest practices or areas logged.

Moreover, with a nominal ban on logging in Thailand since 1989, more open borders with Thailand since 1988, and high world demand for tropical hardwoods, Thai logging companies reputedly are now mining the forests of Burma, Cambodia, and Laos, with or without the permission of central governments or, sometimes, local authorities. Legal concessions in Laos have been granted to a number of Taiwanese, Japanese, and Thai logging companies (Saly Khamsy, Ambassador of the Lao PDR to the United Nations, personal communication, 1991). Technically, these concessions require companies to build roads into the concession, to build or upgrade mills for initial processing in-country, and to replant after harvest. However, boundaries of the concession are not well defined, and there is no mechanism for enforcing compliance with concession agreements. Furthermore, government policy (taxes on logs felled for export have been much higher than those felled for sale or use in the domestic market) encourages false reporting of logging for export. Thus, the government's revenue from logging was not extraordinary, although Lao forests disappeared at ever-increasing rates until the logging ban in 1992.

Some forest-dependent communities of all ethnic groups are being affected by logging. One such village in central Laos reports that enterprise-harvesting activities have included killing or scaring away all forest animals, killing all fish, and destroying other forest foods. Even the ancient, large water animals that may have spiritual powers have been destroyed. These villagers expect drier streams in the dry season and more flooding in the rainy season because logging roads have filled the streams. During the logging period, animals fled from the forest area, fish in ponds and streams were harvested by grenade, and downed timber made it difficult to negotiate forest paths. Besides careless logging practices by the company, loggers are gathering and hunting for their own families as they cut timber (C. Ireson 1989a, 1989b).

On a positive note, these villagers stated that when asked, enterprise employees cut and haul house construction logs and firewood for them and that some roads have been improved. Nonetheless, enterprise harvesting has brought strong negative effects to the lives of these villagers who have depended heavily on forest gathering and hunting as one of the main pillars of their economy. Both women and men gather forest products in this village. Men cut certain varieties of trees searching for insect by-products to be sold to Chinese medicine merchants; women forage more conventionally for food and other products. During the rainy season after logging, plants began to grow again and some animals returned to the village's gathering forest (C. Ireson 1989b, 1991; Plant 1990).

Nonetheless, women's forest-related activities and resources in a number of villages have been impacted by this dramatic increase in logging. Foraging becomes more difficult and less productive. Road construction may attract new settlers who then compete with old residents over use of both forest and crop land. The water supply, both for irrigation and domestic use, may become more erratic as watersheds above the village sources are deforested. Villagers may experience mud slides, other debris torrents, erosion, flooding and local drought, as well as less reliable water supply as a result. Women, helped by their children, must spend more of their time and energy trudging to more distant water sources, while women's dry season gardens may wither and die. Since loggers also harvest nonwood forest crops and destroy ponds and streams in the logged area, village sources of cash from "minor forest products" are also threatened (C. Ireson 1991). Women gather and sell some of these products, like bamboo shoots, cardamom, rattan, fish, and turtles, though men also gather and sell some forest products.

In 1992 and 1993, in an attempt to regain national control and stop illegal logging, the government recentralized budgets and decreed a temporary stop to forest harvesting so that a new forest management system could be organized and implemented (World Bank 1993). The reformulation of forest policy could possibly benefit rural women and all villagers if illegal logging can be contained, if legal loggers must adhere to the terms of their concessions or contracts, if villages are actually ceded village forests and lands to manage with enforceable rights over these forests, and if women within the village participate in decision making about village lands. Government inability to effectively police the new system and the profits to be made from the sale of tropical hardwoods ensure that the destruction of village forests will continue, though perhaps some of the worst abuses may be curbed. Continued forest "mining" will continue to hurt more and more villagers, especially women, who rely on intact forests for part of their livelihoods.

Bolikhamsay Example

All villagers depend, to some extent, on gathering activities, even today. Some villagers, particularly those from wealthier, paddy-farming villages, content themselves with gathering shoots and leaves from the margins of their rice fields or from brush lands near the village, according to mainly ethnic Lao respondents in a study conducted in Bolikhamsay, a central Lao province, during the late 1980s (C. Ireson 1991, 1989a, 1989b).[3] None of the eight villages sampled is wealthy (Map 5.1 includes all eight villages), and in each village some families do not produce enough rice for their family's consumption. These families regularly supplement their rice with forest tubers and other forest products, though they may also work for neighbors to earn the rice they need. During a particularly difficult year of too much, too little, or poorly timed rain, most families must depend on the forest "safety net." Researchers accompanied Phone Sa-at foragers into their gathering forest. The foragers dug a tuber to demonstrate to researchers what they eat when their rice is insufficient. These tubers, they said, are at their largest in April and May, just when village households begin to experience rice shortages.

Village women frequently gather products from the forest. Twenty-five percent of women respondents gather every day, and 75 percent gather at least

PHOTO 6.1 Bolikhamsay women regularly forage for food. This woman from Ban NaO is collecting tender plant stems for her family's dinner.

once a week. Women, alone or in small groups, harvest shoots and leaves while moving steadily from plant to plant. They cut, trim, drop the usable shoot or leaf into their basket, and cut the next plant (see Photo 6.1). Root digging requires more time for each root. A group of women may sing or talk, but they rarely stop working (C. Ireson 1991, 30–31).

TABLE 6.1 Items[a] Commonly Gathered by Bolikhamsay Households

Products Gathered		Households Gathering
English Name	Lao Name	(No.)
Food products:		
Bamboo shoots	*Noh mai*	165
Mushrooms	*Het*	142
Calamus shoots	*Noh boun*	64
Rattan shoots	*Noh wai*	56
Medicinal products:		
Sarsparilla	*Ya hua*	57
Uvaria micrantha	*Kamlang seuakhong*	37
Use products:		
Rattan	*Wai*	55
Elephant grass	*Nya kha*	43
Thitga resin	*Khi si*	40
Bamboo for weaving	*Mai hia*	37
Forest animals:		
Fish/freshwater shrimp	*Pa/Kung*	61
Mouse/rat		56
Birds		50
Squirrel		34

[a]List includes all items gathered by at least 30 households from the combined sample of 200.
Source: C. Ireson 1989b, 36.

Village households reported gathering a great variety of plant foods, medicinal products, items for use, and forest animals. All respondents combined (n=200) reported household gathering or hunting of 141 different types of forest products: 37 food items, 68 medicinal products, 18 products for use, and 18 kinds of animals (C. Ireson 1991, 30). On the average, members of each household studied gathered eight different kinds of items from the forest. Male and female herbalists gather a greater variety of forest products. A number of families sell or barter forest products, most commonly mushrooms, bamboo shoots, resin, rattan, cardamom, freshwater shrimp, or small animals caught or shot by men.

The most common items gathered or hunted are listed in Table 6.1. Composite village lists combining all forest products gathered or hunted by respondents' families in each village reveal that each village gathers at least twenty-eight different kinds of forest products, with the longest listing fifty-

TABLE 6.2 Households Selling or Bartering Forest Products by Category of Product

Category	Households (No.)
Food products	74
Use products	73
Animals or animal products	53
Medicinal products	11

Source: C. Ireson 1989b, 37.

three items. The number of items gathered in each village does not seem to be related to the apparent poverty or wealth of a village, since one of the better off villages gathers the same number of different products as the poorest village.

Many villagers sell or barter forest products to supplement their own agricultural production. Thirty-eight percent of the entire sample, including 120 village households and 80 households of logging enterprise employees, sell or barter these products. As is evident from Table 6.2, forest products are most often gathered for food and for use. Most of the animals collected are also used for food.

Women and their families most commonly sell mushrooms or bamboo shoots; resin, rattan, and cardamon; squirrels, birds, rats, and freshwater shrimp. Most families gather only one kind of medicinal plant, sarsparilla, which is used to make tea or to flavor rice whiskey. Otherwise, the gathering of medicinal plants appears quite specialized and is usually done by an older man or woman in the village. Only one of our respondents gathers medicinal plants regularly and sells nine different varieties (C. Ireson 1989a, 13).

On their most recent forest visit, most respondents reported going with one or two other persons (63 percent), though 13 percent reported going alone and 27 percent went with a larger group (total n=101). Of respondents gathering in a group who reported the gender of their companions, 68 percent reported going only with other women (n=75). Women who reported gathering with others during the week of the interview (n=77) most commonly went with neighbors (43 percent), though others reported going with relatives and neighbors (19 percent), husbands (14 percent), children (10 percent), non-household relatives (9 percent), and other household relatives (4 percent) (C. Ireson 1989a, 13).

The importance of the forest gathering activity of village women is particularly evident in contrast to the forest activity of other women who also live in rural Bolikhamsay, but who are the wives or daughters of salaried employees of logging enterprises. The eighty respondents from rural salaried households included in the larger study were drawn from employees of two companies located in mainly ethnic Lao areas of Bolikhamsay Province. They live in company towns located in the countryside at some distance from other towns and markets. Their living situations are similar in some ways to those of villagers, with similar housing and social customs, but some differences are notable.

Village women clearly gather from the forest and brush land around their village more frequently than do women from salaried families ($t = 3.76$; $p < .001$). Considerably less than half (41 percent) of salaried family women visited the forest in the week preceding their interview, while almost three-quarters (72 percent) of village women had done so. Village families are much more likely than salaried families to have eaten forest products in their meals the day before their interview ($X^2 = 29.11$, $p < .001$). Village women are much more likely than those of salaried families to consider their forest gathering as a "vocation" and to gather more different types of forest products ($t = 6.03$, $p < .001$; $t = 5.27$, $p < .001$, respectively; C. Ireson 1989a, 16–17). Respondents from rural salaried households not only frequent the forest less, they also generally have better living conditions, and their household economies derive from different sources than those of village women.

Differences between women villagers with access to old growth forest and those with access only to young or degraded forest suggest changes in women's economic activities as village forest resources deteriorate. Women with access to old-growth forest forage more frequently, but women without such access sell more types of forest products than do other women. Women without access to old-growth report less rice available for their families than do women with access to old growth. These households are more dependent on less productive upland fields and report a greater variety of nonagricultural income sources including shopkeeping; selling prepared food, drink, crafts, and services; clearing forest; planting tree seedlings; and, of course, selling forest products. In contrast, women with access to old-growth forest rely almost entirely on sales of animals or agricultural produce for their cash needs, although a few sell forest and other kinds of products.

A recent study of Laotian women as shifting cultivators and forest foragers in Luang Prabang Province also found that forest products are important in household food security, supplementing agricultural production in all eight villages studied. All sixty-eight women interviewed from three different ethnic groups (ethnic Lao, Khmu, Hmong) reported that their families gather forest food. All but three said that they eat at least one forest food at every meal. Like many women in Bolikhamsay Province, they collect food in secondary forest, fallow fields, and along streams, walking from thirty minutes to two hours to reach their gathering destination. Interestingly though, half of the Hmong women reported that their husbands were responsible for collecting forest products (Håkangård 1990, 13). During the rainy season, these Hmong women reported that they were too busy maintaining upland field crops to collect forest food. Again, as in Bolikhamsay Province, families with sufficient rice report using forest food as regularly as poorer families.

A number of Luang Prabang women reported that finding food in the forest is more difficult now than it used to be. They offered various explanations including the loss of forest cover, soldiers killing all the deer and other large animals, and an increase in the numbers of people collecting in diminished areas of forest. Although the forest is an important source of food and other products for interviewed women, forest products are less important than agricultural products as a source of income. More important sources of income are wage labor and the sale of pigs, soybeans, corn, sesame, and opium (Håkangård 1990, 14, 19–20).

In short, then, it appears that women's forest gathering, supplemented by men's trapping and hunting, is an important pillar of family and village economy, along with crop production and animal-raising. This support becomes more important during the years when the other aspects of family and village economy are weaker, as in drought or disease years, but the forest is a regular feature of the rural economy in all years. Government logging concessions to foreign timber firms require no mitigation of the effects of logging on village livelihoods. Neither government nor village has effective legal or financial control over logging firm activities nor an effective way of protecting village land rights. The current logging boom is therefore undercutting one of the supports of the household economy in many rural villages. Poorer villagers are more forest-dependent than others, and they are hardest hit by the loss of the village gathering forest.

Impact on Women's Work and Power

Women's forest work, supplemented in some groups by men's hunting or trapping, has been a regular feature of the rural household economy in all ethnic groups and in all time periods under consideration. Especially for poor families or during years of poor harvests, the forest has been an important source of food, medicines, construction and craft materials, and items for sale.

Noi and Phing, two women interviewed initially in the 1980s, gave examples of traditional forest gathering. Noi (profiled in Chapter 1), an ethnic Lao woman deserted by her husband, must rely on her own swidden production and forest product foraging to feed her family of two daughters and a toddler son. She gathers from the forest near her swidden field while her daughters weed. If she needs cash, she carries swidden crops and forest products on her back 13 kilometers to the nearest market. The day before being interviewed she had sold corn, bamboo shoots, and forest leaves. Phing, a Khmu woman, and her husband sometimes go together to the family swidden field.[4] While she works in the swidden he often hunts wild boar and other forest animals, or chops firewood in the forest or from trees cleared from the swidden. Noi, Phing, and their families depend on the forest to provide both food and income. Upland swidden farming households, like those of Noi and Phing, depend more on forest products for their daily needs than do paddy farmers whose source of food is more secure.

While a woman's main income sources are her crops, animals, crafts, and (for some) commerce, women are responsible for family welfare as well as income. Women can only produce an economic "surplus" when their sources of family subsistence are assured. In years when the family rice and cash crops are devastated by disease or natural disasters, or when her products encounter a poor market, she must still ensure family survival. Although she may gain little power from maintaining family subsistence, in difficult years forest products enable her to keep her family alive and, occasionally, to earn money. The forest as a source of family subsistence is available to proportionately fewer Laotian women every year as the current logging boom continues and as a growing population cultivates available brush land more and more frequently.

In short, women with access to both old-growth forest and second-growth areas use forest products to supplement their relatively more adequate subsistence rice crop. Small amounts of family surplus crop production and sale of animals seem to meet these women's minimal cash needs. Women with access only to second-growth areas, on the other hand, may have a somewhat more commercial view of the forest and forest products. Although these women visit the forest less frequently, they are twice as likely to sell what they gather (C. Ireson 1991, 32–34). They describe a conflict between commercial logging and their forest gathering, two different commercial uses of a forest. These women are more likely to participate in other aspects of a market economy as well, through various selling and wage-earning activities. Because their subsistence base is less adequate than that of women in the other group, they have developed alternative ways of supporting their families.

Without longitudinal data, it is hard to know if the subsistence base of women with access only to second-growth areas has always been inadequate or has only recently become so. It is possible that women with access to old-growth forest may have to adopt similar strategies as logging operations remove that source of subsistence. Interestingly, the income sources reported in villages with access only to second-growth areas are mainly exploited by women (selling forest products, selling cooked food or whiskey, or shop-keeping), with the exception of clearing forest and planting seedlings, tasks

PHOTO 6.2 Ethnic Lao women regularly produce cloth for family use. This Houa Phan woman is weaving cloth for work clothes.

open to both men and women. Any changes in the quality of forest available to a village, then, are likely to have effects on women's work. With further forest destruction, more women may market agricultural products or prepared items, or may engage in wage labor, if the local market can support them.

Crafts and Other Home Production

Today, as in the past, few of the goods needed for rural household use can be purchased with the small income obtained from the sale of agricultural surplus or forest products. Most must be made by family members.

Women and men, young and old, contribute to goods production. Traditionally, crafts are produced for respect, cultural identity, and religious observance, as well as for use and income. Women in all three Laotian ethnic groups are responsible for cloth production, but a number of women make other items for sale or barter, including, for example, alcoholic beverages, snack foods, floor mats, and thatch for roofing.

Cloth production was profoundly affected by liberation and socialist reorganization. Ethnic Lao women traditionally weave both silk and cotton textiles for use and for sale, though factory-produced cloth has been also available for purchase in Laos for decades. Rural subsistence households, however, have continued to produce much of their own clothing (see Photo 6.2). Household clothing makers are responsible for the production of family clothing from the planting of a cotton crop through the sewing of the final garment. Some Lao villages traditionally specialize in silk production, with women responsible for most of the production process. Cloth produced beyond family requirements is sold or bartered. Khmu women often trade cotton to a lowland Lao weaver in exchange for cloth. A few acculturated Khmu women weave, but most purchase or barter for cloth. Hmong women traditionally make one elaborate set of clothing for the New Year, demonstrating their skills in stitchery, applique, and batik-making. All of these local products are now encountering competition from imported or local factory-made goods with economic liberalization.

Lao and Khmu women traditionally make alcoholic drink from rice while Hmong women are more likely to use corn for their alcohol-making. Part-time village specialists distill the more potent spirits. Rice or corn wine and spirits are commonly sold or exchanged within the village. Some women make snack foods on special occasions or as a business. Floor mats, thatch, tables, and carrying bags are commonly made by some village women for use and for sale or barter. Interestingly, the production for sale of snack foods, mats, and thatch increased in some villages after economic liberalization, while products based on traditional Lao textile traditions began to enter the international marketplace and fashion scene.

Activity Under Socialist Reorganization

With the accession of the communist government and the severence of trade links with capitalist Asia, women unpacked their stored looms and resumed their traditional cloth-making activities. According to one chronicler of village life near Vientiane, this process had begun by 1974, as U.S. support for import subsidies and foreign exchange collapsed (Barber 1979, 56). With the change in government in 1975, the urban market for silk clothing dried up as free-spending foreigners left, wealthier urbanites fled the country, and those who remained dressed simply. In contrast, demand for cotton cloth and clothing for ordinary wear increased since imported cloth was much less available.

Certain women's cottage industry activities were bolstered by the economic reorganization and crises of the first decade of the Lao PDR. Local textile production was touted as one route to self-sufficiency by the new government (Stuart-Fox 1986a; Adams 1987). In 1975, the new government "waged a relentless attack against all traces of Western decadence" (Christie 1982, 67). Western dress for women was attacked and ethnic Lao women again began wearing the Lao sinh, a traditional handwoven skirt (Ng 1988). Even urban women began weaving again, to provide cloth for their family's clothing, as well as in response to the newly developed market for local cloth, and especially for Lao sinhs. With increased demand and official approval, ethnic Lao women resumed or even increased their production of cotton and cloth, usually working as individuals or with family members. Women of all ethnic groups were encouraged to undertake cotton production and weaving. Since 1975, a few textile factories employing women's weaving skills have been developed in some towns. These factories use more efficient looms to produce goods for sale on the regional market or even for export. One of the earliest United Nations–Lao Women's Union projects in Vientiane supported this governmental goal. The project hired skilled weavers and trained them in dyeing, designing cloth, and weaving with efficient looms. They then continued to work in the project workshop or returned to their nearby homes to work on improved looms producing high-quality textiles for export as well as for local sale. Another textile factory in remote Phong Saly was equipped with flying shuttle looms, which could be mechanized whenever there was diesel fuel to power the town generator (R. Ireson, Quaker Service Laos trip report, 1984).

Phone Thong Textile Cooperative. Phone Thong Cooperative[5] was established in response to the changed political climate and economic opportunities after 1975. The Vientiane neighborhood of Phone Thong was established by war refugees from rural areas of Houa Phan Province. Women from this region are renowned as weavers, but in the Vientiane war economy before 1975, there was no market for their woven products. These women still raised vegetables and small animals near their houses, but they had to rely on their husband's wages to support the family. With the end of the war and the change in government, the Vientiane economy was in shambles. Like other Vientiane families, Phone Thong households began producing more of their own food and goods, while a number of husbands were employed, at very low wages, by the new government. In response to increased demand, these Houa Phan women began weaving again. The new government outlawed the wearing of Western clothes, like jeans, and encouraged the wearing of traditional clothing since cheap imported cloth was no longer available.

The case of Komaly, a younger Phone Thong woman, is illustrative. She had continued her education after moving to Vientiane and had experience working for an import-export company before 1975. She marketed her family's vegetable and cloth production and purchased the silk, cotton, and dye necessary for weaving. Her education and commercial experience were essential during the time of shortages, erratic supply, and limited demand characteristic of the late 1970s. Neighbors soon asked her to handle their marketing also and asked her advice about patterns and colors that would sell well. During this period, the government promoted cooperative work, merchants demanded high prices for raw materials, and the state established import-export companies. In response, Komaly persuaded her weaving relatives and neighbors to form a cooperative work team to fill contracts that she had arranged. By 1979, they began to work as a cooperative, receiving official status the following year. As the workload increased with successful marketing and steady production, the cooperative grew from eleven to twenty members with 200–300 part-time workers. Within five years it had nearly tripled in size and developed specialized units for designing, spinning, weaving, sewing, repair and maintenance, packing, finance, and administration.

While the cooperative was founded by older women, except for Komaly and her sister who were single household heads, the majority of new members were young and many of these were single. While two-thirds were refugees from Houa Phan, the remainder had moved from other provinces. Part-time workers often did not become cooperative members because they had to care for several children, because they held another job during the day, or because they lived outside the town and farmed for most of their living. Komaly or other members recruited these more distant women based on their reputation for distinctive weaving styles.

As the cooperative grew, it diversified its products, mechanized some of the spinning, weaving, and sewing, and bid for large contracts from eastern Europe. While wage rates were low, they were comparable to those paid to civil servants and workers in state enterprises. Women chose to work for the cooperative for the money, for personal satisfaction, and for political correctness. Their wages were crucial to family survival and were mainly spent on food and clothing. Their new earning status did not translate into more help from husbands at home, however. But the cooperative work style was flexible, allowing women to occasionally bring children to the factory and to take time off for family business; thus they could combine their cooperative and their household responsibilities. Phone Thong Cooperative is an example of how the aftermath of the war and socialist economic policies facilitated the integration of rural weavers into a proto-industrial economy with links to international markets. As a result of political and economic changes under socialism, these weavers began learning basic industrial and organizational skills.

Activity Under Economic Liberalization

The opening of borders once again to imported goods, tourists, and foreign capital seems to be changing the income opportunities open to women and displacing some local products. Cheap factory-made cloth is once again beginning to undercut the Lao weaving industry. Some village cotton weavers now rely more on their production of ginned cotton than on finished fabric. Weavers today are most likely specialists who have found or are searching for a local or international market for their products. A few villages or urban workshops like the former Royal weavers living in a village near Luang Prabang, northern Lue (ethnic Lao) weavers, and an artistic weaving workshop in Vientiane have been weaving for the tourist trade, for export, or for exhibition and international sale.

Ethnic Lao weavers continue to provide clothing for their families but modify their cotton- and cloth-producing activities in response to market changes. In 1986, Na Fai village in Luang Prabang Province was well known locally for its cotton cloth. Na Fai women grew cotton, wove for their own families, and traded their cotton goods as far away as Thailand, even before and during the socialist period. They had twelve seamstresses who owned their own sewing machines and who sewed garments to order. By 1990, Na Fai's cotton crop was much larger than before and provided income for many families. Since 1986, the village women's union had obtained from the national women's union both a mechanized cotton gin and an agreement to buy ginned cotton. In 1990 weaving seemed a less important source of income than it was in 1986 (C. Ireson 1990). Some local products besides specialized fabrics are still enjoying successful markets, like mats produced by villages on the outskirts of Vientiane and thatch produced by a village 50 kilometers north of Vientiane.

The likely future for another common woman-run "home industry," home-prepared drinks for public sale, illustrates how imported or factory-made goods can threaten women's income sources. The local rice wine or distilled liquor made by women is still much cheaper than commercially made whiskey, beer, and soft drinks, but richer urbanites, government officials, other rural workers and travelers, and even some villagers purchase commercially made products to serve their guests. One of the first noticeable effects of economic liberalization in rural areas was the availability of Heineken beer even in small outlying district centers (R. Ireson, personal communication, 1988).

Both alcoholic beverages and women's skirts were made and sold locally before the influx of their imported or manufactured replacements. Household goods, agricultural tools, and luxury items are now available for purchase by villagers, but villagers beyond the immediate reach of Vientiane and provincial capitals are still oriented to subsistence production (except for a few large-scale Hmong opium producers). Most villagers, women and men, produce just a few items for occasional sale and, in turn, purchase a few items for family use. Some villagers, though, are no longer able to find a market for the products they once sold.

Lue Weavers, Thatch and Mat Makers, High Fashion.[6] Other villagers, though, increase the production of items they have traditionally produced or sold as they see that market links are now open and private entrepreneurship is no longer politically dangerous. For example, weavers in the former royal weaving village near Luang Prabang city, the former royal capital, are as busy as ever, hosting tourists and weaving and hawking traditional fabric. As part of the standard Laos tour, foreigners regularly fly into Luang Prabang to see several temples, the museum, the former royal Palace, the sacred caves, and this weaving village.

Many ethnic Lao women, besides the royal weavers, are competent at the loom, and Lue women in Luang Prabang Province are particularly well known for their textiles.[7] Na Nyang Tai women make several different kinds of fabric products. Khone Kham weavers are best known for their production of both natural and indigo blue homespun fabric, which women barter for other needed goods.

Na Nyang Tai weavers responded to new market outlets and project inputs by growing cash crops, raising pigs, and weaving more patterned fabric. The market for textiles, though, was still undeveloped in 1990. The provincial women's union was purchasing some of the textiles but could not purchase more without locating a market. As mentioned earlier, a development worker from a different project visited Na Nyang Tai and purchased a lovely fabric at above the market price. She advised the weavers to make more since "people will want to buy them," without being aware of marketing problems. The next project worker to visit that village was confronted with dozens of identical pieces and the expectation that she would purchase all of them at the same above-market price (D.D. Bounyavong, personal communication, 1992). Other Lue villagers have better market connections for their weaving. Weavers in a Bo Keo village on the Mekong River weave for their relatives in northern Thailand. The relatives provide weavers with dyed thread. Weavers then produce contracted items using traditional Lue patterns and techniques, and the relatives sell the products on the Thai tourist market (IFAD 1993).

Like Na Nyang Tai families, Khone Kham villagers are long-time Luang Prabang Province residents, though the village was moved during the war. The women are known among nearby villages for their sturdy dark-blue cloth used throughout the area for everyday work clothes. Like Na Nyang Tai weavers, Khone Kham weavers also produce patterned textiles. Women sell cloth, exchange it for baskets, animals, or other products, and use it in their own families. One Khone Kham woman reports that she gives indigo dyed cloth to a Hmong family living on a nearby mountain ridge in exchange for the pasturing and care of her two cattle, while another exchanges cloth for the raising of two goats by a Khmu woman in a neighboring village. A Khone Kham weaver may produce up to 90 meters of plain white or indigo cloth for sale per year, while also providing all of the laborers in her own family with their work clothing. These fabric production and barter relations were not suppressed by socialist reorganization and seem to have changed little with economic liberalization.

Ban Houei Deua, a recently established Vientiane Plain village mainly inhabited by Khmu migrants from more remote provinces, specializes in producing sheets of thatch. Women cut the heavy grass, while men, women, or older children tie the thatch into sheets for sale. People from other villages and even from as far away as Vientiane travel to Houei Deua to purchase thatch (United Nations Development Program (UNDP 1988). Similarly, women and men in a land-short ethnic Lao and Thai village near Vientiane established a floor mat-making cooperative in the early 1980s, using reeds from a nearby lake and swamp. Mat-making continued to be an important income supplement for villagers in the late 1980s. Both women and men weave mats, though women market the finished products (Maroczy 1987; UNDP 1988). In this and two neighboring villages mat production on the average accounted for about one-quarter of household income in 1987 (Maroczy 1987, Table 28). So far these major income-earning products have not been displaced by factory-made tin roofing or plastic floor mats.

Lao Silk, a weaving and silk fabric production company, was established by a foreign weaver and entrepreneur in response to the incentives of economic liberalization. The owner and manager, Carol Cassidy,[8] has thirty direct-hire employees and about thirty indirect employees, nearly all women. Like Phone Thong Cooperative, Lao Silk uses rural ethnic Lao women's traditional skills to integrate them into the local and international economy. Located in an older French villa and its compound in Vientiane, the Lao Silk "factory" is really a creative workshop filled with looms, spinning wheels, and fabrics on display. Cassidy designs all the looms and fabrics using her European training and traditional Lao design ideas, and assigns each fabric design to a weaver that specializes in that particular technique. The excellent weavers may suggest changes as they also bring their creative skills to the task. Some of the pieces faithfully replicate old designs, while all pieces use Lao design ideas. The main market for these unique and high-quality fabrics is textile museums and the world of high fashion. "Sales" trips are really lecture tours to, for example, a Japanese art gallery, the Los Angeles Art Museum, or the Fashion Institute in New York. Cassidy lectures, exhibits her fabrics, and brings a loom and one or two of her weavers to demonstrate the techniques. One critic says that only Japanese weavers produce such exceptionally high-quality silk textiles, and for a much higher price.

Most of the thirty direct employees of Lao Silk are weavers, trained or retrained to workshop expectations by a highly skilled and creative weaver originally from Sam Neua (Houa Phan Province), although many of them first learned to weave from their mothers as teenagers. The thirty or so indirect employees are sericulturalists from several villages in three northern provinces contracted by Lao middlewomen who provide silk to the specifications of Lao Silk. Silkworm-growing villages receive about $600–$1000 per year from this activity. The families of nearly all direct employees are farmers, with the wife providing the main cash income to the household. Employees often pay for family medical services that family members would not be able to afford without their earnings. One financed her father's cataract surgery, another sponsored an appendectomy, and a third a goiter operation. Because, like many ethnic Lao women, older women employees are often responsible for household finances, they keep the purse and jointly make family financial decisions with their husbands. One younger woman says that while she jointly makes decisions with her husband, he keeps the household money. Older male relatives or husbands often arrive with their wives on payday as they attempt to control the women that out-earn them, though Cassidy delivers the monthly salary only to the worker herself.

Like Phone Thong Cooperative, working conditions enable women to combine some family and work responsibilities. Employees sometimes bring mildly sick children to work and occasionally take time off for family business. The lack of production quotas, a participatory management style by Cassidy and her technical weaving supervisor, and even music to weave by make it a pleasant place to work. There has been no turnover in recent months, except for one recent hire.

Impact on Women's Work and Power

Although some activities that commonly provided women with sources of income are being displaced by cheaper or more desirable imports, other craft, small-scale industry, or factory opportunities are increasing. Weavers who have located a market niche are still weaving profitably. Local, provincial, and even national markets still have demand for mats, roof thatch, and other cheap, locally made products. International links through markets, tourism, and local factories financed by foreign capital support the production of certain kinds of local craft and industrial items. The displacement of women-produced wares by imported and mass-produced goods has been a common occurrence in other countries, as has the increase in cash cropping, tourism, and factory jobs (see Chapter 1). Traditionally, crafts, whether for sale, personal adornment, or use, have often enabled rural women to control some aspects of their lives. Some women, who once exerted control by producing and allocating certain products, may now control the allocation of income from their productive activity, though other women may be displaced entirely.

Economic opportunities with liberalization are available mainly to (1) urban or rural women with access to markets and tourists; (2) market-wise women, usually educated Lao and Thai language speakers; (3) very young women for factory work, though the factory work has low wages, poor working conditions, and very close supervision (see Chapter 1 for other examples); and (4) well-educated women who can work in modern sector businesses and services (as accountant, translator, researcher).

Perhaps the meaning of some types of women's craft production is also changing. For example, Lefferts (1993, 16; see Chapter 3) argues that Tai[9] women "re-produce the means by which all Tai laypeople—men as well as women—obtain salvation" in the textiles worn and used by monks at ordination. Today, however, women may purchase the requisite lengths and types of cloth. Presumably, then, anyone with cash, male or female, could provide the cloth and other accoutrements of an ordination today.

Cassidy's employees provide another example. They are no longer autonomous individual producers as some were when they lived and wove in a rural village. Although the best weavers have license to improvise, they weave to someone else's specifications, using materials and equipment provided by their employer. Like the Phone Thong Cooperative members before them, they have used their traditional skills to enter a more industrial workplace.

Salaried workers, if they maintain control of their earnings, are likely to exercise more power within their families than they did before making such an economic contribution. Cassidy's employees, for example, participate, with their husbands, in financial decision making. Since their salaries, especially those of the excellent weavers, are high compared to other Vientiane area salaries, they actually provide most of the family's cash income.

Marketing

Women producers often actively seek to find or create key market links by selling their own produce, though ethnic Lao women especially may become market women as an occupation. Businesspeople in towns both before and after 1975 are often non-Laotians, but village entrepreneurs and local traders are frequently ethnic Lao women. Nearly all petty and local traders were Lao women. Lowland women traveled into the countryside to purchase goods for sale in these markets, while village women sometimes traveled to such markets to sell village goods and purchase dry goods for sale in small village shops. Traditionally Khmu and Hmong men buy and sell products and goods, though women may barter or sell locally with their fathers' or husbands' permission.

Activity Under Socialist Reorganization

The new government suppressed private enterprise after 1975 and created a state marketing network to replace it. Strictures against individual petty traders were lifted in 1980. Traders in fresh produce again became active, though many were fearful of engaging in such politically incorrect behavior until economic liberalization. State limitations on private commerce had the potential for destroying one of rural women's most important sources of power and autonomy.

A very few women entrepreneurs became managers in the network of state stores and village marketing cooperatives that were established in the late 1970s. Store and marketing cooperative managers were nearly always men. Although young women were often store clerks, the managerial skills of experienced businesswomen and local market women were rarely used and neither the state-run marketing network nor most local cooperative stores functioned well. In 1986, the cooperative store of Na Fai was located in the office of the village agricultural cooperative on the ground floor of an impressive concrete and sawn hardwood house. The floor was covered with new linoleum and the shelves were clean, but the store was practically devoid of goods. All cooperative managers were men.

On the other hand, also in 1986, the store of the Sieng Lom trading cooperative was well stocked with bolts of bright-colored cloth, cooking utensils, rubber sandals, and many other goods. A veteran woman merchant who formerly ran a private store in Sieng Lom was a member of the village cooperative committee and managed the store. Her expertise and organizational ability ensured the regular flow of needed goods into Sieng Lom.

State stores in district and provincial centers carried an erratic supply of household and agricultural goods that could be purchased with Lao currency, rice, or coupons (during the period when the government was paying its employees mainly with coupons, rice, and other foodstuffs). Village buying and selling cooperatives were supposedly linked with the state-run sales network to offer a variety of goods at both levels, but limited village economic activity and lack of coordination doomed this effort. Even as early as 1979, though, Party Secretary Kaysone Phomvihan recognized that "it is inappropriate, indeed stupid, for any party to implement a policy of forbidding the people to exchange goods or to carry out trading" (Chanda 1982, 124).

Activity Under Economic Liberalization

Since the government was not able to develop viable alternatives to private trade, it was recognized by the Fourth Party Congress of 1986 that some capitalism would be necessary. At the same time, local trading cooperatives were de-emphasized. Because of these policy changes, private trade resumed. Formerly entrepreneurial families retrieved their money from various hiding places and began investing, once again, in local businesses. In towns the number of restaurants and small shops increased, while village women once again felt comfortable operating small retail shops in their homes. A potential threat to the status of lowland Lao women proved short-lived as many of these women resumed entrepreneurial activities common to their mothers and grandmothers in previous decades.

When private commerce was again encouraged in the late 1980s, Na Fai once more had working stores. By 1990, several women had established stores in this prosperous village. Starting in the mid-1980s in the cities, businesswomen who had hidden their capital in the 1970s or who had begun receiving remittances from relatives abroad began investing in business activities again. With the changes since 1988, women entrepreneurs have become even more visible, operating city and village stores and market stalls, purchasing goods for sale in market towns, making food or other items for sale, and selling services like sewing.

Even some Khmu and Hmong women have begun selling some of their own products, as their villages became more integrated into local political and market areas (Soumountha Yutitham, Quaker Service Laos project officer, personal communication, 1993). For example, in June and July Hmong women and children from villages in Nong Het (see Map 5.1), an isolated district in Xieng Khouang Province, sometimes carry baskets of ripe peaches on their backs to sell along the only road in the district (see Photo 6.3; R. Ireson 1990, 35). Opium and cattle, the principal sources of Hmong household income, are still sold by men, however (Hkum 1992, 17; R. Ireson 1990, 48–49).

Villages best situated to benefit from market connections are those that have a secure livelihood with food and shelter assured. Villages that have installed amenities that diminish women's drudgery, like a water system and rice mill, may also benefit most from market connections since women will be freer to produce crops, raise animals, or make goods for sale. The ability to make market connections is also limited by lack of infrastructure. Villages connected by river or by road to major market towns may also be better able to make market connections.

Cheng, an ethnic Lao village in a flat and fertile region of Vientiane Province, is among the richest I have seen in Laos. With good road and river transportation and full elementary and middle schools, it is obviously well integrated into the educational and economic infrastructure of the province. Village women are central to this integration. Cheng women regularly sell village produce in Vientiane, transporting their goods in the village-owned truck.

Most Luang Prabang Women's Project villages profiled in Chapter 4 established viable market links after 1988. Successful installation of water systems and rice mills led to labor saving of two to four woman-hours a day per household. This additional time was then available for other activities. Cash crop production increased in many villages as they were given seeds and the likelihood of a market by the provincial agricultural purchasing companies. Na Fai farmers greatly increased their cultivation of cotton when the national women's union provided a cotton gin and promised to purchase the ginned cotton. Small animal production increased in some villages, partly because pigs and chickens were easier to sell as market women resumed traveling to villages to purchase them. Market links to Thailand for Lue textiles, though, have not yet been well developed, so textile production will probably stagnate until the provincial women's union or an entrepreneur is able to make that connection.

On the Road. With the reconstruction of Highway 13 from Vientiane east and south to Paksane, villagers experience a number of changes. Most

PHOTO 6.3 These Hmong women and children of Nong Het carry packbaskets of peaches to sell to travelers along the road in their district. *Source*: Randall Ireson.

important for marketing are increases in vehicle ownership, private travel, production, technology, and commerce. While most technology changes (like hand tractors) benefit men, newly purchased rice mills do save one to two woman-hours per day. As in Luang Prabang project villages, some women use their additional time to produce more goods for market or to go into marketing full-time. Women traders in roadside villages often withdraw from agriculture to staff and stock their store or other businesses. Husbands are often very supportive of this profitable activity, running the store and the household in the wife's absence. These women entrepreneurs have altered their pattern of traditional activities and increased their household decision-making power. A village leader in one of the roadside villages half-jokingly summarizes women's current economic responsibilities: "Women travel more than men. They are selling and buying. They keep the money. They are responsible for the economy. They give money to their husbands when husbands ask for it" (Håkangård 1992, 39). Håkangård (1992, 39) responds that "there is a great deal of truth in his statement[s]. Women's position in the family and in the community has been consolidated and the husbands support and encourage their activities and new knowledge."

The wealthiest villagers "on the road" are best positioned to benefit from opportunities offered by access to the reconstructed road, while about 25 percent of village households are too poor to benefit at all (Håkangård 1992, 3, 35–37). Households with no capital or time to invest in newly available opportunities do not benefit from proximity to the road and sometimes sell their land to urban speculators to meet their subsistence needs, subsequently sinking to the level of landless or nearly landless laborers or sharecroppers. As a result, within-village stratification increases. Further, accessible villages may benefit, but more remote villages do not seem to benefit economically from the road, so differences between accessible and remote villages are exaggerated. Women who are not able to develop new activities in response to opportunities offered by Road 13, however, may experience a heavier workload relative to their husbands who have mechanized some of their agricultural tasks and who may have even left agriculture to their wives as they operate a rice mill, a repair shop, or a vehicle full-time. Similar changes are evident on rebuilt Route 13 north from Vientiane through Vang Vieng and beyond.

Impact on Women's Work and Power

Ethnic Lao women, traditionally the traders, were at risk of losing commercial activities as a source of power and esteem during the years after liberation when government policy mandated the development of only state-run and cooperative stores while curtailing the activities of private merchants. But with economic liberalization in the late 1980s, this group of women resumed their customary trading activities and both villages and towns again had easy access to needed goods. Not all ethnic Lao women benefited from economic liberalization though, as can be seen from the case of Highway 13. Instead, poorer women and women in less accessible villages may not benefit at all from road improvements. Often ethnic minority women, who do not speak the language of commerce (Lao) or who are not culturally authorized to handle money or relationships outside the village, do not benefit from economic liberalization. Also, relaxed import restrictions, the establishment of a manufacturing sector in some towns, and the influx of foreign businesses may displace some rural women's crafts, and the women who sell them, from town markets.

Coordinating Women's Other Activities with
Forest, Craft, and Commercial Activities

Women's forest work, home production, and commercial activities all must be coordinated with women's other activities, including women's domestic responsibilities. An empty granary, however, makes forest gathering imperative, so other work must wait while women gather forest products to meet immediate family needs. They usually do not take their children with them on short forest visits.

Home production enables a woman to combine her family responsibilities with income-earning activities by which she contributes to family welfare. As women produce alcoholic drinks or fermented tea leaves (a Khmu specialty), or weave textiles or mats in the shade under their own house, children often play nearby or sleep in cradles hanging from house joists. Even nursing mothers with several small children can weave or brew at home to earn money. Curious or bored two-year olds, though, can easily burn themselves on a still, catch their fingers in the hard wooden rollers of the traditional cotton gin, or irretrievably tangle the threads of a loom that may have taken days or even months to prepare. Once craft work moves to a more industrial setting in the cities, it is more difficult to coordinate women's housework, child care, and production responsibilities. While a number of government offices have child-care centers, few other workplaces provide this service. Some women-sensitive workplaces like Lao Silk and Phone Thong Cooperative allow women some flexibility (tolerating sick children and time off for occasional family business), but flexibility and employee services are not among the characteristics of the newly established garment factories.

Apparently women employees with families continue to be primarily responsible for housework. They manage with the cooperation of other family members, though they must do additional work when they return home at night. For example, a weaver at Lao Silk whose family is supportive of her work says that in the morning she organizes her family and the items for dinner, which she then cooks on her return in the evening.

Ethnic Lao women design their commercial activities around their other responsibilities. Young women without children are often market vendors, buying goods in their own or nearby village and selling them in a nearby market town. Older women with no young children are often traveling merchants covering a wider area and purchasing village vegetables, animals, forest products, or craft items for sale in a market town or at a border crossing. A woman with young children may run a village store, as long as she can leave her children with someone once or twice a week when she leaves the village to purchase supplies for her store. Women who regularly buy and sell throughout the year may occasionally assist with household agricultural production, but usually their commercial activities replace their participation in farming. Some women store owners, like Somkhouane and a Na Fai seamstress, combine sales with a production activity. In the 1970s, Somkhouane sold groceries and drugstore items, and made noodle soup as well. The Na Fai seamstress, who sewed and cared for her children in her home in 1986, had opened a store in her house by 1990 but still continued to sew as well. She clearly wished to create an economic substitute for agricultural work, which she disliked.

In short, all economic activities must be coordinated with child-care and domestic responsibilities. Home production enables women to care for young children and still be economically active, but young children and domestic activities still require women's time and energy. Forest foraging and commercial activities are less easily combined with child care, but limited commercial activity and short forest trips are still possible for young mothers.

Rural Lao women, then, contribute substantially to household and village economies with their forest, craft, and commercial activities. Although recent changes may be threatening some aspects of women's roles in forest foraging and craft production, they are providing new income opportunities. The "social security" system of the forest may be at risk at the same time as stratification increases. Ethnic Lao women of middle and, especially, upper economic status, by village standards, benefit more from the economic opportunities available in the liberalized economy. A few Khmu and Hmong women are also able to benefit, but most ethnic minority women and all poor women experience little benefit.

Notes

1. A number of examples in this section are drawn from a study of women in forestry in Bolikhamsay Province in central Laos, nearly all of whom were ethnic Lao. More abbreviated reports from Lao, Khmu, and Hmong women in Luang Prabang indicate that, while the products and timing may be somewhat different, rural Luang Prabang women use the forest in much the same way as the women interviewed in Bolikhamsay.

2. Sources of information about the importance of Hmong and Khmu forest activities in recent years are drawn from my research in specific Hmong and Khmu villages in Luang Prabang Province (Phou Thit Pheung, Thin Keo, and Sam Ton) and other sources including LP Rural Micro-Projects (1990, 1991); R. Ireson (1990); IFAD (1993); Alton (1993); Håkangård (1990); and Tayanin and Lindell (1991).

3. Example is drawn entirely from C. Ireson 1989a, though some of these findings are also reported in C. Ireson 1991, especially pp. 30-34. The study focused on rural women in Bolikhamsay Province, a province that had a variety of forest types and three active timber companies at the time of the study in 1989.

4. Phing and her husband live in the Khmu village of Thin Keo, Luang Prabang. She was interviewed in 1986, with a follow-up conversation in 1990. More details are included in Chapter 1.

5. Information on Phone Thong Cooperative is drawn mainly from Ng (1988) with a few additional details drawn from a newsletter article by Adams (1987).

6. Examples are drawn from C. Ireson 1990 and 1992a, and from interviews conducted in May 1993 unless noted otherwise.

7. Lue is a northern ethnic Lao group.

8. Information about Lao Silk from Carol Cassidy was supplemented by employee interviews and workshop observation in 1993 and a mailing from the museum at the Fashion Institute of Technology of New York in 1995.

9. Tai is the larger cultural group including both Thai and all lowland Lao groups.

7

Family, Home, and Children

The authority, power, or autonomy that women manifest in the household is often a reflection of their power in areas such as the economy and education. Women's activities in these other areas connect them to the world beyond the household, even when these activities (like, for example, cottage industry production) occur within the household. On the other hand, women's domestic,[1] child-bearing, and child-rearing activities do not seem to augment women's power. In fact, the time, energy, health, and economic resources women must devote to domestic and child-related activities limit women's access to resources. However, family inheritance patterns and kin relations traditionally may provide resources for ethnic Lao women who continue to reside in their natal communities after marriage (see Chapters 3 and 4). Other women, however, are less likely to be able to draw on economic, social, and even political resources provided by a well-developed network of kin and near-kin. In fact, a number of women experience kin relations as yet another area of subordination, as much of their work is directed by their husbands' mothers. Domestic labor to maintain the daily life of the household, child-bearing and child-caring, and family and kin relations have all been affected in some ways by socialism and economic liberalization.

Socialism introduced changes that had the potential to ease rural women's household and child-care work (rural development, child-care centers) while encouraging continuous child-bearing. The socialist policy of extending schools to all villages, while positive in the long term for girls and women, deprived women of necessary assistance. The ideal socialist family proclaimed by the socialist government, though, probably had little effect in rural areas.

Economic liberalization brought more cash income and development projects to rural areas resulting in some mechanical assistance with household maintenance activities like pounding rice, carrying water, and transporting goods. An embryonic birth-spacing program has the potential to reduce the ill effects associated with continuous child-bearing. The expanding system of schooling and fewer child-care centers, however, may mean that women's child-care responsibilities may increase unless rural women actually have the opportunity to "space" their children. Under both socialism and economic liberalization, the promise of effective rural health care was still empty, with the exception of a few special project areas. Economic growth is already influencing migration from rural to urban areas. Continued migration is likely to change the composition of families in rural areas.

Food, Fuel, and Water:
Household Maintenance Activities

Rural women in Laos, like many other Third World women, are largely responsible for the domestic labor that maintains the daily lives of household members. These domestic activities include processing and cooking food, obtaining fuel, and hauling water.

Food

Food processing includes preparing staple food; processing forest tubers as a staple substitute; preserving fish, meat, and other food by fermenting, drying, or "jerking"; and making alcoholic beverages for household use.

Especially important is the husking, winnowing, soaking, and steaming of rice, the main staple for all groups. Because all Laotian households store rice in its unhusked form, women or older girls must husk rice before cooking it. Some households are able to pay a nearby rice miller for this service, but most use their own labor power. Ethnic Lao and Hmong women husk rice with a foot-driven rice pounder that splits the hulls it strikes, while Khmu women pound the rounded tip of a large hand-held wooden pestle into a large wooden mortar full of unhusked rice for the same effect. The Khmu method requires much more physical effort, but the practice is culturally well entrenched (see Photo 7.1). Interviewed Khmu men said that they sought a wife that hand-pounded rice, so they could be sure that she was industrious. It takes one to two hours a day to husk enough rice for a family of seven. Men husk rice only when female labor is completely unavailable as in the case of childbirth, illness, or desertion. In many households, women or older daughters rise before the rest of the family in order to husk rice. Women then separate the rice from the chaff, tossing and catching it in a circular tray. With each toss, more chaff wafts onto the ground, while the rice kernels drop neatly back into the tray, a process assisted greatly by a breeze.

The rice is then either set aside until needed or immediately washed and, if it is glutinous or "sticky" rice, soaked for several hours before it is steamed. The early morning cook first builds or revives the hearth fire, then brings the steaming water to a boil in a jug-shaped metal pot with a wide funnel-like

PHOTO 7.1 Khmu women husk rice by hand as their children play nearby.

opening. She places a conical basket filled with soaked rice into the pot opening and may cover it. She steams the rice for at least forty minutes and turns the mass with a deft toss at least once during the process. When the rice is fully cooked, she spreads it on a wide board or a woven bamboo tray to release the steam, which would make it too "sticky," rolls it into cylinders, and stores it in woven cylindrical rice baskets to eat immediately or to carry to the field for lunch. The cook steams rice again for dinner. In all, a woman or older girl may spend up to two and a half hours every day husking, washing, soaking, and steaming rice.

Forest tubers are more difficult to prepare than rice and are used only when the family rice supply is exhausted. In one district of Bolikhamsay Province, women reported that this shortage might happen as early as April or May with at least six months remaining until the next rice harvest.[2] These tubers are not immediately edible; they must be peeled, sliced, and soaked in a number of changes of water over a period of several days until poisons in the root are thoroughly leeched out. Then the processed root slices may be boiled or steamed and eaten. Households of all three ethnic groups use forest tubers to supplement an inadequate rice supply.

Hmong households in Laos, which used to depend mainly on corn as their staple, changed to rice during the last century, feeding corn to their livestock and poultry. Nonetheless, they sometimes do eat corn from their own fields when the family rice granary is nearly empty, rather than purchasing rice. Again, women are responsible for grinding the corn into flour or meal (Geddes 1976; Vang Dao 1993).

Basic foods in an ethnic Lao household are rice, *padek,* and *cheo. Padek* is made by fermenting fish with salt and a variety of spices, while *cheo* usually includes liquid fish sauce, ground chili peppers, and, perhaps, other ingredients. *Padek* is made well in advance of its use while *cheo* does not require advance preparation. To make *padek,* women clean, chop, salt, and pack the fish, including bones and skin, into a ceramic jar. They seal the jar with mud or dung and leave the contents to ferment for weeks before using the finished product. Balls of sticky rice can be dipped directly into a bowl of *padek* and eaten, or it may be used as a flavoring for soups, sauces, and green papaya salad. *Padek* made during the rainy season when fish can be easily caught in paddies and rivers can be used throughout the following dry season and is a major source of calcium and iodine in the diet.

I recall one warm noontime when a party of fish sellers arrived on foot in a Khammouane Province village some 20 kilometers from the river. Many of the fish they carried were large and tasty-looking, but were already beginning to rot. Attracted by the excitement and the odor, women throughout the village descended on the tired sellers, purchasing their entire inventory. Then the smells spread through the village as women in each household began to process their purchases. By evening, the odor had subsided as the entire catch was packed in jars for future use.

Buffalo, beef, fish, and other foods may be sun-dried for later eating. While men nearly always slaughter large animals, and either males or females (including children) may catch the fish, women are commonly responsible for preserving food. Red meat may be coated with a sauce for flavoring before drying. Other nonfood products may also be dried, including tobacco after shredding. Both women and men participate in shredding tobacco and in drying the shredded tobacco.

Certain household-made products must always be available for guests. Among the ethnic Lao, an alcoholic beverage is essential to serve their guests, while among the Khmu, fermented tea leaves are *de rigueur.* Women make sure that these household hospitality items are available. To make rice wine, for example, women husk the rice, and then steam the rice, husk, and bran separately. After cooling them, they mix the rice ingredients together with dry yeast cake, pack the contents in ceramic jars, and seal the jars with mud or dung. They leave the jars for three to seven days, depending on the strength and flavor they wish to achieve. When it is needed, the host or hostess breaks the seal and adds water to leach the alcohol from the fermented rice. The host or hostess pokes in long straws reaching to the bottom of the jars and the drinking begins.

Women also prepare daily family meals. Soups, sauces, and roasted food are the most common dishes. Meal preparation usually requires the slicing of ingredients, pounding of spices, and, occasionally, the gutting, plucking, or skinning of a small animal or bird. Interestingly, some groups of Khmu say that men are better cooks than women. Khmu women, though, are commonly responsible for the daily cooking.

Nearly all of traditional women's food preparation tasks have remained unchanged with socialism and economic liberalization with the exception of rice husking. Some agricultural cooperatives during the socialist period received government-supplied rice mills. Later, with the redevelopment of a cash economy as a result of economic liberalization, some prosperous villagers operated rice mills as a private business. Development projects in both periods sometimes also included village rice mills. Only households with sufficient rice for most or all of the year, however, are able to afford (and therefore to support) the use of a mill. Poorer women, then, are less likely to benefit from this important female labor-saving technology.

Fuel

The preparation of dietary staples and most other food requires two other important items: fuel and water. Women of all groups collect fuelwood and haul it back to their kitchens. Ethnic Lao and Hmong men, though more rarely Khmu men, may chop trees into burnable lengths in the forest, upland field, or village, since "chopping with an axe" is a male activity, and they may transport loads of wood from field to village, but ultimately the women, who directly depend on firewood for their cooking, must gather wood when the supply is depleted. Women usually chop and split wood with a machete. Cooper (1984, 137) comments that he observed Hmong women chopping down small trees in the swidden with a machete and splitting fuelwood with an axe, but he could not persuade them to chop down a tree with an axe! City and town dwellers often purchase charcoal to fuel their more efficient ceramic and metal stoves, but few village women have such labor- or fuel-saving devices.

Some long-established villages of paddy-growing ethnic Lao have converted nearby forests into agricultural land or chopped down all of the larger trees. When these nearby sources of wood are consumed, women and other family members must expend more time and energy gathering fuelwood, though residents sometimes plant fast-growing groves of trees or bamboo specifically to meet fuel, construction, or craft needs. Upland farmers use their swiddens as a major source of firewood, even when it is quite a walk from swidden to village (IFAD 1993). Occasionally, villagers with road access may be able to hire a truck or persuade a local logging or government construction crew to haul wood down the road from forest to village. On Sundays, a truck driver may drive his vehicle home to his village where it can be used for a myriad of transportation tasks. Oxcarts are sometimes also used to haul heavy loads. Women have little control over trucks or oxcarts but can persuade men to use them for a big load. Otherwise, women haul wood themselves on their backs, heads, or shoulders, or in a push cart. Since they are ultimately responsible for fuel and food, they must use their own labor and their children's labor.

Water

Most Laotians draw drinking water from surface sources (river, dam reservoir, lake) or unimproved wells or boreholes. In the rainy season, water carriers are more likely to frequent unimproved wells/boreholes (30 percent), while in the dry season they are more likely to resort to surface water (38 percent), though both are major water sources throughout the year. A significant minority (22 percent) of Laotian households draw their water from improved wells/boreholes year-round (e.g., wells lined with concrete rings, surrounded with a concrete apron, and covered with a roof). Less common household sources of drinking water are standpipes, indoor faucets, other kinds of wells, and bottled water (Lao PDR CPC 1993).

Women, assisted by older children, are the regular water carriers for all groups, though everyone who is strong enough occasionally hauls water. Normally water is carried in two buckets or waterproof baskets slung over the shoulder on the ends of a long, flat carrying pole. Smaller children may have smaller buckets and a shorter carrying pole. Some Hmong in a village near Phou Thit Pheung[3] use 1.2 meter-long sections of large diameter bamboo instead of buckets. All nodes, except for one at the bottom that separates each bamboo section, are removed. Several of these are roped together and the water carrier slings them onto her back with a rope harness. This Hmong village is situated high on a ridge but on one of the paved roads constructed with Chinese aid more than twenty years ago. The water source most of the year is located uphill from the village, also along the road. One innovative villager constructed a pickup-like vehicle from wood, complete with steering wheel and bed, to accommodate bamboo water cylinders. Older boys seem to prefer this method of hauling water. Some Khmu water carriers use head straps to haul water-filled bamboo tubes (UNICEF 1991b). Women with access to a paved road often use wheeled carts to haul water-filled kerosene cans or buckets (Trankell 1993, 84).

In a compelling water shortage, men as well as women are pressed into service as water carriers. For example, the water supply of the Khmu village of Sam Ton dries up for two months at the end of each dry season. So every two or three days all able-bodied people in the household trudge to the valley floor thousands of feet below to drink, wash clothes, bathe, and carry several gallons of water back to their waiting dependents.

In nine Laotian villages studied at the end of the dry season when water sources are most likely to dry up, women make three to five water-collecting trips per day to provide household water. Each trip takes from just a few minutes to as long as forty minutes, depending on the village, so a woman with a large household in a village with a distant water source might spend more than three hours per day just collecting water (Hewison and Tunya-vanich 1993, 17). One ethnic Lao village in Luang Prabang Province, in contrast, has three unlined but covered dug wells spaced evenly throughout the village. The wells do not dry up in the dry season and are located 130–200 meters from most houses. Women in this village spend about fifteen minutes on each water-hauling trip and make four trips a day on the average (UNICEF 1991b, C-11). A spring at the foot of the mountain is the only water source for a Khmu village in the same province. While the spring is less than one half kilometer straight downhill from most village houses, the walking path is much longer. Water carriers ladle the water into bamboo tubes using a dipper. Women make about four trips a day of thirty-five minutes each to this lined, year-round water source (UNICEF 1991b, C-16).

Some villages now have more efficient water systems, so villagers only carry water from a dug or drilled well, storage tank, or nearby tap. Another Luang Prabang Khmu village has participated in the women's development project described in Chapter 4. Project activities included, among other things, the installation of a gravity-flow drinking-water system with four water taps spaced throughout the village. Today household water carriers spend only a few minutes for each water-collection trip. They previously spent as much time hauling water as women in the Khmu village described earlier (UNICEF 1991b, C-18). The construction of piped village drinking-water systems accelerated with economic liberalization and the increase in aid from multi-lateral and capitalist donors.

The daily amount of female time and effort required to carry water varies remarkably, from a few minutes in the case of a village with a piped water system to a full day in the case of villages like Sam Ton. Generally, though, villagers carry water from a nearby spring, stream, or river, consuming one to three hours a day of household womanpower.

Other Household Maintenance

Women and girls are entirely responsible for sweeping the house and its surrounding compound, washing dishes, airing bedding, and washing family clothing, though older children and husbands will sometimes wash their own clothes. Women are usually also responsible for the care of sick family members.

"Domestic" Responsibilities in Community and Nation

Nurturing and caretaking are not limited to the household. Now, as before, women prepare food for festivals and village guests. The festivals are still carried out in traditional form, and the guests are often connected with government, as before, though now they are socialist officials rather than representatives of the royal family or Royalist or colonial officials. In 1986 members of the Khone Kham women's union, supposedly part of an organization to "emancipate" women, planted a collective cotton garden so they could use the proceeds for the purchase of plates and utensils to serve guests—hardly an activity demonstrating emancipation! Women are also encouraged to support soldiers with letters and small gifts. Again, the local women's union is often the group that organizes women for these services.

The allocation of domestic responsibility to women has changed little through the periods of socialism and economic liberalization, but a few of women's domestic tasks have become easier or have remained as difficult as a result of government policies or actions. Agricultural cooperatives, rural development projects, and the development of a rural cash economy have resulted in the establishment of rice mills and the construction of piped drinking-water systems in some villages, thereby easing women's daily tasks of rice husking and water carrying.

Birth, Child Care, and Patterns of Work

These domestic and household maintenance activities are often carried out in conjunction with women's other reproductive responsibilities: childbirth, infant care, and childhood socialization. Work patterns and patterns of birth and child care affect each other.[4] Laotian women of all ethnic groups are expected to produce food and other goods for their families, yet because most women between the ages of eighteen and forty-five are pregnant, nursing, and/or responsible for young children, productive tasks shape and are shaped by reproductive events and tasks. Greater detail about Lao women's reproductive lives illustrates some of the constraints on women's work.

Birth Control and Family Spacing

"Four children, two boys and two girls," is the usual ethnic Lao response to a question about desired family size. Hmong women usually want more children. Both Khmu and Hmong parents prefer boys, but ethnic Lao parents welcome both boys and girls. Since childhood mortality is so high, the survival of four children into their teen years generally requires six or more births. A majority of women with three living children and more than 80 percent of women with five or more children would like to stop having children. In addition, more than 70 percent of ever-married women ages fifteen to forty-nine years would like to delay or prevent their next pregnancy (Lao PDR CPC 1993).

In spite of women's strong interest, "birth control" is a nonexistent phrase in official Lao pronouncements today and twenty years ago, though some government officials and urban women are becoming acquainted with "birth spacing" through several small pilot programs. Generally, government policy has envisioned a more developed Laos through the efforts of more workers. The sale of birth-control devices was outlawed until 1988. High fertility was rewarded in some places. In Houa Phan Province, for example, province women's union officials reported in 1985 that government employees received a larger cash bonus for each birth after their third birth. Children are an economic necessity in rural Laos, but the birth-control ban probably contributed somewhat to the maintenance of very high rural birthrates.

A birth-spacing policy was decreed in 1988, about the time that private pharmacies were allowed to operate. Birth control pills, injections, and condoms are now available in private pharmacies while clinics in two Vientiane hospitals have instituted birth-spacing programs (Escoffier-Fauveau, Souphanthong, and Pholsena 1994). There is little public information or education about the availability or use of any birth-control method. A small study of a prosperous rural district in the Vientiane Plain found a 20 percent contraceptive prevalence rate including use of pills, injectables, and IUDs. Ignorance about contraception is still the norm, though, even in this relatively affluent and well-educated (by rural Lao standards) group. Two-thirds of the sample did not know about contraceptive pills and three-quarters did not know about other modern methods (Foley and Vongsack 1991). In more remote rural areas, contraceptive use is virtually nil and the knowledge base is very low.

Ethnic Lao folk knowledge about the uterus and the "fertile period" during a woman's cycle, for example, perpetuates unscientific ideas about conception, while associating the monthly cycle and the womb with symbols of fertility, maturity, nature, and harmonious balance (Escoffier-Fauveau, Souphanthong, and Pholsena 1994, 16–17). None of the interviewed women in this study located the uterus in the middle of the pelvic area. Many said it was off to one side or moved around, and a number thought they had more than one uterus or that the uterus was divided into parts in different locations (Escoffier-Fauveau, Souphanthong, and Pholsena 1994, 22–23). These ethnic Lao respondents used the lotus flower as a metaphor for the uterus. One woman said:

> Every woman has a *dokboua* (lotus flower) at birth. It opens for the first time at menstruation. When it opens, it looks like a "cockscomb" and then the blood will flow for a few days. A woman can become pregnant if she sleeps with her husband just after the periods. (Escoffier-Fauveau, Souphanthong, and Pholsena 1994, 19)

So most ethnic Lao women believe that the fertile period is when the lotus is open, during and immediately following the menstrual flow.

The lotus flower is a symbol of purity and perfect balance. It is also closely associated with the Buddha. Images of the Buddha commonly portray him seated on an open lotus when attaining enlightenment. Like a person, a lotus needs a balanced combination of the four elements (earth, air, water, sunlight/fire) in order to grow. Words used to describe women's monthly cycle suggest the harmony of women with nature. The word for the monthly period means "season" and derives from a Sanskrit word meaning "season under cosmic influence" (Escoffier-Fauveau, Souphanthong, and Pholsena 1994, 16–17). Among the ethnic Lao, then, women's cycle and womb have positive cultural attributes. Unfortunately, midland and upland Lao respondents were too shy to respond to questions about their own reproductive physiology.[5]

Women's use of contraception depends not only on contraception availability, but on lower childhood mortality and female autonomy. Of seventy-two women interviewed from the three major ethnic categories in four provinces, twenty-one were contraceptive users, while forty-three did not use modern methods of contraception (Escoffier-Fauveau, Souphanthong, and Pholsena 1994, 48, 52). Contraceptive users were judged "more autonomous" than were nonusers. That is, they were more likely to have (1) access to information (through greater education, knowledge of Lao language, and freedom of movement), (2) access to household resources (through matrilocal residence and inheritance), and (3) power to make decisions affecting themselves and others (Escoffier-Fauveau, Souphanthong, and Pholsena 1994, 48). Not surprisingly all contraceptive users were ethnic Lao, except one Khmu woman who was married to a Lao. All had attended school, spoke Lao, and most went regularly to the market to buy and sell. They lived matrilocally and most did not feel obligated to bear sons, though they desired sons as well as daughters. All felt that they were within their authority in making decisions to limit their family size. Husbands interviewed acknowledged their wives' decision-making authority. While most of these women were urban residents that would be less likely to view children as necessary family labor, several were from rural areas in Oudomxay Province (Escoffier-Fauveau, Souphanthong, and Pholsena 1994, 49–52).

Nonusers, on the other hand, were more likely to be physically and culturally isolated from information about birth spacing. Half lived in isolated villages with no easy access to district or provincial clinics. The other half, though, lived near such facilities, but none of the medical staff spoke their languages. Furthermore, the Oudomxay Khmu women interviewed worked either in their swidden field or the village, had no access to information about contraception, never went to market, and were therefore dependent on their husbands or husbands' relatives for any purchases including contraceptives. Nearly all the nonusers were midland or upland Lao living patrilocally and were culturally obligated to produce sons (Escoffier-Fauveau, Souphanthong, and Pholsena 1994, 52–57). Few of the interviewed upland or midland women felt that they could choose to limit their fertility, though three young women claimed that they would have a tubectomy after having enough children (Escoffier-Fauveau, Souphanthong, and Pholsena 1994, 56).[6] This study provides an excellent example of how female power affects women's life options. In general, some urbanized ethnic Lao women seem to have the power and information necessary to plan their family size, but few other women have that luxury.

Childbirth

Pregnancy, childbirth, and caring for nursing babies consume enormous amounts of female energy. Inadequate nutrition and short birth intervals ensure that each birth further depletes mothers' bodies as women lose teeth to calcium deficiencies and are always tired from iron-deficiency anemia. Two decades ago the "average" woman married before her seventeenth birthday, bore eight babies, and had at least five living children (C. Ireson 1969). The situation as recorded in small sample surveys is almost unchanged today. The Luang Prabang women I interviewed who were thirty-five or older had, on the average, borne seven babies and still had five living children (C. Ireson 1990). Similarly, Bolikhamsay women who had finished their child-bearing had given birth eight times over a seventeen-year period and had five to six living children (C. Ireson 1989b, 21). As mentioned in Chapter 2, two other sample surveys found that women over fifty had given birth an average of eight to nine times with an average birth interval of less than two years (UNICEF 1992, 98). Khmu women, one study revealed, tended to have the shortest birth interval, in some cases as short as fourteen months (Phanjaruniti 1994, 45). The average age of first pregnancy varies somewhat by ethnic group, according to this study, with Hmong girls becoming pregnant first at sixteen years, Khmu at seventeen, and ethnic Lao at eighteen years (Phanjaruniti 1994, 45). Some women bear as many as twelve children, with twenty-one births being the "record" known to my women's union colleagues. Women in remote areas have more difficulties than those closer to towns. A small study of midland and lowland women in a poor mountainous district of Savannakhet Province estimated that women in that district who married at the average age of seventeen and survived their reproductive years would have the following "average" reproductive experience: twelve to thirteen pregnancies producing nine live births, with only three to four children surviving early childhood (Xenos 1991, 125–26).

High fertility, even with high mortality, does ensure the generational continuity of families and ethnic groups, but at the cost of great human suffering. The cumulative effect of many births, short birth intervals, and increasingly risky births after age thirty-five is high levels of maternal death, depletion of women's bodies, and low birth-weight babies. UNICEF (1991a, 7) estimates that 75 percent of pregnant women are anemic and attribute about 10 percent of maternal deaths to underlying iron deficiency. Poor diet and excessive physical work during pregnancy exacerbate the situation, contributing to "intrauterine malnutrition, fetal loss and low birth weight" (Hort 1991, 3). An estimated 30–40 percent of all births in rural areas produce low birth-weight babies (Kripps 1984, 4).

Especially important in rural areas is the impact of high fertility on women's health, women's productive labor contribution, and the family cycle. Later stages of pregnancy, childbirth and recovery from childbirth, and the nursing and care required by babies interfere with women's ability to produce for subsistence and sale while increasing family subsistence needs. The regular loss of children during early childhood prolongs the "difficult" stage of the family cycle when children are borne and cared for, but are too young to assist with household production (Xenos 1991).

Many pregnant rural women, especially poor women and Khmu women, often work in fields and forest until labor begins, while pregnant ethnic Lao women continue working at their usual tasks, but with less intensity. Over 90 percent of village women give birth at home with the assistance of a family member, though a much higher percentage of urban women give birth in a hospital or at home with the assistance of a trained birth attendant (Hort 1991, 3; Lao PDR CPC 1993). Over one-third of the respondents in a national survey reported that they had no assistance during delivery (Lao PDR CPC 1993). Ethnic Lao and Hmong women are often assisted by husbands, while Khmu women occasionally give birth alone and in the forest. While husbands and older women may prepare necessities and assist with the birth, in no rural group are umbilical cord-cutting instruments sterilized, nor do women regularly receive pre-natal or post-natal care. Informants in two Khmu villages estimated that one-third of village babies die during or shortly after birth (Phanjaruniti 1994, 51). The custom of "lying over the fire" after birth widely practiced throughout Laos legitimates several days of recuperation from childbirth. During this period the new mother and her baby stay in bed with a small fire (or an electric heater in urban areas) lit under the bed while the mother drinks liters of warm fluids every day. Friends and relatives visit the mother and baby in bed. Poor women may return to work a week or two after birth, though most women of all ethnic groups report a month of full rest before returning to work (Phanjaruniti 1994, 53).

Child Care

A mother's burden of domestic and productive work affects how she will carry out her child caretaking responsibilities, particularly in villages or households with precarious food security. Furthermore, a mother's workload affects whether daughters are allowed to attend school.

Mothers have major responsibility for the care of their children, but they most commonly delegate the care of weaned children to an older daughter or the child's grandmother. Older sons and grandfathers occasionally also care for young children (see Photo 7.2). When fathers are home, they often play affectionately with their babies or instruct older children, but take little responsibility otherwise. However, one author reports a different pattern. When a new baby is born into the Hmong families studied, the father takes over the care and instruction of the next youngest child. The child goes everywhere with his or her father. Although sometimes this child must soon yield its place with the father to a younger child, the father often cares for this child until it is five years old (Lemoine 1972, 169–70). However, a more recent study of two Hmong villages in Houa Phan Province does not find that fathers are significant child caretakers (Phanjaruniti 1994).

Infants are carried in cloth slings wrapped around the body of the child carer. The infant's needs are met as soon as they are perceived. Weaned children, however, are expected to meet their own needs much of the time and are not pampered. Babies, sometimes along with an older caretaking child, accompany mothers to the fields, where they can be left in the shade of a small "field house" while the mother works. They are also carried into the forest when mothers gather shoots and leaves, and taken to the garden where there may also be a shady place where they can be left on a mat.

The Houa Phan study finds similar child caregivers for households of each ethnic group (see Table 7.1). By the time a child is three months old, most women have returned to work in field and forest. Poor women may return to work more quickly, carrying the infant with them. All ethnic Lao children in the Houa Phan villages studied attend school, but some care for their younger siblings during school breaks and after school. Women in Houa Phan Khmu villages return to work after about one to two months, leaving the baby with a grandparent or carrying the baby to the fields for up to a year. After that they will leave the weaned child with a relative or older daughter. Most Khmu girls care for children and do household chores rather than attend school. Hmong mothers maintain their primary caretaking role for up to two years,

PHOTO 7.2   This retired Lao Lue man of Khone Kham cheerfully cares for his grandchild.

though an older daughter may accompany the mother and baby to the fields to help with caregiving while the mother works. A child older than two, however, is left in the village with other caretakers. "*Taking care of younger siblings is the main reason that prevents girls from going to school*" (Phanjaruniti 1994, 11; emphasis in original).

TABLE 7.1 Primary Child Caregivers by Age of Child

Age of Child	Primary Caregiver
0 to 3 months	Mother
3 months to 3 years	Grandparent or older sibling (usually female); mother if no grandparent or sibling is available
3 to 6 years	Same as 3 months to 3 years; preschool teacher (if available)
6 to 8 years	Child goes to school or becomes a caregiver

Source: Phanjaruniti 1994, 10.

Infants and children must survive basic home-birthing conditions and gastrointestinal and respiratory illnesses, but they are valued. They serve important family labor and social security functions. They learn early to take care of themselves and to help their parents with household chores by carrying water, stoking the cooking fire, steaming rice, and gathering forest foods (Phanjaruniti 1994, 34). Gender differences in work and play are visible in early childhood. Girls begin simple household work as young as five years and become quite proficient by eight. Girls, more often than boys, carry water, cook, feed poultry, and care for toddlers. Girls may also begin learning to sew at this age, though ethnic Lao girls usually do not begin to weave until they are nearly adolescents. Already girls are beginning to learn how to manage the variety of reproduction, household, and production tasks that will confront them as adults. Boys of the same age, on the other hand, may help by fetching water, forest foods, and wood for toy making. Older Lao boys may begin herding the family water buffalo. Both boys and girls are considered full-fledged laborers in mid-adolescence.

Parents' conceptions of child growth and learning vary by ethnic group, according to Phanjaruniti (1994). A number of Hmong and most Lao parents believe that children's development depends on how they have been trained and taught by their parents, though many also believe that children over age three can develop on their own, learning through friends and the environment. Khmu parents' conceptions of child learning, however, are more related to parents' (especially mothers') needs for assistant workers. These parents are unable to spend much time with their young children and are most concerned about whether and when their children can meet their own needs and begin to carry some of the heavy subsistence work burden (Phanjaruniti 1994, 17–18, 20). Most clearly among the Khmu, a mother's workload affects how she is able to care for her children.

PHOTO 7.3 The cooperative child-care center in Khone Kham enabled some mothers to work without also watching or carrying their children.

Child-Care Centers

The first child-care centers were established under government mandate in province and district center towns for civil servants' children, but village cooperatives were also encouraged to develop cooperative child care. In one district center, I saw smiling, confident five-year olds play circle games in the schoolyard, while, on the other side of town, babies awoke from their naps in the child-care center. In 1985, two young nursing mothers in the cooperative village of Khone Kham cared for their own and others' youngsters in a bamboo building near the center of the village. Hanging crib baskets provided napping space, while children played on bamboo mats, bathed in a metal dishpan, or toddled through a nearby open area under the watchful eye of their supervisors (see Photo 7.3). The children were clean and active, and the centers, while lacking supplies, seemed to provide a safe and acceptable alternative to care by grandparents or older siblings. In the centers with trained workers,

PHOTO 7.4   In nursery schools and kindergartens with trained teachers, young children learn songs and dances celebrating important people in Lao history, like these girls in Savannakhet Province.

children learn cooperation, sharing, and respect for others, as well as learning songs and stories about important figures in Lao revolutionary history (see Photo 7.4).

By 1990, agricultural cooperatives had been abandoned. The child-care centers supervised by young mothers and older grandmothers at Khone Kham and other cooperative villages had disappeared and child caretaking had reverted to traditional forms. Some villagers, though, changed their child caretaking practices as a result of their experience with child-care centers. One Houa Phan Khmu village, for example, had not traditionally used extended family members for child care, but after its experience with a cooperative child-care center, it began using grandparents and other relatives as child caretakers after the cooperative era (Phanjaruniti 1994, 13). Continued development of child-care programs may benefit both girls and women, enabling girls to stay in school and lightening women's heavy and, during the agricultural season, relentless workload.

Relationship of Child Care to Work

In order to carry out all of their activities, women schedule their activities to minimize interference by children. They often labor long hours during the night or early morning during heavy work seasons. For example, Sieng Lom women rise hours before dawn during tobacco season to shred tobacco so children do not interfere or become exposed to the fumes or the sticky tars covering their parents' hands and clothing. Also, during cotton season, the women of Na Fai may spin far into the night while others sleep. Spinning wheels fascinate young children who can easily make a mess of the newly spun thread, so the late night timing of spinning activities avoids this problem. The more noisy tasks of ginning and fluffing, though, must be carried out during the day. One excellent weaver of Na Fai was demonstrating the traditional cotton gin made of two hardwood rollers on a frame with a hand crank. As she began to insert the raw cotton and crank the gin, the lively baby sitting on her lap started to "help" her. She pulled him away from the rollers and back onto her lap several times before quitting in disgust. The incident led to a passionate discussion about the value of a child-care center, an amenity not yet enjoyed by Na Fai women (see Chapters 4 through 6 for other examples).

Childbirth and child care affect women's health and productivity. The most difficult time in the family cycle of two-generation households is when the couple has only young children, but must produce subsistence for themselves and their children. Government policy changes on birth control, banning it after 1975 and then reinstating it in 1988 along with a pilot birth-spacing program, may have affected both women's health and productivity. A well-conceived national birth-spacing program could have dramatic effects on women's lives and perhaps on other problems exacerbated by increasing population density (e.g., decreasing land availability, deforestation, over-hunting). While the decline of cooperatives presaged the opening of economic opportunities to a number of Laotian women, the occasional cooperative child-care center also disappeared, returning child care mainly to mothers and their daughters.

Family, Kin, and Community Relations

Kin groups or the household itself may provide some women with the resources they need to control some aspects of their lives. These resources traditionally may take the form of inheritance, land, labor, or allies in cases of conflict. In Vientiane, the capital city, marriages are solidifying alliances between old and new elites. A number of children of the Party leadership married children of the "old elite" who stayed after 1975, thus consolidating a national elite by uniting politically, economically, and culturally important families (Stuart-Fox 1986b). In rural areas that experienced much migration after the end of the war in 1975, marriages may also serve to link families previously unknown to each other, though there is no research to detail this process.

Traditionally, as noted in Chapter 3, most ethnic Lao women remain in their natal communities after they marry and generally keep the family purse. On the other hand, Khmu and Hmong women nearly always move to their husbands' villages, often living and working under the direct supervision of their mothers-in-law, and usually do not keep the family money. These general marriage patterns have not changed, though changes in ideology, law, and opportunity have impacted some aspects of family and kin relations during the periods of socialism and economic liberalization.

Ideology and Family

Ideals of the new socialist person and the new socialist family have been a regular feature of the socialist revolution in Laos (see Evans 1990, 1–4). The ideal socialist is patriotic, technically and managerially competent, morally upright, and selflessly devoted to the greater social good. Many of the structural changes initiated by the socialist leadership (agricultural cooperatives, state farms, state stores, an extensive bureaucracy) required the existence of these ideal people for success. The creation of socialist families to assist in the evolution of this ideal-type person was assigned to the Lao Women's Association as part of their task to "build socialism." Women were enjoined to be good wives and good mothers. Such a wife or mother, in socialist terms, would foster proper socialist hard work and selflessness among family members, especially her husband, and encourage her children to serve the state and continue their schooling. Women's units in work places and some village women's unions were the main recipients of the campaign for the Three Goods and Two Duties. Husbands were not so easily reached through this campaign, although the campaign included the injunction that the husband should "help" his wife. Needless to say, rhetoric did not change either family structure or behavior. Some laws and changes in opportunities, though, may yet have some effect on families in all three ethnic groups.

Laws, Governance, and Family

Decrees during the socialist period and laws, decrees, and the constitution during the liberalization period contain possible seeds of family change, though enforcement mechanisms are still lacking. During the socialist period polygyny was outlawed, though existing unions were still recognized. The right to divorce was written into law. High bride prices and extravagant weddings were discouraged. In fact, local Party branches sometimes sponsored group weddings of local cadre. Most of these changes continued into the period of economic liberalization. In addition, inheritance law specified that, where no will had been prepared, children should receive equal portions of the estate from their parents, although "all citizens have the right to turn over or bestow or establish a will devolving their properties" as they wish before their death (Inheritance Law, Article 32, 1990). Property law stipulated that, upon divorce, women and men retained rights to the assets they brought to the marriage (either owned before marriage or received as an individual inheritance) and that conjugal property should be equally divided unless there are extenuating circumstances (e.g., misuse of conjugal property).

Polygyny was not unusual among all ethnic groups in the past, but seems to be uncommon today. In six villages studied in Houa Phan Province, only two Hmong men were reported to have two wives (Phanjaruniti 1994, 40). Census data obtained locally for 154 Hmong households in the Nong Het district of Xieng Khouang indicate that only seven of 200 marriages (including husbands and wives of all ages) were polygynous in 1990 (R. Ireson 1990, 16). In Houa Phan, villagers suggested several reasons for the decline in polygyny. First, in 1978 the government initiated a campaign to end polygyny. Second, the decline of opium addiction among men has enabled more men to be effective field workers, making a second wife for farm labor less necessary. Third, having multiple wives advertises a man's wealth. Under socialism it was politically inappropriate to be wealthy. Finally, young people are now included in consultations about their future spouse and are more likely to be satisfied in their marriages (Phanjaruniti 1994, 40).

Although property and inheritance laws now clearly allow for female inheritance and landownership, practices in some villages have abrogated women's traditional rights to land. For example, in one village near Vientiane, village officials registered all land in the name of the household head.[7] Village women, however, had a clear picture of who had inherited the land in this village and who had not (noted by Evans in 1982–83; 1990, 246 n.6). Trankell notices a similar pattern in villages along Route 13 between Vientiane and Paksane. She says that paddy "landholdings are in this village as elsewhere recorded under the name of the male household head, even where it is recognized as female property" (Trankell 1993, 39). Only female household heads, usually widows, have land registered in their own names, Trankell observes. This practice is likely either to provoke future land conflict or to effectively disown female heirs. One of the preceding incidents formally "disowning" Lao women's landholding occurred during the socialist period, while the other was documented during economic liberalization, though it may have occurred earlier.

Socialism and Family

Cooperatives and Family. Traditional authority within the ethnic Lao family was threatened by agricultural cooperativization. Traditionally, the senior economically active man in the household directed the family's agricultural work, particularly work in paddy farming. He controlled the timing of each stage of the process each year, directing the labor of family members as well as family draft animals. Traditionally also, there was a tendency for women to inherit or to eventually accumulate more of the paddy land than their brothers. Brothers often married women in other villages, either receiving a non-land inheritance upon marriage or selling inherited home village land to a resident family member, often a sister. Cooperatives, by usurping the control over agricultural labor and land, often threatened the authority of senior household men or the land rights of senior household women (Evans 1990, 131–32). However, few agricultural cooperatives outside the areas under long-time Pathet Lao governance (Houa Phan, Phong Saly, Oudomxay, Xieng Khouang) actually owned land and buffalo collectively. In cooperatives along the Mekong River, though, owners of land, buffalo, and other "means of production" committed their productive resources to the cooperative for as long as they were members and were given work points in return (Evans 1990, 91–94). Some village men were able to mitigate their loss of control over household labor by becoming members of the cooperative's governing committee, an option rarely open to landowning women who truly did lose control of their land when they joined the cooperative. Since agricultural cooperatives were implemented mainly in paddy farming villages, cooperative organization may have had little effect on traditional family and kinship relationships in Khmu or Hmong villages.

Traditionally, women's and men's labor in the household has been complementary. Each needed the other in order to create an economically (as well as socially) viable unit. Cooperatives offered one way for women-only or men-only households to survive in rural areas. Noi (profiled in Chapter 1), a swidden farmer and single mother, is responsible for all the work that is necessary to keep her family alive. Noi earnestly explained to an interviewer in 1986 that her hope for a better life lies in the organization of a cooperative with a child-care center. Then her child would have proper care during the day and she could exchange her labor for labor at tasks she now finds difficult. She also would not need the ten children she now desires to help with agricultural and household tasks. Unfortunately for women like Noi, agricultural cooperatives were not very successful and were abandoned in the late 1980s by nearly all cooperative villages.

Literacy, Education, and Family. Early goals of the new government included the equal development of town and countryside with schooling and health care available to all. While health-care initiatives did not bear fruit, the adult literacy campaign and the construction of rural schools did begin to make literacy and educational opportunities available to a larger number of rural residents. The rural expansion of schooling has continued with increased foreign development assistance from capitalist and multilateral sources since the mid-1980s.

For years some rural children, mainly ethnic Lao boys, left home after completing their studies at the local school to continue their education in towns, cities, and even in other countries. While an educated son may return to his natal village for a while, he more likely will obtain a job. In fact, this is one of the most common aspirations rural parents have for their children (Phanjaruniti 1994). This male mobility pattern affects ethnic Lao family structure very little, since young men customarily leave their home village to "travel" and often marry and reside in their wives' villages. The family structure of Khmu or, especially, Hmong families would be more strongly affected by this mobility, but not all the sons of one family are encouraged to continue their education. One or more are selected to remain a farmer and care for their parents. These sons do not continue their schooling.

Ethnic Lao girls have been more likely than girls of other ethnic groups to take advantage of available schooling, while few Hmong girls do so. The schooling of Khmu and Hmong girls is of low priority for families because (1) unmarried girls are valuable laborers and (2) any investment in a girl's education is lost to her natal household since her labor and education benefit her husband's family, not her natal family. Educational investment in girls would pay off only if educational costs could be recouped in an increased bride price. So far, education does not seem to enter bride price negotiations, and bride prices have reportedly been declining under pressure from local government, particularly during the socialist period. However, the number of Laotian girls receiving some education is increasing. More young women are literate in Lao and knowledgeable in basic arithmetic, skills needed to convert economic change into personal opportunities.

Effects of Economic Liberalization on Families

Opportunities that are already beginning to affect some rural families include those for education as already discussed and for alternate economic activities like marketing, trucking, wage work, and factory work in cities. Economic opportunities that withdraw one or more household adults from agricultural work or which draw migrants to or from rural areas can have a dramatic effect on the power and authority of adult family members, the division of labor between them, and the composition of the family itself. Håkangård and Trankell, viewing the same reported changes in households along Route 13, came to different conclusions about the implications of these changes for women. Håkangård (1992) emphasized the opportunities that a number of women were able to create for themselves, as rice mill owners, as storekeepers or small-scale merchants, and as producers of goods for sale. Trankell (1993), on the other hand, focused on the greater number and more lucrative opportunities available to men.

Håkangård describes the changes in household division of labor accompanying women's successful shopkeeping activities. Husbands often assist in the business and take care of children and domestic responsibilities during their wives' regular trips to purchase more goods. Not only did these successful small-scale merchants divest themselves of their work in paddy and swidden, traditionally carried out under the supervision of their husbands with husbands selling any surplus rice, they also gained more mobility, financial decision-making power, and assistance with their nonproductive domestic work. Both husbands and wives were happy, though, because the household was more financially secure (Håkangård 1992, 39). The economic success of a woman shopkeeper or merchant translates into a secure position as a decision maker in the household as well as the business, with more sharing of domestic work.

On the other hand, poor women and women whose husbands left agriculture often had more difficult lives. The workload of both groups of women increased. Poor women had to work harder to pay for land rental (in either money or rice), as well as to produce enough food for household needs. Their husbands were in equally more difficult work and financial straits (Trankell 1993). Poor women continued carrying a heavy domestic workload. A number of men have left traditional agriculture to take advantage of a variety of opportunities available to them, especially in commercial mechanized agriculture, transport, and long-distance marketing. As men specialized, the women in their households became completely responsible for supervising and implementing family food production.[8] Some of these women farmers were able to sharecrop their land so others produced some of the household rice needs, or to hire agricultural laborers, if their husbands' ventures were successful and if their husbands shared their profits with their households.

Finally, the reconstructed road did not help with transportation needs in the village and farm, the hauling and carrying most often done by women. Even though women might now be able to travel to Vientiane in ninety minutes rather than three or four hours, in many households they are still responsible for up to four hours of work per day hauling water and firewood under the same conditions as before (Trankell 1993, 84). In the most prosperous families, though, new products ease even this burden. One woman reports, for example, that she now has an "electric cooker" and does not use firewood anymore (Håkangård 1992, 30).

Improved transportation along Route 13 has not increased geographic mobility in roadside villages. Most villagers maintain their rice fields while searching out and developing other income-earning opportunities like temporary wage labor and production and sale of products made from local goods (baskets, mats). Only a few villagers commute to Vientiane daily for work. The area is experiencing in-migration rather than out-migration. In the seven villages studied, a total of seventy-eight families have moved in during the last two years, while only three families have moved out (Håkangård 1992, 29). In addition, twenty-five road construction workers married girls in these villages, and half of these young men have quit construction work to become farmers. None of the women or men interviewed wanted to move. One village man reports that his village is "good because it is easy to find food and catch fish. There are plenty of . . . things and it is not far from the big road" (Håkangård 1992, 29). His is the village that experienced the most in-migration during the previous two years! In short, many traditional family patterns are being maintained in the villages along the road, even though the division of labor has shifted in some families, sometimes in ways that enable women to exercise more power in their households and more autonomy in their communities.

The survey did not identify the number of farm family offspring that had left the village for education or for work in Vientiane. It is possible that poor women's work burden is heavier because some young women are migrating to Vientiane for work in Vientiane garment factories and other growing industries and services. The growth of industry and business in Vientiane is not lost on villagers in the nearby hinterland. They often have access to radios, televisions, and relatives in the capital city for information. Although wages are very low and working conditions are poor in most of these new jobs, young women from the countryside are apparently attracted by these new opportunities. This is a new phenomenon, but if large numbers of young women leave the countryside, rural ethnic Lao family structure will truly be forced to change. There may be few young women to "recruit" young men into aging village households and lives of farming. Farm family self-sufficiency in rice may be threatened, while old people, perhaps caring for their grandchildren, may be supported by remittances from their urban working children. So far, though, major changes apparently have not disrupted the domestic and family lives of most rural ethnic Lao women.

Impact of Changing Opportunities on Khmu and Hmong Families

Ethnic Lao women are better positioned to take advantage of opportunities offered by economic liberalization (see Chapter 4), but a few Khmu and Hmong women are beginning to exploit commercial opportunities as well. This may, in turn, affect the division of labor and decision making within their families. Khmu and particularly Hmong family structures were altered in the early socialist period when marriage of multiple wives became illegal. Two other current or impending changes will potentially affect Khmu and/or Hmong family structure in the future: the education of girls and the development of independent income sources for some women. These changes may enable Khmu and Hmong women to develop some areas of autonomy within the household.

In short, while traditional family patterns are still intact, a number of factors seem to be affecting family and kin relations. Laws affecting polygynous marriage and girls' increasing literacy and school attendance seem likely to have a positive effect on women's domestic power. Socialist ideology about the "ideal socialist family" and economic opportunities that may affect geographical mobility and the division of labor by gender may have had both positive and negative effects on women's access to resources in the family. Finally, land registration practices that appear to disenfranchise female heirs and the diversion of girls' time from family labor to schooling may negatively affect the domestic power of adult women.

Conclusion

Women's domestic power as decision makers or as directors of domestic activities is often a reflection of their activities and resources in other arenas. Child-bearing and domestic activities are essential to household continuity and functioning, and require much of women's time and energy. But in all ethnic groups these activities are devalued and do not contribute to women's autonomy, power, or authority in or out of the domestic sphere. Traditional family organization and kin networks can subordinate or support women's control of domestic resources.

While ethnic Lao men are still the formal heads of households, temples, and villages, some level of female authority and even extra-household leadership is currently evident in many households and villages, as it has been traditionally. It is still the case, though, that Lao women exercising more intra-household (and even extra-household) power are often those living in their natal communities and older women in established and prosperous families.

Khmu women still have few areas of autonomy or power that might enable them to exercise domestic power and decision making. The involvement of some Khmu women in development projects, education or literacy training, and sales of their own or others' production may eventually enable more of these women to function with some level of autonomy within the household. Most Khmu women, however, are hampered by their weak position as in-marrying spouses and by a level of poverty that requires them to devote all of their energy to day-to-day subsistence. It may be possible for a few Khmu women leaders to emerge from traditional sources: female shamans or female relatives of Lao-assimilated Khmu leaders.

The authority of men over women continues to be a constant theme in Hmong social organization. Men's monopoly on power is so complete that even women's union projects meant to empower women are often channeled through the village head (see Chapter 8 for an example). Girls' power still seems limited to one or two years of sexual autonomy. A Hmong woman's powerlessness in her household after marriage is reinforced by her position as a laborer in her husband's family fields and by her importance as a producer of children for his clan. The limited power of the mother-in-law—to direct the training and domestic labor of her sons' wives—does not generalize to arenas beyond the household. A few Hmong women are "called" to be shamans, but this does not seem to have a positive effect on Hmong women in general. Girls' education, women's literacy training, and women's control of some income through sales of household production seem paltry tools to breach men's firm control of household women. Young wives suffering at the hands of their husbands or in-laws still commit suicide, a "solution" that only underlines their continued domestic powerlessness.

Significantly, the basis for and forms of Laotian women's domestic power may have shifted, first with socialism and now with economic liberalization. Commercial activity, perhaps coupled with production for sale, seems to be the major source of women's domestic power today. But it may be that the ideology of gender equality, women's greater "public" visibility as cooperative members, and the activities of the Lao Women's Union workers—all clearly legacies of the socialist period—have facilitated the development of women's power in a variety of other arenas. Women are freer to engage in these economic activities if they have access to some labor-saving technologies, such as piped water systems and rice mills, that reduce their otherwise heavy household maintenance workload. They may also be more competent entrepreneurs with some education. This shift is more evident among ethnic Lao women but may also be occurring among women of other ethnic groups. Today, younger, more-educated women who are exploiting a variety of economic opportunities and perhaps even "spacing" their children are also likely to share family decision making with their husbands.

Women in all groups are still more responsible than men for everyday domestic tasks. Some of these tasks, particularly rice milling and water carrying, have been alleviated by rice mills or water systems, respectively. These improvements are nearly always the result of improved infrastructure or direct project assistance to the villages. Such improvements, which began in a few villages before 1988, have markedly increased because of more village-oriented foreign assistance to governmental units like the Lao Women's Union. As was demonstrated in Chapter 4, ethnic Lao women are better positioned to use these amenities to increase their own production and, as a result, to augment their own resources.

Frequent child-bearing, deliberately fostered under socialism, still depletes women's energy and ensures that nearly all younger women care for infants and young children. The few autonomous and literate rural women who use contraceptives demonstrate that high fertility among the ethnic Lao could drop markedly with simply the continuation of trends already under way: enrollment of girls in schools and expansion of embryonic birth-spacing programs, especially if advertised widely on radios, televisions, and traveling video shows.

Child care, while shared with cooperative child-care centers in a few villages during the socialist period, continues to be primarily the mother's responsibility. Furthermore, some child caretakers (older daughters) are now students for part of the workday.

Family and kin relations are changing somewhat under the influence of changing laws, governmental practices, economic activities, and the increased availability of schooling. Fewer polygynous marriages, girls' increasing school attendance, and the increasing diversity of rural economic activities empower some women, though the partial loss of a daughter's labor power and land registration in the male name disadvantage some women in new ways. The development of the national Lao Women's Union reflects these changes in rural women's power but also enables some women to take advantage of economic, educational, and social changes.

Notes

1. While the domestic/public model of female subordination is still a powerful model in social anthropology, it has come under attack. In particular, it has been attacked for the assumed "naturalness" and universality of the mother-child unit, and for the arbitrary division between domestic or private and public that may be easy to see in Western societies, but which may not exist in other societies. See Moore (1988, especially 21–24, 31–35) for useful reviews of the discussion and debate surrounding this theoretical position. I do not emphasize this model since "public" and "domestic" spheres overlap in village Laos.

2. Another study in neighboring Savannakhet Province found that villagers collect wild yams for consumption when no other food is available (Douangdara et al. 1991, 60).

3. Phou Thit Pheung is profiled in Chapter 4.

4. Oakley (1974), Rosaldo (1974), Sacks (1979), and others (see Moore 1988 for review) associate women's subordination with child-bearing and child-rearing.

5. Unfortunately, local male interpreters were used in highland villages.

6. Sacks (1979) notes that women's lack of power is strongest in societies where the role of "wife" is more salient than the role of "sister". In the upland and midland Lao groups surveyed for contraceptive use, the role of "wife" clearly predominates, determining the nature of women's other daily relationships. In matrilocal ethnic Lao groups, however, women are embedded in a network of relationships with their own relatives. While the husband-wife relationship is important, it is but one of several important role relationships enacted every day.

7. Land is always registered in a man's name, unless there is no man in the household.

8. See Chapter 5 for further discussion of the feminization of agriculture.

8

Politics of Gender and Development: Transformation of the Lao Women's Union

The Lao Women's Union (LWU) formally organizes women at all levels, providing them with resources and authority through political education and projects, and sponsoring activities that empower women. As a result the women's union has been able to provide some alternative sources of political power to replace the informal power and traditional functions that were displaced by the consolidation of the state and by increasing formalization of political and social activities. The evolution of the Lao Women's Union mirrors some of the changes in rural women's lives since 1975.

Liberation of Laotian women, as in several other socialist revolutions, was initially subordinated to other nation-building tasks.[1] The Lao Women's Union is one of several national mass organizations. It is ostensibly responsible for women's mobilization to support Party and national goals and for women's emancipation. That is, the union has been responsible for women's political education, and for advising and recruiting women from capital city civil servants to remote village subsistence farmers to build a new socialist society. With increasing foreign aid and economic liberalization in the late 1980s, the women's union was able to broaden its official programs to include training and assistance projects targeting village women. Before the founding of the Lao PDR in 1975, the precursor Lao Patriotic Women's Association organized women to support the revolution. The association was initially established by the wives of revolutionary leaders, some of them leaders in their own right.[2]

The royalist-socialist coalition government of 1973–75 was gradually dominated by the socialists, reflecting the outcome of the war in Vietnam and Cambodia as well as in Laos. Many Women's Association employees moved to Vientiane, along with other Pathet Lao employees, administrators, and Party members. The Lao People's Democratic Republic was officially established on December 2, 1975. The strengthening of women's unions at all levels occurred after the main push to consolidate communist administrative control over the entire country. In the early years of liberation, many soldiers were demobilized, and internal refugees returned to their former villages or established new villages near their old homes. Provincial and district Party organizations and administrative committees were organized and began functioning. Village administration was similarly reorganized and political education began at all levels. Collective work groups were instituted in many villages as precursors to village agricultural and marketing cooperatives. Village marketing cooperatives collectively bought tools and items needed in household and farming activities and sold mainly rice. Agricultural cooperatives, and the work groups that organizationally preceded such cooperatives, were almost entirely devoted to paddy rice farming. The consolidation of the Pathet Lao military and political victory in 1975 and the establishment of functioning government throughout the nation were tremendous tasks, especially since the country had never before been unified under any government with an effective presence at the village level in all regions (R. Ireson 1988).

The result was increasing formalization of power even at the village level with men assigned positions of responsibility in the newly created structures, often taking over functions previously informally carried out by women, such as conflict resolution and commercial activity. Since 1975 a number of groups have been formally organized: village administrative committees, village cooperatives, Party organization to the grassroots, state-run or state-controlled marketing, and projects run by government officials or technicians. Few members of these "official" groups and almost none of their leaders have been women, nor has there been pressure to include women or women's viewpoints in their decisions and activities. Thus, as the new government matured, it marginalized women.

Organizing Women During the Socialist Period

The fledgling administration, anxious to begin governing, appointed Dr. Outhaki head of health services for Vientiane Province in one of its first appointments in November 1975. Since this unit did not exist, she spent six months hiring staff, locating supplies, planning, and organizing activities and facilities. She supervised the staff and activities of the provincial hospital and district clinics. In addition, she organized training courses in nutrition, sanitation, and women's and children's health, often planning and implementing these programs with the Vientiane Women's Association. For the first few years of her tenure as health director, Dr. Outhaki also participated in the governing committee of this association. To lighten the work of her staff, the central health office provided child care for more than twenty children, though as the staff aged, the need for such service declined.

Supplies, medicines, and equipment were always in short supply, yet during the decade-and-a-half of her service as head of Vientiane Province health department, and then of the Vientiane municipality health department, she reports that disease and infant mortality declined markedly, though perhaps mainly in the municipality (Outhaki Choulamany, personal communication, 1993).

Lao Women's Association officials also began working in a completely changed context in 1975 as "the Lao revolution shifted from the stage of national democratic revolution to socialist revolution" (LWU and Boupha 1984, 21). At that point the Lao Women's Association, as a mass organization of the Party, became a "component part of the proletarian dictatorship [and] a body which rallies and educates the Lao women of all ethnic groups and social strata to carry out the tasks of national defense and socialist transformation and construction, advancing toward communism" (LWU and Boupha 1984, 30). National liberation and Pathet Lao governmental control had been won in military and political battles, but the tasks of creating, defending, and governing a new socialist nation still remained. The Party directive to the women's association—to "build socialism through national defense and socialist transformation and construction"—is a clear indicator that women were expected to labor in the public sphere, as well as in the domestic sphere, particularly in support of the military and projects of national priority. In this new stage, the main functions of the women's organization were to educate women of various ethnic groups in order to raise their socialist consciousness and knowledge in all fields; to bring into full play their right to (collective) mastery in the management of the economy, the state, and society; and to bring about equality between women and men and to truly emancipate women (LWU and Boupha 1984, 22).

Like other citizens, a woman educated in socialism and working together with other like-minded women would be able to carry out the three aspects of this new stage of revolution: socialist economic transformation, scientific and technological development, and ideological and cultural metamorphosis (Phomvihan 1984, 7).[3] In 1982, Kaysone Phomvihan, General Secretary of the Party, also said that

> In the new revolutionary stage, work among women is aimed at achieving equality between men and women, real liberation for women, thus enabling them to contribute to the building of socialism. We should assist our women through education work, to enhance their political consciousness, their knowledge in all fields, promote their role of mastery, participate in social activities and in the management of the affairs of the country, especially in jobs suitable to women such as those in health services, education, and so on. (Phomvihan 1982)

The Party realized that without the occupational contributions of women, the country would be able neither to "liberate the production forces [nor] to consolidate and perfect the new relations of production" (Phomvihan 1984, 7), though Phomvihan's limited vision of women's "real liberation" is also evident in this speech. Throughout the writings and speeches of this period, lowland Lao women's traditional commercial skills are ignored or indirectly denigrated, though the agricultural skills and labor of women of all ethnic groups are emphasized. While not mentioning women's traditional marketing role, Phomvihan lectures, "All Lao women must thoroughly understand that the individual economy, the capitalist economy are the very roots of women's poverty and backwardness; it is only socialism that can provide such fundamental conditions as socio-economic, material and spiritual conditions for the actual emancipation of women" (Phomvihan 1984, 8). On the other hand, he praises women for their agricultural work.

> Our women . . . have taken an active part in rehabilitating production in hard conditions, in building irrigation works, multiplying crops, applying new techniques to agricultural production, practicing intensive farming, and increasing production output. Especially our women are very active in the movement of agricultural cooperativization. (Phomvihan 1984, 3)

Problems During the Socialist Period

In spite of women's collective and individual efforts before 1975, the members of the Lao Women's Association brought many unresolved problems with them to Vientiane and, on their arrival, encountered a wary populace that had lived under Royalist control and influence during the American war years. Nonetheless, the Lao Women's Association continued its organizational and educational activities and, with the First Women's Congress in 1984, became the Lao Women's Union. Even after 1984, though, problems of sexism, organizational structure, and technical skills remained.

Sexism

Sexism persisted, perpetrated by both men and women. The General Secretary of the Party revealed that "there are comrades in Party and administrative committees at different levels who . . . disregard women and do not pay . . . attention to . . . developing the great abilities of women" (Phomvihan 1984, 7). Similarly, many women are still "strongly affected with inferiority complex[es], with the tendency to depend on others, and fail to make progress . . . to become mistresses of society and to materialize equality between men and women" (Phomvihan 1984, 7). Furthermore, the emphasis on women's family roles in the Three Goods and Two Duties slogan of the women's union (details follow) was hardly a program for revolutionary change in gender roles.[4]

The paucity of women in management and administrative positions illustrates this sexism (Phomvihan 1984, 10). Only in Phong Saly and Houa Phan, that is, in the old liberated zones, can the women's association point to managerial participation. Boupha (LWU and Boupha 1984, 11) notes that in these two provinces "more than 100 women . . . have taken part in the managerial boards and auditing commissions of agricultural cooperatives." Although many women joined agricultural cooperatives as full members, outside the old liberated zones men almost completely monopolized cooperative control. In 1984 there were four female members of the fifty-three-member Party Central Committee (Stuart-Fox 1986a, 90), whereas in 1993 there were four women members among fifty-five, though two of them were alternates rather than full members (Vongsack, personal communication, 1993). In 1984 all of the leaders at all the three levels of national government were men (Stuart-Fox 1986a, 90).[5] Even at the level of ministry department director or vice-director, proportionately few women were represented: 8.0 percent in the Ministry of Agriculture, 7.7 percent in the Ministry of Health, and 9.8 percent in the Ministry of Industry (M. Viravong 1987, Table 5; 1982 statistics from the Lao Women's Union). Similarly, only eight women, all of them national or provincial women's union presidents or committee members, were elected to the eighty-five-member National Assembly in 1992 (Vongsack, personal communication, 1993; Ng, personal communication, 1993). One of these women, however, the Luang Prabang Women's Union president, was the most popular candidate in the province (Vongsack).

Weak Organizational Structure

Weakness in the organizational structure of the women's association persisted in the successor Lao Women's Union. Having struggled to organize and educate women's sections in all administrative units in the liberated zones and then in the contested areas, the association was not equal to the task of establishing a viable organization throughout the entire country. Phomvihan (1984, 4) criticized the women's union in 1984, saying that the "development of the women's organization has not kept up with the rapid growth of the revolution, and . . . its organizational system has not been perfected yet." In his critique, he also noted that the "Union, at all levels, must improve its style of work, broaden its sphere of activities, . . . observe the principle of collective leadership and individual responsibility, . . . and strengthen its relationship[s] with various branches of the State" (Phomvihan 1984, 16).

The Lao Women's Union acknowledged that the "Union's activities still lack in forms which are suitable to women of various ethnic groups, different age groups and strata, and in some places the women's movement is still discontinuous, not far-reaching and widespread, and even tapering off" (LWU and Boupha 1984, 19). The organization was still to be organized and administered from the top down according to the principles of "democratic centralism" (LWU and Boupha 1984, 31). The 1984 Political Report of the Lao Women's Union recognized that the union must expand its national-to-grassroots organizational system under the guidance of trained and motivated cadre in order to facilitate timely dissemination of Party and union directives and resolutions from the center to the grassroots (LWU and Boupha 1984, 31). By 1986, the Lao Women's Union had established a network of women's unions in villages of all provinces, though often the local unions existed only on paper. Each province had a women's union, with representatives at the district level to work with village unions.

Few Technical Skills

Women's association and women's union cadre lacked technical skills. This limited the effectiveness of women's organizers and managers. Although some women's union workers are highly skilled, like the two doctors discussed in Chapter 2, most were not. In 1984, the Party encouraged the women's union to better select and train its workers (Phomvihan 1984, 11). Phomvihan (1984, 9) urged women's union organizers to avoid "appeals with mere empty words"; to incorporate political education in specific economic, cultural, and social activities; and to solve women's specific difficulties, although most women's union workers were not qualified to offer specific training or skills to village women.

In all fairness, it must be noted that the women's organization had been expected to mobilize women to defend the country and to build socialism with little specific direction and with no budget to support women's activities. The Lao Women's Union has had a small staff, few government-supplied resources, and, not surprisingly, little political influence.[6]

Ideology: Three Goods and Two Duties

Women were authorized by Party policy and directives to improve their lives and their status, but by 1984 most women still were not exercising their rights or respecting their own capabilities, and women and men still were not equal. Members of the Women's Association Central Committee observed this and, at the First Women's Congress coined the motto regarding women's "Three Goods and Two Duties" in order to clarify the rights, responsibilities, and capabilities of good socialist women (Vongsack, personal communication, 1993).

The Three Goods include being a good citizen, a good mother, and a good wife. The Two Duties are those of national defense and socialist construction, and of women's emancipation. A good citizen studies and practices Party policies. A good citizen must learn how to read and write. Good mothers "acquire knowledge and correct viewpoints . . . [to take] good care of their children . . . in order to bring about changes in each family" since parents are children's first teachers (LWU and Boupha 1984, 28). A good mother encourages her children to study and to work responsibly; she supports her daughters' further education, rather than withdrawing them from school to do household and farm work; a good mother protects her health by having only four children (Vongsack, Khone Kham Women's Union lecture, 2 June 1986). A good wife builds a socialist family based on "conjugal love, monogamy, [and] non-exploitation; . . . a type of family in which both husband and wife work and help each other to make progress, set good examples . . . and abide by the Party policies and State laws" (LWU and Boupha 1984, 28). A good wife corrects her husband when he errs and encourages him to contribute his share to the building of a correct family life (Vongsack, Khone Kham Women's Union lecture).

Women's first duty—of national defense and socialist construction of the country—entails encouraging brothers and husbands to enlist in the army or other defense units, supporting those engaged directly in national defense, or volunteering for service in the army or other defense units. Socialist construction involves working for the socialist transformation of the economy and public services as well as the rebuilding of physical facilities destroyed or delayed by war. Billboards found in nearly all provincial capitals illustrate some of the forms "socialist construction" can take. "Work to construct reliable irrigation systems to grow and raise enough food," enjoins the billboard in front of the province party secretary's house in Sam Neua, the capital of Houa Phan Province, as stalwart billboard women help build an irrigation canal. "Lead in producing goods for market," advises a Vientiane city billboard picturing textile factory women workers as they spin, weave, and display finished lengths of cloth. "Studying is patriotic," asserts a billboard at a busy five-way intersection in Vientiane, as the female middle-school teacher depicted on the billboard addresses her class. Teaching, by implication, is also patriotic.

Women's second duty—of emancipation—was poorly elaborated and specified, though the achievement of equal rights with men seemed to be a central part of this duty. The Three Goods and Two Duties were meant as a tool to help women eliminate old habits and ways of thinking and to encourage them to study, learn, and increase their knowledge and skills so that they could then exercise their rights as citizens equal to men. Women's union activities ideally should provide women with the means to improve their lives and status.

Activities of the Lao Women's Union

The main activity of the national Lao Women's Association during this period was to organize and register as many members as possible in as many different units as possible. By 1984 the Lao Women's Association registered more than 426,000 members (the 1985 census indicates there were 975,139 women between the ages of fifteen and sixty-four in the entire country) in Party and state organizations, in units of the armed forces, in factories, enterprises, and cooperatives, and in villages. The association claimed more than 16,750 officers in local women's associations, 500 district cadres, and 160 provincial and national workers (LWU and Boupha 1984, 17). The main activities of the national association other than organizational ones were studying Party policy, celebrating festive days in ways that highlighted patriotic socialist traditions and specific examples of model women, and publishing the magazine *Lao Women*, beginning in 1979.

Some local women's unions carried out similar activities. By 1986, most village unions, if they actually met as a body, had studied[7] the Three Goods and Two Duties. Activities beyond study included traditional group activities of women and adolescent girls, such as preparing food and serving drinks for visiting dignitaries, a central activity of the Sieng Lom Village Women's Union near Luang Prabang city. Some unions carried out activities not traditional in an organized group, like jointly cultivating a 3-hectare cotton field or assisting with irrigation system construction as the Khone Kham Village Women's Union did in the central part of Luang Prabang Province. All active unions assisted the families of female-headed households, especially the families of absent soldiers or government cadre, or sent gifts or letters to soldiers. Merely belonging to a local women's union, learning the Three Goods and Two Duties, cooking for and serving guests, and supporting soldiers or women in need did not constitute the "concrete revolutionary actions" called for by Party Secretary Kaysone. While individual local unions did periodically cooperate to build infrastructure or to produce cooperatively, the national women's union was not yet able to offer a long-term plan to meet its stated goals.

With Kaysone Phomvihan's official admonition (1984, 9, 16) to the Lao Women's Union to broaden its sphere of activities, to avoid empty appeals, and to promote concrete revolutionary actions; with 1984 Party approval of a training center for Union cadre (Phomvihan 1984, 11); and with the Union's interest in seeking training help from "fraternal socialist countries" (LWU and Boupha 1984, 32), the stage was set for further change in the women's union. Two other developments, barely noted in the 1984 Union Political Report, also signaled a new direction for the Lao Women's Union. The Lao Women's Union magazine, *Lao Women*, was published with the assistance of United

Nations Children's Fund (UNICEF), while the United Nations Development Programme began in the early 1980s to support the development of a comprehensive Lao Women's Union textile project-producing export-quality textiles. Other women's union training and village development projects began in the latter part of the 1980s supported by other foreign donors.

Only two international non-governmental organizations (NGOs) sponsoring development activities in the mid-1980s worked in villages in the Lao hinterland. Their representatives, working in outlying areas with officials from ministries or committees as diverse as agriculture, health, education, and social welfare, saw that women's needs and voices were ignored by most officials. Meetings to gather information and to plan projects with village, district, and provincial officials were attended almost entirely by lowland Lao men.[8] Resulting projects such as small irrigation systems and appropriate technology prostheses for handicapped veterans responded to male concerns and needs.

In response to visits by NGO representatives to women's unions, union officials produced lists of wished-for items to help them carry out their Party-mandated tasks of political education, socialist construction, and women's emancipation. These lists included tin roofing and cement to build child-care centers, sewing machines, and, for the national union, a car to transport delegations of visiting foreign women. None of these requests were anchored in programs that might have developed women's skills or increased village production or quality of life. So international development agencies found it difficult to justify support to women's unions, while the unions struggled to meet their goals of socialist construction and women's emancipation with few resources or specific programs.

The year after the First Women's Congress, the president of the Luang Prabang Province Women's Union presented three written project proposals to a visiting representative of an NGO. The union proposals not only contained the usual wish list of supplies but also contained preliminary ideas for women's development activities in the province. The head of the Women and Child Protection Department of the national women's union subsequently expressed interest in exploring village women's needs in Luang Prabang Province in greater depth, perhaps with the hope of generating "concrete revolutionary actions" among women's unions in Luang Prabang and sparking NGO interest in women's project development. In an intensive two-week period of travel by jeep and boat, the national department head (Dr. Davone), the NGO representative (the author), and the Luang Prabang Women's Union president met with village administrative committees and local women's unions in several districts of the province. The team interviewed numerous women in their homes or field huts and discussed village needs and project ideas with provincial administrative and women's union officials. The final morning of the project development trip, after the project team had written a draft project document based on their joint experiences, Dr. Davone received project approval from the provincial party secretary and the provincial governor, who sent his approval with protestations of good will to the entire project development team. After two weeks of working together, both women's union officials and the NGO representative better understood how development activities tailored to village women's needs and interests might actualize union goals of socialist construction and women's emancipation. I, as the NGO representative, had also become more knowledgeable about women's union goals as I listened to discussions and lectures led by the union department head, while women's union officials had been exposed to a new method of learning about village women's needs, interests, and capabilities (C. Ireson 1987). The resulting project served as a pilot project of women's union/ development agency cooperation not only for its sponsors but for other agencies and women's unions. Elements of this project approach were modified and adapted by others as the ideas of Lao Women's Union leaders expanded to encompass development activities.

The development of such a model was important for two reasons: rural development was still relatively new in socialist Laos, but there were numerous examples of development projects that had no sustained impact because project decision makers had not included women. For example, the Forest Development and Watershed Management Project (1983–89)[9] trained 985 policy makers, administrators, technicians, forestry students and workers, and village leaders and workers in improved upland land use (i.e., agroforestry, fruit and forest plantation, watershed protection) with associated technologies. Very few of those trained were women. Instead, the project hired women workers to establish and maintain many aspects of the "demonstration" fields and orchards. These workers received no technologically improved tools, no special training, no consideration of their reproductive responsibilities (no child care or health care), and no salary. Instead they received food rations. Potential male workers had refused to work for no salary. These women workers were so invisible that an evaluation of their contribution to the project was not even included in the terminal project report. Also, women were rarely represented in village management committees overseeing project activities in their own villages. The terminal project report states that project progress and achievements were highly satisfactory, yet after seven years there was no discernible impact on the upland land management practices of villages in Luang Prabang Province. The trained men did not share their training and technology with other members of their families, so the women (who have major responsibilities in upland farming systems and in fruit production) continued their work and farm management as before. This project had increased some women's workloads, while reinforcing women's secondary status.[10]

Women's Organizations and Economic Liberalization

By the time of the Second Women's Congress in 1988, the New Economic Mechanism, designed to convert the subsistence or "natural" economy of most of the Lao PDR to a market economy, had been proclaimed by the Fourth Party Congress. Decrees, laws, and structures had been developed to begin this transition. Household commodity production and marketing entered the national scene as legitimate economic activities, while national prosperity and affluence were institutionalized as Party goals (Phomvihan 1988, 1, 5, 7). At the same time, development assistance from United Nations agencies, Western nations, and non-governmental organizations was increasing, though aid from fraternal socialist countries had already begun to decline.

At the Second Women's Congress, Party Secretary Kaysone noted the continued burdens of Lao women of all ethnic groups: heavy work loads, discrimination, insufficient child care, too many births too closely spaced (Phomvihan 1988, 3). He encouraged the Lao Women's Union to continue working to develop commodity production further, while working closely with grassroots groups and cultivating more competent women's union workers (Phomvihan 1988, 5–6). He urged the LWU to participate in the creation of laws to benefit women and children, as well as to observe the laws that were on the books (Phomvihan 1988, 5).

The Lao Women's Union had begun to solve difficulties and create jobs for rural women, according to its 1988 political report (LWU 1988). Elements of several projects were mentioned in the report, including a weaving training center and labor-saving amenities like rice mills, drinking water systems, and child-care centers (Part 1:7). Further, the union's Central Committee had learned that close contact with ordinary women in local women's unions was essential for union work: as women's union committees "must be cognizant of the thoughts, aspirations and level of women" so these can be conveyed to the upper levels of the union and to the Party and the state (Part 2:4, 5, 15). Future directions for the women's union until the Third Women's Congress included new emphases on basic education, socioeconomic production, birth spacing, and development projects in cooperation with fraternal socialist countries and international organizations (Part 2:4–8, 9–11). The Central Committee also enjoined women to build basic infrastructure by contributing to the construction of roads, irrigation systems, schools, hospitals, child care centers, and kindergartens (Part 2:16).

Differences between the General Party Secretary's addresses in 1984 and 1988 reflect the changes in policy and in the international and domestic climate for Lao women's development, while the two political reports demonstrate an expansion of women's union activities to include concrete development projects, as well as political education and organizational growth, supported by modification in the Three Goods and Two Duties slogan. Already, by 1986, an important LWU representative to an international meeting was touting small-scale development projects for women (Vongsack 1986, 2, 4). With the Second Women's Congress in 1988, the role and authority of the LWU were unchanged, but development projects became a legitimate part of LWU activities (LWU Women and Child Protection, Training, and Development Department group discussion, 1993).

By 1988, the Lao Women's Union had begun development projects with the support of UNICEF, the American Friends Service Committee, and the Japanese Volunteer Center. The LWU Protection, Training, and Development Department gradually expanded to include training and development activities under the visionary leadership of Dr. Davone and her small staff. By 1993 this department managed nearly a dozen projects with a specific staff person assigned to coordinate and manage each project, though most project activities are under the direct supervision of specific provincial women's unions. Many national women's union activities have been reoriented to support this new focus on development as the union receives recognition for its effective response to Party policies on socioeconomic development.

Lao Women's Union Development Activities and Staff

The Lao Women's Union sponsors and coordinates integrated rural development projects, a family planning project, national textile projects, and training at the national and provincial levels. During conversations and interviews with several staff members and two vice-directors of the LWU Women and Child Protection, Training, and Development Department, LWU leaders and staff members described example projects and activities, discussed changes in the LWU since 1975, and shared their observations of changes in village life in successful project villages.[11] Some of them also recounted their personal changes as women's union and development workers.

Integrated Rural Development Projects

Sirikit began planning projects in Sayabouli and Bolikhamsay Provinces in cooperation with Save the Children Fund-Australia (SCFA) in 1990. That year the joint LWU-SCFA planning team visited and chose village project sites and sought funding. In 1991 the planning team worked with the two provincial women's unions and constituted provincial oversight committees with representatives from district women's unions, provincial agriculture, health, and education sections, and the provincial governing committee. The unions and the provincial committees, facilitated by Sirikit and supported by the SCFA representative, designed the projects. The plans were returned to the national women's union for acceptance and an agreement was signed. This is now a common procedure for the union.

According to Sirikit, this women's union project offers three main types of assistance to both villagers and women's union staff: grants for village water supply, paddy construction, and reforestation of watersheds providing the source of village water; revolving funds for community rice banks, fruit trees, fish-raising in ponds or paddies, organic fertilizers and pesticides, silk weaving, garlic cultivation, or medicines; and technical training for villagers and women's union staff in relevant activities (e.g., alley cropping, fruit tree propagation), using trainers and demonstration villages available in Laos, and training of national, provincial, and district-level women's union staff on similar topics in neighboring countries. A specific villager is responsible for coordinating and reporting on each part of the village project. This is not only a women's project. Village meetings include both women and men; men are sometimes the village coordinators or record-keepers for a specific project activity, especially when no village women are literate or when no woman yet knows enough about the activity. Project staff have found that women do speak out in mixed meetings.[12] The project supports eight model development villages in Sayabouli Province. These villages are implementing several activities, while five other villages are carrying out one or two activities with project support.

One midland Lao project village of shifting cultivators had only two families cultivating paddy rice, relates Sirikit. Before beginning project activities, villagers had no fruit trees except for three coconut trees and grew some vegetables in their distant upland fields. The village experienced serious shortages of both rice and water, and most people were covered with rashes from poor hygiene. The installation of a piped domestic water system reduced rashes. With an assured water supply in the village, residents then set to work to improve their food production by planting fruit trees and bio-intensive gardens near their homes and by digging and stocking fishponds. Eighteen more families prepared and began leveling paddy fields, while community members contributed to a relatively low-interest rice bank for loans to those who were still rice-short at the end of the next cropping season. The project trained a village midwife, a competent and intelligent older woman, who successfully coordinated project activities in the village.

A second village required few material inputs from the project. After project staff discussed village development in general and generated village ideas for possible improvements, villagers themselves developed a fish pond by diverting a nearby stream and stocking it with native fish that they caught themselves. Because the village was Hmong, it was not possible to involve the women in project discussions or decision making, according to Sirikit, and the project team worked through the village head. The village head, though, reports that men now help women by caring for children sometimes and by hauling firewood, activities that they did not do before. Sirikit was especially impressed that these villagers required only knowledge, not material inputs, in order to improve their situation.

Sirikit was not always oriented toward improving village lives and livelihoods. In fact, she was an urban girl who led a childhood of study and play. Her parents did not require her to do any household or farming chores, though she continued her studies until she graduated from high school. She began working for the LWU in 1981 translating documents and letters. One international organization representative remembers that she also gracefully served tea to union visitors. Fashion and fun, tempered with a desk job at the LWU, seemed most important to her. But her life changed when she decided to work in the development department of the LWU. On her first visit to the countryside as a development facilitator, she saw the difficult conditions her countrywomen experienced daily, and she decided that it was her duty to help improve village conditions. She says that at first her husband and friends did not believe that she actually hiked for hours up steep mountains and down muddy hillsides to reach isolated project sites and assisted with training programs in distant centers. With strong motivation, subsequent training, and practical project experience, she has become an excellent project facilitator.

While Sirikit has changed since she began her women's union work in 1981, she has also seen several changes in the LWU itself. In earlier years, the union taught the Three Goods and Two Duties, hosted international visitors who wanted to see the situation of women in Laos, and received "gifts" from international agencies. Since 1989, she says, the union has planned and facilitated a variety of small development projects. Each staff person has her own area of project responsibility and authority, but all learn from one another's experiences.

Khamphone, like Sirikit, began working at the LWU in 1981 and both are now enthusiastic proponents of village development. Khamphone inherited project coordination for the early "model" Luang Prabang Women's Union project in 1991 and a related project based on the same model in neighboring Oudomxay Province. Training problems arose in the Luang Prabang project. Village women were inadequately trained in the maintenance of village facilities like drinking water systems and rice mills. Ultimately, as provincial officials began to allow private entrepreneurship, most of the mills were leased by village unions to private individuals to operate for profit. Also, the province women's union project coordinator retired in the middle of the project without training her successors. Khamphone appreciates the value of widely available training for both village women and women's union staff. With a recent increase in staff and with recent experience and technical training, Luang Prabang Women's Union staff can better and more frequently conduct project training courses and administer project activities. In some cases, training alone is enough to foster village development. Khamphone herself is also interested in receiving further technical training.

In one Luang Prabang project village, a Hmong village like the one in Sirikit's project, a training team explained how to integrate fishponds, animal-raising, and vegetable gardening so that animal manure fertilizes the garden and feeds the fish, and water from the pond irrigates the garden. After three short visits to this remote village, including training sessions for women as well as men, Khamphone reports that there is now an abundance of fish and nearly all families have fishponds and gardens.

The Oudomxay Women's Union project benefited from "lessons" learned from the initial Luang Prabang women's project. Khamphone has seen dramatic improvements in village living conditions in Oudomxay project villages. Previously, for example, twenty village families might experience severe rice shortages, whereas now only a few families are rice-short. In the past, people of all ages died, but now only the elderly die. Villages are cleaner as livestock is fenced out of the village. In two Khmu project villages, Khamphone reports that change is visible. Children continue their education in both villages. In one village, residents have replaced their small bamboo and thatch houses with larger wooden houses, and the ample school is filled with students. In the other village, women and children used to wait in line for water, but now, with a piped water system, water is available not only for household uses but also for the numerous fishponds and vegetable gardens. The village is experimenting with a small irrigated area of dry season rice and with permanent upland fields. No babies died during 1992, and wives now have enough leisure to rest during the latter stages of pregnancy. Men are very supportive in Oudomxay project villages. Many Khmu and some Hmong women have studied Lao as part of their project activities, and many village women now have the ability and confidence to lecture about village development and lead demonstration tours, even to illustrious visitors like government officials and international guests.

Khamphone herself taught primary and middle school for ten years in Xieng Khouang Province before she was transferred to a military school in Vientiane. The school had no day-care facilities, however, so she transferred to the women's union where she did office work until her youngest child entered school in 1991; she then transferred to the Protection, Training, and Development Department. She has attended two short courses and one conference to build her technical skill in village-level development and project administration.

Khamla began doing women's union work in Houa Phan in 1969, unlike Sirikit and Khamphone who began women's union work well after the communist national government was established. Khamla's main tasks in Houa Phan were to inform women about Party policies and resolutions and to motivate them to implement Party teachings. When she moved to Vientiane in 1975, she continued doing the same kind of work but with more emphasis on improving women's knowledge and evaluating the strengths and weaknesses of women's work for their own family and for the community. Both the activities and the ways of thinking of women's union cadre began to change after 1975. In recent years, though, the change in the women's union has been more striking, Khamla reports. Women's union staff are now expected to study and to develop their own expertise. Training is also a central part of all development work. For example, through increased knowledge of improved techniques, technologies, and markets, farmers and handicraft producers can increase their production, learn how to market their products, and thereby increase their income. Successful farmers and other village producers are, in turn, very effective development agents themselves and contribute toward changing village ways of thinking about production and subsistence, according to Khamla's observations.

A Birth-Spacing Project

Women are shy when discussing sex, but many are very interested in controlling their fertility, according to **Boun Song**, LWU project officer for a birth-spacing program that recently expanded from one pilot district near Vientiane city into four districts of Luang Prabang Province.[13] She herself still has not completely overcome her own shyness, she says, but she prepares informational brochures on various birth-control methods and regularly discusses birth-spacing and birth-control methods individually or with large groups of women. A project medical team visits project villages monthly. Boun Song reports that, in order to enter the program, a woman must learn about the program herself and must interest her husband in birth-spacing. Then a medical team member talks to the couple, educating them both about their options. When the couple makes a decision, the wife is examined by a team member. Intra-uterine devices (IUDs) and birth-control pills are most popular. An IUD is inserted during the physical exam, if appropriate. The sale of IUDs, pills, and condoms is heavily subsidized, but the cost still requires some commitment of resources for ordinary villagers. An IUD insertion costs $.70, a month's supply of pills costs $.14, and condoms cost $.03 each.[14] "This program is too late! I already have too many children," say some older women when they learn of the program. The project document reports that 17.6 percent of reproductive-age couples use some form of birth control, though that figure appears impossibly high for rural couples not conveniently located near a city or the Thai border.

The assignment of Boun Song to the LWU is a result of party and union efforts to improve the number of young and well-trained staff members in women's unions throughout the country. Boun Song studied in Moscow before spending two years learning office management in Australia. When she returned, she was assigned to the LWU. Now she manages a project rather than an office.

Textile Preservation and Production: A National Project

Bandith has several jobs within the LWU Women and Child Protection, Training, and Development Department. She is a deputy department director with supervisory responsibility for the "Art of Silk," an LWU textile project.[15] With the opening of the Lao PDR to international trade, tourism, business, industry, and natural resource exploitation, the flow of antique treasures out of the country increased. Buddha statues, religious artifacts, ritual items, and traditional textiles were lost almost daily, sometimes through sale, usually at ridiculously low prices paid to the owner, and sometimes through theft from unguarded religious shrines. The export of these traditional works of art is often facilitated by Lao businesswomen, legitimately operating in the new market economy. This LWU project works to preserve traditional Lao textiles against these new threats and to provide production and market opportunities for an ancient Laotian craft. The project maintains a textile gallery and a shop in Vientiane.

The LWU collection and display of traditional textiles draw from various regions and ethnic groups in the country. Some pieces are estimated to be 150 years old, while others are recent re-creations of ancient designs. One of the tapestries housed at the "Art of Silk" won second prize at a regional competition in Chiangmai, Thailand, in 1992. The sales outlet at the "Art of Silk" sells a variety of both silk and cotton textiles produced by weavers from throughout the country. Weavers use traditional designs but may use either natural or chemical dyes. Profits from sales are returned to the weaver. Bandith trains local weavers in the use of natural dyes, quality control, and marketing, often relaying traditional knowledge of natural dye plants from weavers in one area of the country to those in another.

Since Bandith began working with the LWU in 1975, she has seen marked changes in rural areas as farmers in some areas, often with the help of development projects, begin to exert more control over their own lives and production, for example, by raising chicken and fish, and by contributing to a village rice bank to draw on in years when their family is short of rice. Some Lao families are now controlling their family size and composition by participating in family-spacing programs, though these programs are limited to just a few areas. She herself now understands the basics of development, including how to share responsibility with local women's unions and how to cooperate with an international organization to design and implement a development program.

Training

Khamman, deputy director for training, makes requests to donor agencies for women's union staff to study, and approves all training programs. Sometimes she herself will handle the initial training of women's union staff in an inexperienced province, conducting an orientation to development, though she takes some specialists with her as well even for the initial training. She at times conducts training programs in the Party-approved LWU Training Center on the outskirts of the city of Vientiane. She joined the ranks of the LWU in 1984, at first teaching about the Three Goods and Two Duties. In 1991 she transferred into the Protection, Training, and Development Department and traveled on a development-oriented study tour to Thailand. She says that in order to develop the country, both villagers and government workers must develop.

Since joining the LWU, she has seen a number of changes, both in the union itself and in villages participating in women's union programs. Women's union staff previously trained village women in theory only. Their advice was not based on specific technical training, and they were unable to transmit useful knowledge to the women. Now, however, women's union staff members oversee technical training for village women and have specific and useful advice for local women's unions. Women's union project activities now enable women to generate income by, for example, growing cash crops or processing food for sale. A number of women's union staff are studying language now, especially English, to facilitate cooperation with international agencies. The LWU now has more work and fewer staff members, but the workload is not too heavy because current staff are better trained and prepared. Finally, the LWU has a new unit, the "Art of Silk."

In project villages, Khamman has seen an increase in paddy farming; improved sanitation as livestock are fenced out of the village; development of weaving among midland Lao women; better village access because of road construction (usually by villagers), which has resulted in more village markets; and a large increase in the number of television sets in the countryside. In one village, four families with thriving project-related pig-raising and weaving businesses cooperated to purchase and install a small hydropower generator on a nearby stream to power their television sets and to enable the women to weave at night. Foreign companies have had both positive and negative effects on rural villages. With a market for rice, she says, villagers are more likely to grow dry season rice. Some villagers can also now afford to purchase goods produced locally by foreign companies. But many villagers are unhappy with the dramatic increase in logging that is driven by easy access to the world timber market and the many concessions granted to foreign logging companies. Recent policy changes, though, may give more forest responsibility to villagers, she says. As far as Khamman knows, the LWU has no responsibility for the welfare of women workers in private factories.

In addition to these project examples and activities reported by staff and deputy directors of the LWU Protection, Training, and Development Department, the women's union facilitates several other projects, each with its own effects on village life and the national union activities, including other integrated village development projects, training center programs, and projects supported by additional international agencies.

In short, long-time LWU staff have seen development become a centerpiece of women's union activities during the late 1980s and the 1990s, expanding the earlier political education and mobilization functions of the Lao Patriotic Women's Association and the Lao Women's Union of the 1970s and early 1980s. Some staff members see development as a political activity that actualizes current Party and government policy and LWU goals. For example, when asked to define the Three Goods and Two Duties, several in a 1993 LWU group discussion said that one of the duties is now to *develop* women, rather than to emancipate them! In dozens of project villages, LWU staff members have observed that village project activities allow women and men to exert more control over their own lives by increasing their agricultural production, by reducing the labor required for everyday survival, by improving sanitation and health, by controlling the size of their family, by increasing cooperation between women and men, by encouraging education of women and children, by increasing women's confidence and status, and by increasing household income.[16] Finally, experienced LWU staff report that they themselves are better trained and more effective now than they were just a few years ago.

Transformation of the Women's Union

The organization of Laotian women has evolved from groups of soldiers' mothers to an agency of rural and national development as well as of political education. The official communist women's organization began as a women's auxiliary of the Party, became a more active agency of political education and exhortation to national socialist construction and defense during the heat of war, and continued to organize and educate for Party and government goals in the early years of the national communist government. The women's union has evolved from the pre-1986 top-down organization that taught Party policies and programs and the union's own political program of the Three Goods and Two Duties and sought "gifts" from foreign aid organizations. Now it has become an organization that is developing useful technical skills and knowledge in both its staff and in project participants and is encouraging village initiative and leadership in the design and implementation of development projects. At various times women's organizers have been able to reach women farmers, foragers, and factory workers, as well as ministry and other government workers.

At each stage of its evolution, the LWU was blessed or limited by culturally acceptable women's roles and by the prevailing political and economic structures, events, and policies. Socialist Laotian women's individual and organizational power appears most evident during two periods: in Houa Phan during intense American bombing and equally intense struggle for revolutionary victory when women's skills and courage were essential, and today as the LWU manages small-scale externally funded projects that visibly improve the lives and livelihoods of ordinary people in a variety of ethnic groups and economic conditions.

The reputation of the Lao Women's Union as a small, ineffective, under-funded, and politically weak body, acquired during the first decade of nationhood, has been changing as national women's union officials receive financial and program support from international organizations, and the nationwide women's union network begins to effectively involve numerous women at the grassroots through successful development projects.

Village Implications

LWU-sponsored development projects in rural villages often transform the village women's union into a viable organization, make women's work visible to the entire community, and authorize village women to work directly with government officials and technicians. As one of several "mass organizations" with a network reaching the village, a woman's representative sometimes is included in the village administrative committee, a structure that replaced the former role of village headman. Other such representatives may include youth and elders.

There is potential for women's union officers, at least in effective local unions, to be from families that are better off than the village norm. The most effective women's unions are those whose leaders are assertive and committed to improvement. Unmarried young women or women burdened by several young children, disease, or poverty are not effective union officers. The leaders need not be literate, though they are seldom effective unless aided by literate and competent deputies. Thus, healthy women at the height of their own family authority (middle age), not burdened by an everyday struggle for survival, and from families at the height of their labor power (with children old enough to work) are more likely to be effective leaders of women's unions. Under traditional subsistence-oriented economic conditions, the ascendancy of these families is temporary and they are allied by kinship, neighborliness, and traditional labor exchange networks to families at other stages of development and other levels of socioeconomic status in the village. Labor exchange and other kinds of unpaid neighborly help, though, are often replaced by wage labor as the village economy "develops" and becomes more monetized and market-oriented (see Håkangård 1992 and Trankell 1993 for examples). Thus, LWU village-level development projects have the potential to improve the lives of most village women and other household members, while crystallizing incipient class differences within the village.

Province Implications

The increased capability and authority of women in project villages are reflected also in changes in women's union credibility in the province and in the nation. The Luang Prabang Women's Union evolved from a weak and marginal organization into a self-sufficient, somewhat effective and respected organization in the province as it carried out projects with local women's unions, beginning in 1987. Provincial respect developed as the union became the source of project goods and the facilitator of other provincial assistance to villages. In the process, the province union developed working relationships with other units of provincial government, like the health section, the maintenance section, and the province governing committee.

National Implications

The political influence of the national women's union may have increased along with its increased resources, program effectiveness, and respect in province and village. For example, while national political deliberations are not public, it appears that the women's union, along with demographic projections by the national statistical unit, may have had some part in convincing the Party and the Council of Ministers to lift its prohibition against birth control and to approve the initiation of a birth-spacing program.

The women's union official responsible for most women's union development projects until 1993, Davone Vongsack, the head of the Protection, Training, and Development Department, was elevated to the status of alternate Central Committee member at the March 1991 Party Congress, potentially giving the women's union greater voice in national decision making. Unfortunately for the LWU, she was also given a major post within the Party, so now has little time for her women's union work.[17]

The Lao Women's Union is gradually moving toward actualizing its goals through development activities, a process that was fully acknowledged at the Third Women's Congress in 1993. The new women's union development orientation and its newly acquired political representation at the highest level of the Party may actually improve women's lives, or at least temper the nega-tive effects of burgeoning capitalist development. Economic liberalization, coupled with local examples of village development, may also make it increas-ingly possible for village women to improve their technology, increase their production, locate markets for their products, and otherwise improve their lives. Units of government like the women's unions or, potentially, Laotian non-governmental organizations, may be able to facilitate these processes. But continued authoritarian governmental and Party political control limits the decision-making capability of these groups.

The changes in the Lao Women's Union prior to 1975, through the socialist period, and into the current period of economic liberalization reflect (as well as affect) the changes in rural women's lives through those three time periods. Rural women traditionally had few formal rights and no national organization or network. During the wars before 1975, many women either supported revolutionary efforts or coped with war in ways that sometimes gave them temporary control over resources while dramatically increasing their workload. During the socialist period, ethnic Lao women lost an important source of economic power as private entrepreneurship was closely controlled. But the work of women in cooperative villages became more visible, as women cooperative members received work points in their own right. Some cooperatives even sponsored child-care centers to enable women to be even more productive workers. Finally, during the current period of economic liberalization women have regained the option of developing their own commercial and entrepreneurial ventures, an option pursued by a number of ethnic Lao and a few minority women. However, the nominal supports of rural cooperatives, work points and child-care centers, are gone as both paddy labor and child care have reverted to households once again. The legal equality of women and men, now enshrined in the constitution and in political ideology, is an important legacy of the socialist period that may continue to affect rural women's lives.

As rural women's situation changed after 1975 with socialism and economic liberalization, so too did the Lao Women's Union. It began as almost a "women's auxiliary" of the Lao Communist Party and reflected women's traditional nurturing and family roles. In wartime, however, it became more active, moving into some nontraditional activities, much as rural women did, either as revolutionaries or as their households' primary farmers. With the end of the war in 1975, active and qualified women's union members were appointed to a variety of responsible governmental positions, while the women's union itself was given a share in the job of consolidating a new nation. The limited focus of women's unions on child-care centers for governmental workers and on creating a nominal network of local women's unions was replaced in less than a decade by more active women's unions oriented toward local development controlled by village women in cooperation with village administrative committees and supported by the socialist ideology of gender equality. With economic liberalization local women's union projects freed women's time and energy for a return to entrepreneurial activities, enabling a number of women to develop their own economic sources of power. As local projects succeeded, the Lao Women's Union prospered as an organization. The Lao Women's Union too increased its access to economic resources during this process as it became increasingly able to channel funds from foreign donors to local development projects. During the first decade of socialist rule, the Lao Women's Union benefited from an ideology of gender equality and an obligation to "mobilize women," but, without actual economic resources and knowledge, it was unable to develop an effective program. Now, with more economic resources, a stronger organizational base in a number of active provincial and village women's unions, and somewhat better trained workers, the Lao Women's Union is a more effective organization than it was in the past. Not surprisingly, though, women's union projects are more likely to be effective in ethnic Lao villages, though minority villages also participate. Thus, changes over time in the Lao Women's Union parallel the changes experienced by rural women during the same time periods.

Notes

1. For a Cuban example see Randall (1981) and for an example from the former USSR see Lapidus (1978).

2. See Chapter 2 for more historical details.

3. The three aspects are often referred to in Party and government documents and in speeches by the code words "the three revolutions" (Doré 1982).

4. Stuart-Fox (1986a, 90) also notes the lack of change in the status of women in Lao society in the first ten years of communist government.

5. The three levels, as described by Stuart-Fox (1986a, 72–74), are the "inner cabinet" comprised of the chairman and five vice-chairmen of the Council of Government (also known as the Council of Ministers), the ministers and state committee chairmen, and associated vice-ministers and vice-chairmen of national ministries and state committees.

6. For accounts of the greater political influence of the Vietnamese Women's Union see Eisen (1984).

7. "Studying", in this context, often refers to listening while someone else reads from a document provided by the central government or the Party.

8. During this same period, ethnic minorities were nearly excluded from the embryonic development process. See C. Ireson and R. Ireson (1991) for more information.

9. The Forest Development and Watershed Management Project was funded by the United Nations Development Programme, executed by the Food and Agriculture Organization of the United Nations, and implemented by the Lao Ministry of Agriculture.

10. The critique is by Sisouvanh (1992).

11. Information about project examples and project officers is based on interviews of Lao Women's Union staff members conducted in May 1993, unless otherwise noted.

12. Women's silence or murmured acquiescence was a problem for earlier women's projects.

13. This officially entitled "Birth-Spacing Program" is supported by the Family Planning International Assistance (FPIA). Birth control was prohibited by the newly established communist government. Government leaders are still wary of population control but acknowledge the value of allowing several years between each pregnancy for women's health and productive capacity, and for child survival.

14. Estimated per capita income is less than $200/year (see Chapter 2 for details).

15. The "Art of Silk" is supported by UNICEF and the Swedish International Development Authority (SIDA).

16. UNICEF alone reports sponsoring LWU projects in about eighty villages in several provinces, while Quaker Service Laos (QSL) sponsored nearly 30 project villages in Luang Prabang and Oudomxay Provinces (personal communications, 1993). In addition, Save the Children Fund-Australia and the Japan Volunteer Center (JVC) have recently sponsored or are currently sponsoring numerous other LWU village projects. Also, other foreign donors sponsor village projects involving provincial and local women's unions but work at the national level with a particular ministry (like the Ministry of Education or the Ministry of Agriculture and Forestry) rather than with the LWU.

17. Dr. Davone was appointed assistant to the director of the Party and Government Control Committee, a powerful internal ethics commission.

9

Rural Laotian Women: Work, Power, and Development

Socialist reorganization and economic liberalization have both affected rural women's traditional sources of power. Macro-level policies, structures, and programs have affected many of women's power bases, while changes in women's traditional economic power have mutually influenced their domestic and other types of power. Because religion, culture, and kinship continue to affect the ways in which women change their lives in response to these macro-level forces, women of different ethnic groups respond differently to political and economic changes. The transformation of the women's union throughout the country reflects the influences of these macro-level political and economic forces. The Lao Women's Union has facilitated the empowerment of some groups of women by sponsoring local women's union projects that relieve women's daily domestic chores, and that support women's production and local political authority. The consequences of changes in women's economic power are not yet clear, but life choices appear to be wider for many women, while rural economic production and trade appear to be increasing.

Most policies, programs, and structures developed during the period of socialist reorganization affected rural women's sources of power for a few years, but some continue to have an effect even today. Paddy farming women's participation in agricultural cooperatives and participants in the few active village women's unions became more visible locally as workers and active community members, supported by the communist ideology of gender equality. The increased visibility of women and their work seems to be continuing into the present period. Policies of national sufficiency in cloth production and in a return to the traditional female skirt enabled women weavers to earn some income from their craft, but this market niche contracted after economic liberalization. Resettlement and "no swidden" policies were initiated during the socialist period and continue today. These

two policies affect all upland dwelling people and therefore have a disproportionately negative impact on ethnic minority women and men. Official
strictures against private entrepreneurship, on the other hand, had a
disproportionately negative effect on ethnic Lao women who abandoned
marketing and production for sale. While socialist endorsement of child-care
centers assisted some women, most women were not civil servants or
cooperative members and therefore did not benefit. The ban on birth control
maintained the nearly continuous physical drain on women's bodies and
energy required by frequent pregnancies and births. Similarly, other socialist
policies and programs did little to reduce women's domestic and reproductive
responsibilities.

Some elements of women's more "public" presence continued into the
period of economic liberalization, such as constitutionally mandated though
not yet enforceable gender equality, and women's visible participation in
community groups. Women's active public presence may mitigate or at least
postpone some of the negative effects of "development" on women now so
apparent in other capitalist Southeast Asian countries. Some aspects of
economic liberalization clearly benefit rural women, at least in the short term.
Access to markets and "modern" agricultural inputs improves the likelihood
that women live in rice-sufficient households, enabling these women to
produce and market other crops and goods, at least if these crops or goods are
not undercut by more cheaply produced imports. Increased road construction
has improved the market access of some women, though facilitating logging
of forests important for local subsistence. Factory work in urban areas has
drawn some young women from rural areas into towns. Continued population
pressure on the limited swidden area and logging of primary forests threatens
the subsistence base and the "social security system" of the poorest women,
even while women in more accessible areas with more secure sources of
subsistence and income are taking advantage of a variety of new opportunities
available with economic change. Thus, inequalities are increasing, with poor
women, ethnic minority women, and women in less-accessible villages
benefiting less or being harmed by the effects of economic liberalization. Often
even these women may experience small improvements with, for example, the
installation of a piped drinking-water system or a rice mill. Without other
improvements (rice sufficiency, access to markets), however, poor, isolated, or
ethnic minority women cannot translate this lighter domestic workload into
increased power in domestic or other arenas.

In short, then, the basis for and forms of women's power have shifted with
legacies from the socialist period and opportunities opened by decreasing
domestic labor, increasing availability of markets for some women's products,
and the increasing visibility of female actors in some rural communities. While
the main beneficiaries seem to be ethnic Lao women from rice-sufficient
households in more accessible villages, some women from other groups are

beginning to market their own produce as well. Some other positive results are also likely to develop in the near future as more girls are educated and as birth-spacing programs, birth-control technologies, and rural health care become more widely available. Thus economic liberalization, after a period of socialism, appears to be having some positive effects on a variety of rural women.

However, one cannot ignore the damaging effects of dynamic capitalist development in neighboring countries. National governmental policy seems insufficient to limit this damage in Laos. A variety of groups of women are likely to be negatively affected by booms in tourism, with the associated sex industry and growth in AIDS victims; in natural resource development and depletion, with the associated environmental harm; and in urban low-wage industries, with the associated urban migration, labor abuses, and pollution. Further, the feminization of agriculture, especially if few resources are invested in this sector, is likely to marginalize older rural women in a relatively nonproductive sector while younger women migrate to urban areas for the bright lights and low-wage jobs. The empowerment of some women as producers, income earners, and decision makers in their households and even in their communities seems insufficient protection against future exploitation of many women by the underregulated, well-organized, and economically powerful multinational companies now beginning to operate in Laos. The Lao Women's Union (LWU) similarly is unlikely to provide any protection against abuses. In fact, LWU staff have no knowledge of or programs for urban women workers and in-migrants.

This focus on rural women and women's power adds to our understanding of development and change in Laos by enabling us to look beyond the some-times rapid and superficial changes in the capital city, Vientiane, to the rural areas that are home to most Laotians. Focusing explicitly on women enables us to look behind the aggregate statistics and rapid urban changes to the places inhabited by most Laotians and to the people responsible for the daily well-being of nearly all family members. This focus draws us to consider who determines what development is, and who benefits from specific development policies, programs, and structures. It further enables us to see that development effective at the local level requires local control and that development exclud-ing important groups like women is likely to fail.

What are the implications of this study for future research as well as for future policy and program development? First, policies and practices that seem to have little to do with women like the "no swidden" policy or the practice of allowing ill-controlled logging actually may have quite dramatic effects on rural women and their ability to produce for their families. Second, policies intended to increase the country's level of development may actually require more from women than from men.

This study is based on the existing information and the author's own studies about Laotian rural women and, as a result, illuminates the shortcomings in these data. Available information is mostly qualitative and based on a patchwork of small regionally and ethnically specific studies of certain aspects of village life, usually designed for project purposes. Most available quantitative data are not complete or accurate, and sometimes do not include women as a separate category. Samples have not been representative, though research sites have been scattered throughout the country. Nonetheless this quantitative information does identify some important issues. Systematic social, demographic, and economic data on Laotian villages, including gender stratification and division of labor, ethnic variation, and village, household, and intra-household responses to national and regional changes, could better inform national policies, provincial implementation, and local program development.

Despite the shortcomings in knowledge and data, the changes in rural women's lives since 1975 illustrate important mechanisms by which women's lives are both improved and harmed by "development." National and even international policies, structures, and programs directly affect the lives and traditional sources of power of rural women. Although women's organizing to maintain or modify their bases of economic power does seem to enable them to control some aspects of development, greater local and national efforts and stronger international networks will be necessary in the face of Laos' increasing integration into the global capitalist economy.

References

Acharya, Meena. 1983. *Women and the Subsistence Sector: Economic Participation and Household Decisionmaking in Nepal.* Washington, D.C.: World Bank.

Adams, Nina. 1987. "Women's Cooperatives in Laos." *Indochina Newsletter* 44:1–3.

Adams, Nina, and Alfred McCoy, eds. 1970. *Laos: War and Revolution.* New York: Harper Colophon.

Alton, Charles. 1993. *Land Use Planning Prototype.* Unpublished. Vientiane: Lao-Swedish Forestry Programme 1991–95, Shifting Cultivation Sub-Programme.

Asian Development Bank (ADB). 1989. "Education Sector Study." Advisory Technical Assistance Project, Asian Development Bank.

Atkinson, Jane. 1991. "How Gender Makes a Difference in Wana Society." In Jane Atkinson and Shelly Errington, eds. *Power and Difference: Gender in Island Southeast Asia.* Stanford: Stanford University Press.

Ayabe, Tsuneo. 1961. *The Village of Ban Pha Khao, Vientiane Province.* Laos Project Paper no. 14. Los Angeles: Department of Anthropology, University of California.

Bacdayan, Albert. 1977. "Cooperation and Sexual Equality Among the Western Bontoc." In Alice Schlegel, ed. *Sexual Stratification: A Cross-Cultural View.* New York: Columbia University Press.

Barber, Martin. 1979. "Migrants and Modernisation—a Study of Change in Lao Society." Ph.D. diss., University of Hull.

Barkow, Jerome. 1972. "Hausa Women and Islam." *Canadian Journal of African Studies* 6:317–28.

Barnes, Sandra T. 1990. "Women, Property, and Power." In Peggy R. Sanday and Ruth G. Goodenough, eds. *Beyond the Second Sex: New Directions in the Anthropology of Gender.* Philadelphia: University of Pennsylvania Press.

Belsky, Jill, and Stephen Siebert. 1983. "Household Responses to Drought in Two Subsistence Leyte Villages." *Philippine Quarterly of Culture and Society* 11:237–56.

Benería, Lourdes, and Gita Sen. 1986. "Women's Role in Economic Development." In Eleanor Leacock and Helen Safa, eds. *Women's Work.* South Hadley, Massachusetts: Bergin and Garvey.

Benería, Lourdes, and Martha Roldan. 1987. *Crossroads of Class and Gender: Industrial Homework, Subcontracting, and Household Dynamics in Mexico City.* Chicago: University of Chicago Press.

Berval, René. 1959. *Kingdom of Laos.* Saigon: France-Asie.

Blumberg, Rae Lesser. 1978. *Stratification: Socioeconomic and Sexual Inequality.* Dubuque, Iowa: William. C. Brown.

Blumberg, Rae Lesser. 1988. "Income Under Female vs. Male Control: Hypotheses from a Theory of Gender Stratification and Data from the Third World." *Journal of Family Issues* 9.1:51–84.

Blumberg, Rae Lesser. 1991a. "Income Under Female Versus Male Control: Hypotheses from a Theory of Gender Stratification and Data from the Third World." In Rae L. Blumberg, ed. *Gender, Family, and Economy: The Triple Overlap.* Newbury Park, California: Sage.

Blumberg, Rae Lesser. 1991b. "Women and the Wealth and Well-being of Nations: Macro-micro Relationships." In Joan Huber, ed. *Macro-micro Linkages in Sociology.* Newbury Park, California: Sage.

Blumberg, Rae Lesser. 1995. "Introduction: Engendering Wealth and Well-Being in an Era of Economic Transformation." In Rae Lesser Blumberg, Cathy Rakowski, Irene Tinker, and Michael Monteón, eds. *EnGENDERing Wealth and Well-Being.* Boulder, Colorado: Westview.

Boserup, Ester. 1970. *Women's Role in Economic Development.* New York: St. Martin's Press.

Boua, Chanthou. 1981. *Women in Kampuchea.* Unpublished. Bangkok: UNICEF.

Boua, Chanthou. 1982. "Women in Today's Cambodia." *New Left Review* 131:44–70.

Boua, Chanthou, and Ben Kiernan. 1987. *OxFam America's Aid Program in Babong Village, Kampuchea.* Unpublished. New South Wales, Australia: Department of History and Politics, University of Wollongong.

Bouavonh and Chantheum Latmani. 1994. "Commentary on Transitional Period of Economy of the Three Countries: Lao, Vietnam, and China." Unpublished paper, workshop on Women in Socio-Economic Transitions. Bangkok: Chulalongkorn University and the University of California.

Boulding, Elise. 1983. "Measures of Women's Work in the Third World: Problems and Suggestions." In Mayra Buvinic, Margaret A. Lycette, and William Paul, eds. *Women and Poverty in the Third World.* Baltimore and London: Johns Hopkins University Press.

Bourdet, Yves. 1990. "Laos: Macroeconomic Performance and Economic Policy." Unpublished.

Branfman, Fred. 1978. *The Village of Deep Pond: Ban Xa Phang Meuk.* Asian Studies Committee Occasional Papers Series no. 3. Amherst: University of Massachusetts.

Brown, MacAlister, and Joseph J. Zasloff. 1986. *Apprentice Revolutionaries: The Communist Movement in Laos, 1930–85.* Stanford: Hoover Institution Press.

Brownmiller, Susan. 1994. "Women of Vietnam: After Socialism, Fighting Sexism." *The Nation* 259.3:82–84.

Bunster, Ximena, and Elsa Chaney. 1985. *Sellers and Servants: Working Women in Lima, Peru.* New York: Praeger.

Chafetz, Janet S. 1991. "The Gender Division of Labor and the Reproduction of Female Disadvantage: Toward an Integrated Theory." In Rae L. Blumberg, ed. *Gender, Family, and Economy: The Triple Overlap.* Newbury Park, California: Sage.

Chagnon, Jacqui, and Roger Rumpf. 1982. "Education: The Prerequisite to Change." In Martin Stuart-Fox, ed. *Contemporary Laos—Studies in the Politics and Society of the Lao People's Democratic Republic.* St. Lucia, Queensland: University of Queensland Press.

Chanda, Nayan. 1982. "Economic Changes in Laos, 1975–1980." In Martin Stuart-Fox, ed. *Contemporary Laos—Studies in the Politics and Society of the Lao People's Democratic Republic.* St. Lucia, Queensland: University of Queensland Press.

Chansina, Kou, Terd Charoenwatana, Harold McArthur, Bounmy Phonegnotha, and Goro Uehara. 1991. "The Agroecosystem of Ban Semoun." In *Swidden Agroecosystems in Sepone District, Savannakhet Province, Lao PDR.* Report of the 1991 SUAN-EAPI-MAF Agroecosystem Research Workshop, Savannakhet Province. Khon Kaen, Thailand: SUAN Regional Secretariat, Khon Kaen University.

Charlton, Sue Ellen M. 1984. *Women in Third World Development.* Boulder, Colorado: Westview.

Cheesman, Patricia. 1988. *Lao Textiles: Ancient Symbols—Living Art.* Bangkok, Thailand: White Lotus.

Cheng, Nivana, and Ek Praney. 1994. "Transition Period of Economy/War: Lack of Adequate Attention on the Behalf of the Policy Maker on Women's Issues." Unpublished paper, workshop on Women in Socio-Economic Transitions. Bangkok: Chulalongkorn University and the University of California.

Chi Do Pham. 1992. "Economic Reforms in the Lao PDR: Current Trends and Perspectives." Unpublished. Vientiane: International Monetary Fund.

Chinchilla, Norma. 1990. "Revolutionary Popular Feminism in Nicaragua: Articulating Class, Gender, and National Sovereignty." *Gender and Society* 4.3:370–97.

Christie, C.J. 1982. "Nationalism and the Pathet Lao." In Martin Stuart-Fox, ed. *Contemporary Laos—Studies in the Politics and Society of the Lao People's Democratic Republic.* St. Lucia, Queensland: University of Queensland Press.

Collins, Jane Fishburne. 1974. "Women in Politics." In Michelle Rosaldo and Louise Lamphere, eds. *Women, Culture, and Society.* Stanford: Stanford University Press.

Condominas, Georges. 1970. "The Lao." In Nina Adams and Alfred McCoy, eds. *Laos: War and Revolution.* New York: Harper and Row.

Condominas, Georges. 1977. *We Have Eaten the Forest.* New York: Hill and Wang.

Cooper, Robert G. 1983. "Sexual Inequality Among the Hmong." In John McKinnon and Wanat Bhruksasri, eds. *Highlanders of Thailand.* Kuala Lumpur: Oxford University Press.

Cooper, Robert. 1984. *Resource Scarcity and the Hmong Response.* Singapore: Singapore University Press.

Cooper, Robert. 1986. "The Hmong of Laos: Economic Factors in Refugee Exodus and Return." In Glenn L. Hendricks, Bruce T. Downing, and Amos S. Deinard, eds. *The Hmong in Transition.* New York: Center for Migration Studies of New York.

Croll, Elisabeth. 1986. "Rural Production and Reproduction: Socialist Development Experiences." In Eleanor Leacock and Helen Safa, eds. *Women's Work: Development and the Division of Labor by Gender.* South Hadley, Massachusetts: Bergin and Garvey.

Curtin, Katie. 1975. *Women in China.* New York: Pathfinder Press.

Davison, Jean. 1988. "Land Redistribution in Mozambique and its Effects on Women's Collective Production: Case Studies from Sofala Province." In Jean Davison, ed. *Agriculture, Women, and Land.* Boulder, Colorado: Westview.

Deere, Carmen. 1988. "Rural Women and Agrarian Reform in Peru, Chile, and Cuba." In June Nash and Helen Safa, eds. *Women and Change in Latin America.* South Hadley, Massachusetts: Bergin and Garvey.

Deere, Carmen Diana, Peggy Antrobus, Lynn Bolles, Edwin Melendez, Peter Phillips, Marcia Rivera, and Helen Safa. 1990. *In the Shadows of the Sun: Caribbean Development Alternatives and U.S. Policy.* Boulder, Colorado: Westview.

Dixon, Ruth. 1976. "Measuring Equality Between the Sexes." *Journal of Social Issues* 32.3:19–32.

Dixon, Ruth. 1982. "Women in Agriculture: Counting the Labor Force in Developing Countries." *Population and Development Review* 8.2:539–66.

Dommen, Arthur. 1964. *Conflict in Laos: Politics of Neutralization.* New York: Praeger.

Doré, Amphay. 1982. "The Three Revolutions in Laos." In Martin Stuart-Fox, ed. *Contemporary Laos—Studies in the Politics and Society of the Lao People's Democratic Republic.* St. Lucia, Queensland: University of Queensland Press.

Douangdara, Onechanh, Keith Fahrney, Herri Y. Hadikusumah, Bounkhouang Khambounhouang, Thong Et Phayvanh, A. Terry Rambo, Bounchine Sidavong, and Tran Duc Vien. 1991. " Bou Houay Loua: The Agroecosystems of a Lao Theung Community." In *Swidden Agroecosystems in Sepone District, Savannakhet Province, Lao PDR.* Report of the 1991 SUAN-EAPI-MAF Agroecosystem Research Workshop, Savannakhet Province. Khon Kaen, Thailand: The SUAN Regional Secretariat, Khon Kaen University.

Dunnigan, Timothy. 1982. "Segmentary Kinship in an Urban Society: The Hmong of St. Paul, Minneapolis." *Anthropological Quarterly* 55.3:126–34.

Ebihara, May. 1974. "Khmer Village Women in Cambodia: A Happy Balance." In Carolyn Matthiasson, ed. *Many Sisters: Women in Cross-cultural Perspective.* New York: Free Press.

Ebihara, May. 1990. "Return to a Khmer Village." *Cultural Survival* 14.3:67–70.

Ebihara, May M., Carol A. Mortland, and Judy Ledgerwood, eds. 1994. *Cambodian Culture Since 1975: Homeland and Exile.* Ithaca, New York: Cornell University Press.

Ehlers, Tracy. 1990. *Silent Looms: Women and Production in a Guatemalan Town.* Boulder, Colorado: Westview.

Eisen, Arlene. 1984. *Women and Revolution in Viet Nam.* London: Zed Books.

Errington, Shelly. 1991. "Recasting Sex, Gender, and Power: A Theoretical and Regional Overview." In Shelly Errington and Jane Atkinson, eds. *Power and Difference: Gender in Island Southeast Asia.* Stanford: Stanford University Press.

Escoffier-Fauveau, Claire, Kopkeo Souphanthong, and Phonethep Pholsena. 1994. *Women and Reproductive Health in the Lao PDR: An Anthropological Study of Reproduction and Contraception in Four Provinces.* Unpublished. Vientiane: Save the Children Fund/UK and United Nations Development Programme.

Evans, Grant. 1990. *Lao Peasants Under Socialism.* New Haven, Connecticut: Yale University Press.

Evans, Grant. 1991 "Planning problems in peripheral socialism: the case of Laos." In Joseph J. Zasloff and Leonard Unger, eds. *Laos: Beyond the Revolution.* New York: St Martin's.

Evans, Grant. 1995. *Lao Peasants Under Socialism and Post-socialism.* New Haven, Connecticut: Yale University Press.

Evans, Grant, and Kelvin Rowley. 1984. *Red Brotherhood at War.* London: Verso.

Far Eastern Economic Review (FEER). 1993. *Asia Yearbook.* Hong Kong: Review Publishing.

Far Eastern Economic Review (FEER). 1994. *Asia Yearbook.* Hong Kong: Review Publishing.

Far Eastern Economic Review (FEER). 1996. *Asia Yearbook.* Hong Kong: Review Publishing.

FBIS (Foreign Broadcast Information Service). 1990. "*Pasason* Carries Text of Draft Constitution." *FBIS-EAS* 90–113:41–48. June 12, 1990. (Text translated from *Pasason*, Vientiane: Lao PDR, June 4, 1990, pp. 1–3.)

Fernández-Kelly, Patricia. 1982. *For We Are Sold, I and My People: Women and Industry in Mexico's Frontier.* Albany: State University of New York Press.

Foley, P.J., and Davone Vongsack. 1991. *Demographic and Health Survey: Xay Thani, Vientiane Prefecture.* Unpublished. Vientiane: Family Planning International Assistance.

Fortmann, Louise, and Dianne Rocheleau. 1985. "Women and Agroforestry: Four Myths and Three Case Studies." *Agroforestry Systems* 2:253–72.

Friedl, Ernestine. 1975. *Women and Men: An Anthropologist's View.* New York: Holt, Rinehart and Winston.

Fuentes, Annette, and Barbara Ehrenreich. 1983. *Women in the Global Factory.* Institute for New Communications Pamphlet no. 2. Boston: South End.

Funk, Ursula. 1988. "Land Tenure, Agriculture, and Gender in Guinea-Bissau." In Jean Davison, ed. *Agriculture, Women, and Land.* Boulder, Colorado: Westview.

Geddes, William Robert. 1976. *Migrants of the Mountains—the Cultural Ecology of the Blue Mieo (Hmong Njua) of Thailand.* Oxford: Clarendon Press.

Geertz, Hildred. 1961. *The Javanese Family.* New York: Humanities Press.

Ghosh, Bahnisikha, and Sudhin Mukhopadhyay. 1988. "Gender-Differentials in the Impact of Technological Change in Rice-Based Farming Systems in India." In Susan Poats, Marianne Schmink, and Anita Spring, eds. *Gender Issues in Farming Systems Research and Extension.* Boulder, Colorado: Westview.

Giele, Janet, and Audrey Smock, eds. 1977. *Women: Roles and Status in Eight Countries.* New York: Wiley.

Håkangård, Agneta. 1990. "Women in Shifting Cultivation: Luang Prabang Province, Lao PDR." *Development Studies Unit Report no. 18.* Stockholm: Department of Social Anthropology, Stockholm University.

Håkangård, Agneta. 1992. "A Socio-Economic Study of Villagers, Transport and Use of Road 13S, Lao PDR." *Development Studies Unit Report no. 23.* Stockholm: Department of Social Anthropology, Stockholm University.

Halpern, Joel. 1958. *Aspects of Village Life and Culture Change in Laos.* New York: Council on Economic and Cultural Affairs.

Hanger, Jane, and Jon Moris. 1973. "Women and the Household Economy." In Robert Chambers and Jon Moris, eds. *Mwea: An Irrigated Rice Settlement in Kenya.* Munich: Weltforum Verlag.

Hecht, Susanna, A.B. Anderson, and P. May. 1988. "The Subsidy from Nature: Shifting Cultivation, Successional Palm Forests, and Rural Development." *Human Organization* 47.1:25–35.

Hewison, Kevin, and Nongluk Tunyavanich. 1993. "Socio-cultural Aspects of Water Supply and Environmental Sanitation in Nine Villages in the Lao PDR." *Thai-Yunnan Project Newsletter* 23:13–21.

Heyzer, Noeleen. 1986. *Working Women in South-East Asia: Development, Subordination, and Emancipation.* Milton Keynes, England: Open University Press.

Hkum, Seng. 1992. *Baseline Economic and Opium Survey: Nonghet District, Xieng Khouang Province.* Xieng Khouang Development Programme. Unpublished. Project UNDCP/OPS Lao/91/551-3.

Hoang Thi Lich. 1994. "Rural Women in Socio-economic Changes in Vietnam." Unpublished paper, workshop on Women in Socio-Economic Transitions. Bangkok: Chulalongkorn University and the University of California.

Hoffer, Carol. 1974. "Madam Yoko: Ruler of the Kpa Mende Confederacy." In Michelle Rosaldo and Louise Lamphere, eds. *Women, Culture, and Society*. Stanford: Stanford University Press.

Hort, Krishna. 1991. *Mission Report: Maternal and Child Health, Lao PDR*. Unpublished. Bangkok: World Health Organization.

Huber, Joan. 1991. *Macro-micro Linkages in Sociology*. Newbury Park, California: Sage.

IFAD (International Fund for Agricultural Development). 1993. "Bokeo Food Security Project—Beneficiary Needs Assessment." Unpublished. Rome: IFAD.

Iinuma, Takeko. 1992. *Country Gender Analysis for the Lao People's Democratic Republic*. Stockholm: Swedish International Development Authority and Graphic Systems.

Ireson, Carol. 1969. "Nutrition Survey of Six Lao Villages." Unpublished. Vientiane: International Voluntary Services.

Ireson, Carol. 1987. "The Advantages of Small Scale People-oriented Development: The American Friends Service Committee Experience in Laos." Unpublished paper, Fourth Annual California Universities Conference on Southeast Asia; Rethinking Development in Southeast Asia. Berkeley.

Ireson, Carol. 1989a. "Friendly Forest: Forest Gathering and the Subsistence Food System of Rural Lao Families." Unpublished paper, Annual Meetings of the Rural Sociological Society, Seattle, Washington.

Ireson, Carol. 1989b. *The Role of Women in Forestry in the Lao PDR*. Unpublished. Vientiane: SilviNova Forestry Consultants with the National Institute for Social Sciences, the Swedish International Development Authority, and the Department of Forestry of the Ministry of Agriculture.

Ireson, Carol. 1990. *Evaluation Report: Lao Women's Project, "Improving Labor Productivity of Luang Prabang Women."* Unpublished. Philadelphia: The American Friends Service Committee.

Ireson, Carol. 1991. "Women's Forest Work in Laos." *Sociology and Natural Resources* 4:23–36.

Ireson, Carol. 1992. "Changes in Field, Forest and Family: Women's Work and Status in Post-Revolutionary Laos." *Bulletin of Concerned Asian Scholars* 24.4:3–18.

Ireson, Carol, and Randall Ireson. 1991. "Ethnicity and Development in Laos." *Asian Survey* 31.10:920–37.

Ireson, Carol, Randall Ireson, Chareundi Vansi, Kham-One Keopraseut, Chansouk Meksavanh, and Tou Meksavanh. 1988. "Cooperation Patterns in Pre-1975 Rural Laos." Research project sponsored by the Indochina Studies Program of the Social Science Research Council. Archived in the Indochina Studies Program Grant Collection of the Library of Congress.

Ireson, Randall. 1988. "Laos: Building a Nation Under Socialism." *Indochina Issues* 79:1–7.

Ireson, Randall. 1990. "Hmong Farming Systems and Social Organization in Nong Het District; Xieng Khouang." Unpublished. Rome: International Fund for Agricultural Development, Xieng Khouang Agricultural Development Project Report.

Ireson, Randall. 1991. "Hmong Demographic Changes in Laos: Causes and Ecological Consequences." Unpublished paper, Annual Conference of the Northwest Regional Consortium for Southeast Asian Studies, Eugene, Oregon.

Ireson, Randall. In press 1996. "Invisible Walls: Village Identity and the Maintenance of Cooperation in Laos." *Journal of Southeast Asian Studies*.

IUCN (International Union for Conservation of Nature and Natural Resources). 1988. *Draft Technical Report: Shifting Cultivation in Laos.* Unpublished. Switzerland: IUCN.

Jacobs, Susie, and Tracy Howard. 1987. "Women in Zimbabwe: Stated Policy and State Action." In Haleh Afshar, ed. *Women, State, and Ideology.* London: Macmillan.

Johnson, Stephen. 1992. "Laos in 1991: Year of the Constitution." *Asian Survey* 32.1:82–87.

Kabilsingh, Chatsumarn. 1991. *Thai Women in Buddhism.* Berkeley, California: Parallax Press.

Kandiyoti, Deniz. 1989. "Book Reviews." *Signs* 14.4:939–42.

Kaufman, Howard. 1956. *Village Life in Vientiane Province.* Unpublished. Vientiane: United States Operations Mission to Laos. (Published in 1961 as Laos Project Paper no. 12. Los Angeles: Department of Anthropology, University of California.)

Keen, F.G.B. 1978. "Ecological Relationships in a Hmong (Meo) Economy." In Peter Kunstadter, E.C. Chapman and Sanga Sabhasri, eds. *Farmers in the Forest: Economic Development and Marginal Agriculture in Northern Thailand.* Honolulu: University Press of Hawaii.

Keyes, Charles F. 1984. "Mother or Mistress But Never Monk: Buddhist Notions of Female Gender in Rural Thailand." *American Ethnologist* 11.2:223–41.

Khin Thitsa. 1980. *Providence and Prostitution: Image and Reality in Buddhist Thailand.* London: Change International Reports.

King, Marjorie. 1979. "Cuba's Attack on the Second Shift, 1974–1976." In Latin American Perspectives, ed. *Women in Latin America: An Anthology.* Riverside, California: Latin American Perspectives.

Kirsch, Thomas. 1985. "Text and Context: Buddhist Sex Roles/Culture of Gender Revisited." *American Ethnologist* 12.2:302–20.

KPL News Agency. 21 July 1990. Vientiane.

Kripps, Robert. 1984. *Nutrition Services in the Lao PDR.* Vientiane: World Health Organization.

Kruks, Sonia, Rayna Rapp, and Marilyn Young. 1989. *Promissory Notes: Women in the Transition to Socialism.* New York: Monthly Review Press.

Kumar, Shubh. 1978. "Role of the Household Economy in Child Nutrition at Low Incomes: A Case Study in Kerala." Department of Agricultural Economics Occasional Paper no. 95. Ithaca, New York: Cornell University.

Lamphere, Louise. 1977. "Review Essay: Anthropology." *Signs* 2:612–27.

Lao PDR. 1985. Population Census. Vientiane: National Committee of Plan.

Lao PDR. 1986. *Report on the Economic and Social Situation, Development Strategy, and Assistance Needs,* Vol. I. Geneva: United Nations Development Programme. (Prepared for the Asian-Pacific Round Table Meeting.)

Lao PDR. 1987. "Documents Prepared for the [UN-sponsored] Country Review Meeting." Unpublished. Vientiane.

Lao PDR. 1995. "Country Paper." Paper presented at the Fourth World Conference on Women. Beijing: United Nations. September.

Lao PDR CPC (Committee for Planning and Cooperation). 1993. *Living Conditions in Lao PDR: Basic Results from Two Sample Surveys Carried Out 1992–1993.* Vientiane: National Statistical Center.

Lao Women's Union (LWU). 1988. "Political Report of the Central Committee to the Second National Congress of the Lao Women's Union." Unpublished. Vientiane, Lao PDR. October 13.

Lao Women's Union (LWU) and Khampheng Boupha. 1984. "Political Report by the Constituent Committee for the Lao Women's Union to the First National Congress of Lao Women." Unpublished. Vientiane, Lao PDR (unofficial translation).

Lapidus, Gail Warshofsky. 1978. *Women in Soviet Society: Equality, Development, and Social Change.* Berkeley: University of California Press.

Le Thi Nham Tuyet. 1994. "Some Key Problems Confronting Vietnamese in the Current Process of Renewal and Open-door Policy in Vietnam." Unpublished paper, workshop on Women in Socio-Economic Transitions. Bangkok: Chulalongkorn University and the University of California.

Leacock, Eleanor. 1978. "Women's Status in Egalitarian Society: Implications for Social Evolution." *Current Anthropology* 19.2:247–255.

LeBar, Frank M. 1965. "Ethnographic Notes on the Khamu." Unpublished notes on research in Thailand under the auspices of the National Research Council.

LeBar, Frank M., Gerald C. Hickey, and John K. Musgrave. 1964. *Ethnic Groups of Mainland Southeast Asia.* New Haven, Connecticut: Human Relations Area Files Press.

Lederman, Rena. 1990. "Contested Order: Gender and Society in the Southern New Guinea Highlands." In Peggy R. Sanday and Ruth G. Goodenough, eds. *Beyond the Second Sex: New Directions in the Anthropology of Gender.* Philadelphia: University of Pennsylvania Press.

Lefferts, Leedom. 1993. "Women Weaving and Monks: Textiles of Tai Buddhism." Paper presented at the County Museum, Los Angeles, California.

Lemoine, Jacques. 1972. *Un Village Hmong Vert du Haut Laos.* Paris: Centre National de la Recherche Scientifique.

Lepowsky, Maria. 1990. "Gender in an Egalitarian Society: A Case Study from the Coral Sea." In Peggy R. Sanday and Ruth G. Goodenough, eds. *Beyond the Second Sex: New Directions in the Anthropology of Gender.* Philadelphia: University of Pennsylvania Press.

Liemar, Lisa Marie, and Michael Price. 1987. "Wild Foods and Women Farmers: A Time Allocation Study in Northeast Thailand." Unpublished paper, conference of the Association for Women in Development. Washington, D.C.

Lim, Linda. 1981. "Women's Work in Multinational Electronics Factories." In Roslyn Dauber and Melinda Cain, eds. *Women and Technological Change in Developing Countries.* Boulder, Colorado: Westview.

Lim, Linda. 1982. *Women in the Singapore Economy.* Singapore: Economic Research Centre Occasional Paper no. 5, National University of Singapore.

Lindell, Kristina, Hakan Lundstrom, Jan-Olof Svantesson, and Damrong Tayanin. 1982. *The Kammu Year: Its Lore and Music.* Malmo and London: Curzon Press.

Longhurst, Richard. 1982. "Resource Allocation and the Sexual Division of Labor: A Case Study of a Moslem Hausa Village in Northern Nigeria." In Lourdes Benería, ed. *Women and Development: The Sexual Division of Labor in Rural Societies.* New York: Praeger.

Lovelace, George. 1991. "Background." In *Swidden Agroecosystems in Sepone District, Savannakhet Province, Lao PDR.* Report of the 1991 SUAN-EAPI-MAF

Agroecosystem Research Workshop, Savannakhet Province. Khon Kaen, Thailand: The SUAN Regional Secretariat, Khon Kaen University.

Luang Prabang (LP) Rural Micro-Projects. 1990. "Sector Review of Luang Prabang Province." Technical Report no. 1. Vientiane: Lao PDR and the Commission of European Communities.

Luang Prabang (LP) Rural Micro-Projects. 1991. "Appraisal of Nam Dong Micro-Project Area." Technical Report no. 2. Vientiane: Lao PDR and the Commission of European Communities.

Luang Prabang (LP) Rural Micro-Projects. 1993. "Options for Upland Soil Conservation." Technical Note no. 6. Vientiane: Lao PDR and the Commission of European Communities.

Maroczy, Magda. 1986. "Women in Food Production, Report on the Findings of a Socio-economic Survey in Three Provinces of the Lao People's Democratic Republic." Unpublished. Vientiane: FAO Project TCP/Lao/4405.

Maroczy, Magda. 1987. "Report on Socioeconomic Survey of Three Villages in Vientiane Province, PDR Lao." Unpublished. Vientiane: FAO Project TCP/Lao/6653.

Mather, Celia. 1982. *Industrialization in the Tangerang Regency of West Java: Women Workers and the Islamic Patriarchy.* Center for Sociology and Anthropology Working Paper no. 17. Amsterdam: University of Amsterdam.

Maynard, Paul, and Polachart Kraiboon. 1969. "Evaluation Study of the Muong Phieng Cluster Area." Unpublished report prepared for the USAID Mission to Laos. Menlo Park, California: Stanford Research Institute.

McFarland, Joan. 1988. "Review Essay: The Construction of Women and Development Theory." *Canadian Review of Sociology and Anthropology* 25.2:299–308.

Mencher, Joan. 1988. "Women's Work and Poverty: Women's Contribution to Household Maintenance in Two Regions of South India." In Daisy Dwyer and Judith Bruce, eds. *A Home Divided: Women and Income in the Third World.* Stanford: Stanford University Press.

Miegs, Anna. 1990. " Multiple Gender Ideologies and Statuses." In Peggy R. Sanday and Ruth G. Goodenough, eds. *Beyond the Second Sex: New Directions in the Anthropology of Gender.* Philadelphia: University of Pennsylvania Press.

Mies, Marie. 1988. "Introduction." In Marie Mies, Veronika Bennholdt-Thomsen, and Claudia van Werlhof, eds. *Women: The Last Colony.* London: Zed.

Ministry of Agriculture and Forestry, Lao PDR. 1989. "Development Strategies on Shifting Cultivation Stabilization and Environment Protection." Unpublished paper, symposium on Forestry and Environment, Vientiane.

Ministry of Agriculture and Forestry, Lao PDR. 1990. *Tropical Forestry Action Plan: Main Report.* Vientiane: Ministry of Agriculture and Forestry.

Moore, Henrietta. 1988. *Feminism and Anthropology.* Minneapolis: University of Minnesota Press.

Moser, Carolyn O.N. 1987. "Mobilization is Women's Work: Struggles for Infrastructure in Guayaquil, Ecuador." In Carolyn O.N. Moser and Linda Peake, eds. *Women, Human Settlements, and Housing.* London and New York: Tavistock Publications.

Moser, Carolyn O.N. 1993. *Gender Planning and Development: Theory, Practice, and Training.* London and New York: Routledge.

Mukherjee, Chanda, and A.V. Jose. 1982. *Report of a Survey of Rural Households in the Hat Xai Fong District in Vientiane Province of the Lao People's Democratic Republic.* Bangkok: Asian Employment Programme, International Labor Organization (ILO)—ARTEP.

Ng, Shui Meng. 1988. "The Beginning of Small Enterprises in Laos: The Phonetong Women's Weaving Cooperative." In Noeleen Heyzer, ed. *Daughters in Industry.* Kuala Lumpur: Asian and Pacific Development Centre.

NULW (National Union of Lao Women). 1989. *Status of Women: Laos.* Social and Human Sciences in Asia and the Pacific, RUSHSAP Series on Monographs and Occasional Papers no. 29. Bangkok: UNESCO Principal Regional Office for Asia and the Pacific.

Ngaosyvathn, Mayoury. 1990. "Individual Soul, National Identity: The Baci Soukhuan of the Lao." *Sojourn: Social Issues in Southeast Asia* 5.1:283–307.

Ngaosyvathn, Mayoury. 1993. *Lao Women: Yesterday and Today.* Vientiane: State Publishing Enterprise.

Oakley, Ann. 1974. *The Sociology of Housework.* New York: Random House.

Ong, Aihwa. 1985. "Industrialization and Prostitution in Southeast Asia." *Southeast Asia Chronicle* 96:2–6.

Ong, Aihwa. 1987. *Spirits of Resistance and Capitalist Discipline: Factory Women in Malyasia.* Albany: State University of New York Press.

Ong, Aihwa. 1989. "Center, Periphery, and Hierarchy: Gender in Southeast Asia." In Sandra Morgen, ed. *Gender and Anthropology: Critical Reviews for Research and Teaching.* Washington, D.C.: American Anthropological Association.

Orr, Kenneth. 1966. "Research Memorandum: The Lao Farmer and the Proposed Artificial Fertilizer Program in Laos." Unpublished. Vientiane: Research and Evaluation Branch, Program Office, USAID/Laos.

Ortner, Sherry, and Harriet Whitehead. 1981. "Introduction: Accounting for Sexual Meanings." In Sherry Ortner and Harriet Whitehead, eds. *Sexual Meanings.* New York: Cambridge University Press.

Pelzer, Kristin. 1994. "Research Issues—Vietnam." Unpublished paper, workshop on Women in Socio-Economic Transitions. Bangkok: Chulalongkorn University and the University of California.

Pelzer-White, Christine. 1987. "State, Culture, and Gender: Continuity and Change in Women's Position in Rural Vietnam." In Haleh Afshar, ed. *Women, State, and Ideology.* London: Macmillan.

Perez, Daniel. 1989. *Assessment of MCH Services in Four Provinces of the Lao PDR.* Vientiane: UNICEF.

Phanjaruniti, Somporn. 1994. "Traditional Child Rearing Practices Among Different Ethnic Groups in Houaphan Province, Lao PDR." Unpublished. Vientiane: UNICEF.

Phimmachanh, Binh. 1994. "Rural Development in the Lao People's Democratic Republic." Talk at the East-West Center sponsored by the Center for Southeast Asian Studies, University of Hawaii, and the Indochina Initiative, East-West Center. Honolulu, Hawaii, June 9.

Phomvihan, Kaysone. 1982. *Political Report at the Third LPRP Congress.* Vientiane, Lao PDR.

Phomvihan, Kaysone. 1984. "Address to the First National Congress of the Lao Women's Union." Unpublished. Vientiane, Lao PDR (unofficial translation).

Phomvihan, Kaysone. 1988. "Address to the Second National Congress of the Lao Women's Union." Unpublished. Vientiane, Lao PDR.

Phongpaichit, Pasuk. 1982. *From Peasant Girls to Bangkok Masseuses.* Geneva: International Labor Organization.

Plant, Rod. 1990. "Results from the Follow Up to the Women in Development Study in Bolikhamsay Province." Vientiane: Swedish International Development Authority.

Plant, Rod. 1991. *Borikhamxai: A Provincial Support Programme. A Report to the SIDA/DCO Office.* Unpublished. Vientiane: Swedish International Development Authority.

Population Crisis Committee. 1988. "Country Rankings of the Status of Women: Poor, Powerless, and Pregnant." Population Briefing Paper no. 20.

Potter, Sulamith. 1977. *Family Life in a Northern Thai Village.* Berkeley: University of California Press.

Proschan, Frank. 1993. "Kmhmu." In Paul Hockings, ed. *Encyclopedia of World Cultures, Vol. V, East and Southeast Asia.* Boston: G.K. Hall.

Quaker Service Laos (QSL). 1992. *Report on Women's Development Project in Oudomsay, October 1991 to September 1992.* Unpublished. Vientiane: QSL.

Randall, Margaret. 1979. "We Need a Government of Men and Women . . . ! Notes on the Second National Congress of the Federación de Mujeres Cubanos, November 25–29, 1974." In Latin American Perspectives, ed. *Women in Latin America: An Anthology.* Riverside, California: Latin American Perspectives.

Randall, Margaret. 1981. *Women in Cuba: Twenty Years Later.* New York: Smyrna Press.

Rietmeyer, Fons. 1988. "Socio-Economic Survey of the Urban Area of Vientiane Prefecture." In *Schéma Directeur et d'Aménagement Urbain de Vientiane, Rapport Final.*

Rogers, Barbara. 1980. *The Domestication of Women: Discrimination in Developing Societies.* London: Tavistock.

Roldan, Martha. 1988. "Renegotiating the Marital Contract: Intrahousehold Patterns of Money Allocation and Women's Subordination Among Domestic Outworkers in Mexico City." In Daisy Dwyer and Judith Bruce, eds. *A Home Divided: Women and Income in the Third World.* Stanford: Stanford University Press.

Rosaldo, Michelle. 1974. "Women, Culture, and Society: A Theoretical Overview." In Michelle Rosaldo and Louise Lamphere, eds. *Women, Culture, and Society.* Stanford: Stanford University Press.

Rosaldo, Michelle. 1980. "The Use and Abuse of Anthropology: Reflections on Feminism and Cross-cultural Understanding." *Signs* 5.3:389–417.

Sacks, Karen. 1974. "Engels Revisited: Women, the Organization of Production, and Private Property. In Michelle Rosaldo and Louise Lamphere, eds. *Women, Culture, and Society.* Stanford: Stanford University Press.

Sacks, Karen. 1979. *Sisters and Wives: The Past and Future of Sexual Equality.* Westport, Connecticut: Greenwood.

Salter, Richard, Bouaphanh Phanthavong, and Venevongphet. 1991. "Planning and Development of a Protected Area System in Lao PDR: Status Report to Mid-1991."

Unpublished. Vientiane: Forest Resources Conservation Project, Lao/Swedish Forestry Cooperation Programme.

Samuelsson, Rolf, and Thongphachanh. 1979. "Swidden Agriculture in One District in Central Laos." Unpublished. Vientiane: SIDA.

Sanday, Peggy Reeves. 1981. *Female Power and Male Dominance: On the Origins of Sexual Inequality*. Cambridge: Cambridge University Press.

Schenk-Sandbergen, Loes, and Outhaki Choulamany-Khamphoui. 1995. *Women in Rice Fields and Offices: Irrigation in Laos: Gender Specific Case-Studies in Four Villages*. Heiloo, The Netherlands: Empowerment.

Schlegel, Alice. 1977. "Toward a Theory of Sexual Stratification." In Alice Schlegel, ed. *Sexual Stratification: A Cross-Cultural View*. New York: Columbia University Press.

Sen, Gita, and Caren Grown. 1987. *Development, Crises, and Alternative Visions: Third World Women's Perspectives*. New York: Monthly Review Press.

Sirisambhand, Naphat. 1991. "Gender Relations and Changing Rural Society." *Journal of Social Research* 14.2:19–28.

Sisouvanh, Boun Louane. 1992. "Women in Development in Laos." Lectures at Willamette University and Chemeketa Community College, January 31.

Sivard, Ruth. 1985. *Women: A World Survey*. New York: United Nations.

Smalley, William. 1964. "The Khmu." In Frank M. LeBar, Gerald C. Hickey, and John K. Musgrave, eds. *Ethnic Groups of Mainland Southeast Asia*. New Haven, Connecticut: Human Relations Area Files Press.

Smock, Audrey Chapman. 1977. "Conclusion: Determinants of Women's Roles and Status." In Janet Giele and Audrey Smock, eds. *Women: Roles and Status in Eight Countries*. New York: Wiley.

Sonephet, Southaly. 1994. "Rural Development in the Lao People's Democratic Republic." Talk at the East-West Center sponsored by the Center for Southeast Asian Studies, University of Hawaii and the Indochina Initiative, East-West Center. Honolulu, Hawaii, June 9.

Sonnöis, Brigitte. 1990. "Women in Cambodia: Overview of the Situation and Suggestions for Development Programmes." Unpublished. Phnom Penh: Redd Barna-Cambodia.

Stavrakis, Olga, and Marion Marshall. 1978. "Women, Agriculture, and Development in the Maya Lowlands: Profit or Progress?" Unpublished paper, International Conference on Women and Food, Tucson.

Steinberg, David. 1987. *In Search of Southeast Asia: A Modern History*, 2nd rev. ed. Honolulu: University of Hawaii Press.

Stockard, Jean, and Miriam Johnson. 1992. *Sex and Gender in Society*, 2nd ed. Englewood Cliffs, N.J.: Prentice Hall.

Stromquist, Nelly. 1989. "Recent Developments in Women's Education: Closer to a Better Social Order?" *Women and International Development Annual* 1:103–30.

Stuart-Fox, Martin. 1980. "The Initial Failure of Agricultural Cooperativization in Laos." *Asia Quarterly* 4:273–99.

Stuart-Fox, Martin. 1986a. *Laos: Politics, Economics, and Society*. London and Boulder: Pinter and Rienner.

Stuart-Fox, Martin. 1986b. "Politics and Patronage in Laos." *Indochina Issues* 70:1–7.

Stuart-Fox, Martin, and Mary Kooyman. 1992. *Historical Dictionary of Laos*. Metuchen, N.J. and London: Scarecrow.

Taillard, Christian. 1974. "Les Berges de la Nam Ngum et du Mekong—Systèmes Économiques Villageois et Organisation de L'espace dans la Plaine de Vientiane (Laos)." *Etudes Rurales* 53–56:119–68.

Taillard, Christian. 1989. *Le Laos—Stratégies d'un Etat-tampon.* Montpellier: Reclus.

Tanner, Nancy. 1974. "Matrifocality in Indonesia and Africa and Among Black Americans." In Michelle Rosaldo and Louise Lamphere, eds. *Women, Culture, and Society.* Stanford: Stanford University Press.

Tapp, Nicholas. 1989. *Sovereignty and Rebellion: The White Hmong of Northern Thailand.* Singapore: Oxford.

Tapp, Nicholas. 1993. "Hmong." In Paul Hockings, ed. *Encyclopedia of World Cultures, Vol. V, East and Southeast Asia.* Boston: G.K. Hall.

Tayanin, Damrong. 1994. *Being Kammu: My Village, My Life.* Southeast Asia Program Series no. 14. Ithaca, New York: Southeast Asia Program, Cornell University.

Tayanin, Damrong, and Kristina Lindell. 1991. *Hunting and Fishing in a Kammu Village.* Malmo and London: Curzon Press.

Thao, T. Christopher. 1986. "Hmong Customs on Marriage, Divorce, and the Rights of Married Women." In Brenda Johns and David Strecker, eds. *The Hmong World.* New Haven, Connecticut: Council on Southeast Asia Studies, Yale Center for International and Area Studies.

Tinker, Irene. 1990. "The Making of a Field: Advocates, Practitioners, and Scholars." In Irene Tinker, ed. *Persistent Inequalities: Women and World Development.* New York: Oxford University Press.

Tinker, Irene, and Michèle Bramsen. 1976. *Women and World Development.* Washington, D.C.: Overseas Development Council under the auspices of the American Association for the Advancement of Science.

Trankell, Ing-Britt. 1993. "On the Road in Laos: An Anthropological Study of Road Construction and Rural Communities." *Uppsala Research Reports in Cultural Anthropology no. 12.* Uppsala, Sweden: Department of Cultural Anthropology, Uppsala University.

Tripp, Robert. 1981. "Farmers and Traders: Some Economic Determinants of Nutritional Status in Northern Ghana." *Journal of Tropical Pediatrics* 27:15–22.

UNDP (United Nations Development Program). 1988. Project Document, "Rural Household Production." Project Number LAO/88/016/A/01/31. Unpublished. Vientiane: UNDP.

UNESCO. 1985. *Diagnostic du Système Éducatif de la R.D.P. Lao 1984/85.* Projet LAO/82/010. Unpublished. Vientiane: UNESCO.

UNICEF. 1991a. *From EPI to Primary Health Care: Proposed Strategy.* Unpublished. Vientiane: UNICEF.

UNICEF. 1991b. *Rural Water Supply and Sanitation in the Lao PDR: A Framework for a New Decade.* Unpublished. Vientiane: UNICEF.

UNICEF. 1992. *Children and Women in the Lao People's Democratic Republic.* Vientiane: UNICEF.

UNIDO (United Nations Industrial Development Organization). 1992. *Opportunity Studies for Small and Medium Scale Agroindustries in the Mekong Area, Kingdom of Thailand and Lao PDR.* Terminal Report Vol. II. UNIDO.

United Nations. 1991. *The World's Women 1970–1990: Trends and Statistics.* New York: United Nations.

United Nations. 1995. *The World's Women 1970–1995: Trends and Statistics.* New York: United Nations.

Van Esterik, Penny. 1982. "Laywomen in Theravada Buddhism." In Penny Van Esterik, ed. *Women of Southeast Asia.* Center for Southeast Asian Studies Occasional Paper no. 9, DeKalb, Illinois: Northern Illinois University.

Vang Dao. 1993. *Hmong at the Turning Point.* Minneapolis: WorldBridge Associates.

Vang, Lue, and Judy Lewis. 1984. *Grandmother's Path, Grandfather's Way: Hmong Preservation Project—Oral Lore, Generation to Generation.* San Francisco: Zellerbach Family Fund.

Viravong, Maha Sila. 1964. *History of Laos.* New York: Paragon Book Reprint Co. (Translation by U.S. Joint Publications Research Service.)

Viravong, Manivone. 1987. "Role of Lao Women in Rural Development." Unpublished conference paper, Tashkent, Uzbekistan.

Viravong, Manivone. 1995. "Women, the Family, and Economic Transitions in Laos." Paper presented at the NGO Forum, Fourth World Conference on Women. Beijing. September.

Vongkhamchanh, Phouy, and Jan van der Heide. 1989. "Land Use in Forestry: Discussion Paper for the Tropical Forestry Action Plan of the Lao PDR." Unpublished. Vientiane: Department of Forestry, Ministry of Agriculture and Forestry, Lao PDR.

Vongsack, Davone. 1986. Presentation at the Women in Development section, Second Round Table of the Least Developed Countries of Asia and the Pacific. Geneva: United Nations.

Vongsay, Phoneprasith. 1994. "Impact to Women Concern During This Time of Rapid Economic Transition." Unpublished paper, workshop on Women in Socio-Economic Transitions. Bangkok: Chulalongkorn University and the University of California.

Weiner, Annette. 1986. "Forgotten Wealth: Cloth and Women's Production in the Pacific." In Eleanor Leacock and Helen Safa, eds. *Women's Work: Development and the Division of Labor by Gender.* South Hadley, Massachusetts: Bergin and Harvey.

Weller, Robert. 1968. "Employment of Wives, Dominance, and Fertility." *Journal of Marriage and Family* 30:437–42.

Westermeyer, Joseph. 1982. *Poppies, Pipes, and People: Opium and Its Use in Laos.* Berkeley: University of California Press.

Whyte, Robert Orr, and Pauline Whyte. 1982. *Women of Rural Asia.* Boulder, Colorado: Westview.

Winzeler, Robert. 1982. "Sexual Status in Southeast Asia: Comparative Perspectives on Women, Agriculture, and Political Organization." In Penny Van Esterik, ed. *Women of Southeast Asia.* Center for Southeast Asian Studies Occasional Paper no. 9, DeKalb, Illinois: Northern Illinois University.

Wolf, Diane. 1992. *Factory Daughters: Gender, Household Dynamics, and Rural Industrialization in Java.* Berkeley: University of California Press.

World Bank. 1988. "Lao People's Democratic Republic Economic Memorandum, Report No. 7188-LA." Unpublished. Washington, D.C.: World Bank.

World Bank. 1990. *Women in Development: A Progress Report on the World Bank Initiative.* Washington, D.C.: World Bank.

Wulff, Robert. 1972. *A Comparative Study of Refugee and Nonrefugee Villages; Part I: A Survey of Long-Established Villages of the Vientiane Plain.* Vientiane: Embassy of the United States of America, USAID Mission to Laos.

Wyatt, David K. 1984. *Thailand: A Short History.* New Haven, Connecticut: Yale Press.

Xenos, Peter. 1991. "Demography and Health Issues." In *Swidden Agroecosystems in Sepone District, Savannakhet Province, Lao PDR.* Report of the 1991 SUAN-EAPI-MAF Agroecosystem Research Workshop, Savannakhet Province. Khon Kaen, Thailand: The SUAN Regional Secretariat, Khon Kaen University.

Xiong, May, and Nancy Donnelly. 1986. "My Life in Laos." In Brenda Johns and David Strecker, eds. *The Hmong World.* New Haven, Connecticut: Council on Southeast Asia Studies, Yale Center for International and Area Studies.

Index

About the Book and Author

After the Vietnam War, socialist governments ascended to power in all the countries of the former Indochina. In Laos, more than a decade of socialist reorganization was followed by economic liberalization in the late 1980s. Laotian women had traditionally sustained the household and local economy with their work in field, forest, and family, but political and economic changes markedly affected the context of rural women's prevailing sources of power and subordination. Socialist policies, for example, curtailed women's commercial activities while recognizing women's work in agriculture and child care.

In this richly detailed volume, Carol Ireson draws on ten years of fieldwork and research to explore this metamorphosis among Laotian women. Throughout she poses questions such as: What has happened to women's traditional sources of control over their own and others' activities since the 1975 socialist revolution? Have their traditional sources of power or autonomy expanded or contracted as changing conditions have allowed other groups to appropriate women's traditional resources and roles? Have the dramatic changes had different effects on rural women of differing ethnic backgrounds and varying economic means?

Focusing on women from three major ethnic groups—the lowland Lao, the Khmu, and the Hmong—Ireson examines the different ways they have responded to political and economic changes. She shows us that the Laotian experience reveals in microcosm the processes of change toward specialization and integration of women's work into national and global economies and explains how this shift deeply affects women's lives.

Carol J. Ireson is professor of sociology at Willamette University.

DATE DUE

JUN 28 '99	

BRODART, CO. Cat. No. 23-221-003

35068125